Emerson's Impact
on the
British Isles and Canada

Emerson's Impact
on the
British Isles and Canada

BY

William J. Sowder

LONGWOOD COLLEGE
Farmville, Virginia

The University Press of Virginia
Charlottesville

Library of Congress Catalog Card Number: 66–25469

Printed in the United States of America

To the memory of my beloved brother
ROBERT WALKER SOWDER, 1915–1963

Preface

A NUMBER of critics have made use of British periodical literature in dealing with Emerson. Townsend Scudder, in *The Lonely Wayfaring Man: Emerson and Some Englishmen,* writes of the American during his visits to England and uses letters, biographies, many newspapers, and a few periodicals. Naturally, biographers of Emerson have been interested in his reputation in Great Britain, and Ralph L. Rusk has been especially diligent in using periodicals for glimpses of him while he was on the tour of 1847–48. Clarence Gohdes is another critic who has found in periodicals good material on American writers in nineteenth-century England.[1] No one, however, has dealt exclusively or even extensively with Victorian journals in attempting to establish Emerson's impact on the British.

The reasons for this neglect are fairly easy to discern. First, as Gohdes writes, Emerson received more attention from English periodicals than any other American writer.[2] Second, no adequate bibliography of these articles exists. Third, the number of British periodicals in the latter part of the nineteenth century was enormous, especially if one includes, as I have, those of Scotland, Ireland, and Canada. Anyone dealing with these journals will therefore have to be content with less than full coverage. Yet so important is this literature that the attempt is well worth making: William Frederick Poole, John Morley, and Walter Graham all have attested to its importance, and Hugh

---

[1] Scudder (New York, 1936); Rusk, *The Life of Ralph Waldo Emerson* (New York, 1949), pp. 337, 352, 354; Gohdes, *American Literature in Nineteenth-Century England* (New York, 1944). Throughout the book references are grouped. In all cases the references in the notes follow the order of the citations, quotations, and paraphrases in the text. Occasionally there are more references than quotations because different critics said essentially the same thing.

[2] P. 138.

Walker very well summed up their comments when he wrote concerning the nineteenth century, "The age of periodical literature has come." [3]

One cannot use this literature, however, without a measure of caution. Both Graham and Walker point out that it is often biased, and editors and critics writing in such diverse periodicals as the *British Controversialist,* the *Journal of Sacred Literature,* and the *Bookman* have noted the same characteristic.[4] In order to discover the truth concerning Emerson's impact, one should know something of the prejudices of these periodicals. In addition, one should know something of the writers of the articles. The latter factor poses a problem. During much of the period under study, articles were contributed anonymously, and a majority of them have remained anonymous.[5] Even when the writer is identified, he is often so obscure that nothing can be learned about him. Yet the picture is not altogether dim. Professor Walter E. Houghton is now working on the identification of contributors to thirty-five of the principal Victorian quarterlies and monthlies and has generously shared his information with me.[6] Then, too, the authors of these pieces usually hew to the line set by the journals for which they write: to know the bias of the writer is generally a matter of knowing editorial policy.[7] Pertinent information has been given

[3] *Poole's Index to Periodical Literature* (New York, 1882), I, pref., p. iv; Edwin M. Everett, *The Party of Humanity* (Chapel Hill, N.C., 1939), pref., p. v; Graham, *English Literary Periodicals* (New York, 1930), p. 390; Walker, *The Literature of the Victorian Era* (Cambridge, Eng., 1910), p. 935.

[4] Graham, p. 284; Walker, pp. 936–37; BritC, May–Dec. 1850, pref., p. iii; B. Harris Cowper, "Notice," JSL, 5th ser. II (1867–68); Thomas Seccombe, "Liberal Leaders in Literature," *Bookman*, XXIX (Jan. 1906), 166.

[5] Many of the periodical editors do not now know who their contributors were. See Leslie A. Marchand, *The Athenaeum: A Mirror of Victorian Culture* (Chapel Hill, N.C., 1941), p. 67; Francis E. Mineka, *The Dissidence of Dissent* (Chapel Hill, N.C., 1944), p. 177; *Complete List of Articles Published in the* Dublin Review *between 1836 and 1936* (London, 1936), publisher's note.

[6] Professor Houghton's book, *The Wellesley Index to Victorian Periodicals: Identification of Authors with Tables of Contents in British Monthlies & Quarterlies, 1824–1900,* published in August 1966 by the University of Toronto Press, came out too late for me to use.

[7] One writer who found conformity to *Spectator* policies intolerable was the brilliant radical G. H. Lewes. He resigned and (with Thornton Hunt) established the *Leader* in order to say what he pleased (Francis Espinasse, *Literary Recollections and Sketches* [London, 1893], p. 653).

on the journals under survey and (whenever possible) on the critics.

The book, which covers the years 1840–1903, with a few references to later articles, is organized around Chapters I, II, and V. In these chapters Emerson's reputation is traced step by step and changes occurring in that reputation are noted. Reasons for the changes are also suggested. Chapter I, which shows the early Victorians struggling with Emerson, covers the decade between the publication of *Nature* in 1836 and the tour of 1847–48. Chapter II gives Mid-Victorian reaction to works like *Representative Men, English Traits,* and *The Conduct of Life.* Chapter V tells of the first two decades of evaluation after Emerson's death in 1882. These are the years of the masterful articles by Matthew Arnold, Leslie Stephen, and the American Henry James, as well as the biographies of James Elliot Cabot, Oliver Wendell Holmes, and Richard Garnett.

Although critics were interested in nearly all aspects of Emerson's life and career, their attention centered on his philosophy, religion, and literary style and on his reputation and influence in both the British Isles and America. These subjects give topical unity to the chapters just mentioned and are much used in three additional chapters dealing with subjects of special inquiry.

Chronology has largely been discarded as a means of organizing Chapters III, IV, and VI. Throughout the century Emerson's poetry was poorly received: *May-Day and Other Pieces* was, according to Victorian critics, no more impressive than *Poems.* Yet these critics made an interesting and laudable attempt to come to grips with this poetry, and Chapter III treats this struggle. Emerson's religious and philosophical views were accorded pretty much the same welcome as his poetry. Yet two small sects—the Secularists and the Theosophists—were highly enthusiastic over those views; Chapter IV brings their enthusiasm to a focus. No book on Emerson is complete without some account of his friendship with Carlyle; in Chapter VI that friendship is shown through the eyes of the periodical writers. Chapter VII presents a short summary of Emerson's influence on British Victorians, with emphasis on his reputation at the turn of the century.

Whenever possible, I have merely selected and arranged, leaving the critics to speak in their own words. These critics are not all British: included are Americans like Moncure D. Conway and Henry

James, who spent much of their lives in England, and Parke Godwin, the American socialist. I have not hesitated to include these foreign writers so long as their work appeared in British periodicals: they too contributed to Emerson's impact on the British Isles and Canada. By retaining the critics' own words, I hope to point up the changing religious, intellectual, and cultural trends over the three generations ruled by Victoria—trends that had a decided effect on the appraisal of Emerson. The comments of some of these Victorians on Emerson are as good as any ever made. Emerson would not, I think, object to my procedure: he believed in letting a man speak for himself.

It is a pleasure to express gratitude to Albert F. Moe, researcher in lexicographical matters, who gave me many useful suggestions with regard to the manuscript, and to Caroline Sherwood Peck, who made the index. A research grant from Longwood College helped me to obtain necessary material; in addition, the College, using private funds, defrayed part of the cost of publication. Chapter I appeared in a slightly different form in *PMLA* and Chapter IV in the *New England Quarterly*. They are used here by permission of the Modern Language Association and the *Quarterly*.

W. J. S.

Farmville, Virginia
July 25, 1965

Contents

Key to Abbreviations

Academy (Ac)
Academy and Literature (AcLit)
All the Year Round (AYR)
Annual Register (AnnualR)
Athenaeum (Ath)
Belford's Monthly Magazine (Belford's)
Bentley's Miscellany (Bentley's)
Biblical Review and Congregational Magazine (BibRev)
Blackwood's Edinburgh Magazine (Blackwood's)
British and Foreign Evangelical Review (BFER)
British Controversialist (BritC)
British Quarterly Review (BQR)
Broadway (Bwy)
Broadway Annual (BwyA)
Canadian Magazine (CanM)
Canadian Methodist Magazine (CMM)
Chambers's Edinburgh Journal (Chambers's)
Christian Observer (ChO)
Christian Remembrancer (ChR)
Church Quarterly Review (CQR)
Congregationalist (Cst)
Congregational Review (CongR)
Contemporary Review (ContR)
Cooper's Journal (Cooper's)

Cosmopolis (Cos)
Douglas Jerrold's Shilling Magazine (Jerrold'sS)
Douglas Jerrold's Weekly Newspaper (Jerrold'sW)
Dublin Review (DubR)
Dublin University Magazine (DubUM)
Eclectic Review (EcRev)
Edinburgh Review (EdRev)
Eliza Cook's Journal (Cook's)
English Review (EngR)
Examiner (Ex)
Foreign Quarterly Review (FQR)
Fortnightly Review (FR)
Fraser's Magazine (Fraser's)
Gentleman's Magazine (GentM)
Great Thoughts (GT)
Hogg's Instructor (Hogg's)
Howitt's Journal (Howitt's)
Intellectual Repository and New Jerusalem Magazine (IRNJ)
Journal of Sacred Literature and Biblical Record (JSL)
Ladies' Companion and Monthly Magazine (Ladies')
Leisure Hour (LeisH)
Literature (Lit)
Literary Gazette (LitG)
Literary World (LitW)

Littell's Living Age (Littell's)
London and Westminster Review (LWR)
London Quarterly Review (LQR)
London Review (LondR)
Lotus Journal (Lotus)
Macmillan's Magazine (MM)
Macphail's Edinburgh Ecclesiastical Journal and Literary Review (Macphail's)
Manchester Quarterly (ManQ)
Methodist Magazine and Review (MMR)
Modern Review (ModR)
Monthly Magazine (MonM)
Monthly Review (MR)
Murray's Magazine (Murray's)
National Magazine (NatM)
National Reformer (NatRef)
National Review (NatRev)
New Century Review (NCRev)
New Dominion Monthly (NDomM)
New Monthly Magazine (NMM)
New Quarterly Review (NQR)
North British Review (NBrR)
Notes and Queries (Notes)
Our Corner (OC)
Oxford and Cambridge Magazine (OCM)

Palladium (Pm)
People's Journal (People's)
Primitive Methodist Quarterly Review (PMQR)
Prospective Review (ProsR)
Public Opinion (PubO)
Quarterly Review (QR)
Reasoner (Reas)
Review of Reviews (RR)
Saturday Review (SatR)
Scottish Review (ScR)
Secular Review (SecR)
Sharpe's London Journal (Sharpe's)
Spectator (Sp)
Tait's Edinburgh Magazine (Tait's)
Temple Bar (TBar)
Theosophical Review (TheosR)
Theosophical Siftings (TheosS)
Times Literary Supplement (TLS)
T. P.'S Weekly (T. P.'s)
University Magazine (UM)
Wesleyan-Methodist Magazine (Wes-Meth)
Westminster Review (WR)
West of Scotland Magazine-Review (WScM)
Whittington Club and Metropolitan Athenaeum Gazette (Whit)

Emerson's Impact
on the
British Isles and Canada

The Early Victorians

THE years 1840–50 were important ones in Anglo-American cultural and intellectual relations, for during that period American writers began to be read widely in England. Before that time books had been too expensive for almost everyone except the great readers or the greatly prosperous; in the 1840's, however, a combination of circumstances led to a revolution in English reading habits. Circulating libraries had been in operation in England for some years, but in 1842 Mudie's for the first time made available to all literate Englishmen the literature of the world. More important perhaps than the libraries were the cheap reprints, at first sold mainly in the newly built and overflowing railway stations but later found in bookstalls throughout the country.[1] Commenting on Slater's shilling edition of Emerson's *Orations, Lectures, and Addresses,* the *Critic* wrote, for example, that "the work itself must be familiar by name to *all* our readers, but probably it has been out of the reach of many of them. It is not so now. The poorest may possess it." [2] Ironically enough, the appearance of Emerson and many other Amer-

[1] Richard D. Altick, *The English Common Reader* (Chicago, 1957), pp. 295–96. Francis Espinasse borrowed Emerson's works from Mudie's, and the first work which Mudie published on his own was "Emerson's *Essay,* which he called *Man Thinking*" (Amy Cruse, *The Victorians and Their Reading* [Boston, 1936], p. 310). George Willis Cooke in *A Bibliography of Ralph Waldo Emerson* (Boston, 1908, p. 66) gives the date of *Man Thinking* as 1844, but on p. 73 he records that Emerson's "Man the Reformer" was published by Mudie as early as 1841.

[2] Nov. 15, 1849, p. 526. For more on the cheap press, see *Critic,* Dec. 15, 1849, p. 573, in addition to *The Complete Works of Ralph Waldo Emerson,* ed. Edward Waldo Emerson (Boston, 1903–4), IV, 196 (hereafter cited as *Works*), and Altick, pp. 277–93 *passim.*

ican authors in these cheap reprints was due as much to defective international copyright laws as to a demand for their books. British publishers discovered that under certain conditions they could bring out the works of foreign writers without remuneration, and after 1839 they took full advantage of this knowledge.[3] Emerson tried to outwit the infringers by sending the manuscripts of *Essays, Second Series,* and *Poems* to England prior to bringing the volumes out in America,[4] and Carlyle used the Preface to the *Second Essays* to draw and quarter the pirates. Emerson's precautions and Carlyle's strictures were of little avail: at about the same time that *Poems* came out, Orr and Company was issuing a pirated edition of *Essays, Lectures, and Orations.*[5] Although evasion of copyright laws cannot be condoned on ethical grounds, it had one happy result: the pirated editions were cheap, and their wide sale along with legitimate reprints and the circulating library made accessible for the first time large quantities of American books to a wide British public. From 1840 to the end of the century England read more books by American writers than by all Europeans, and, fortunately for this study, all the major works received critical appraisal in British periodicals.[6]

Channing, Irving, and Cooper were the first American writers to gain much attention, and Emerson's contemporaries Harriet Beecher Stowe and Longfellow were frequently discussed. But it was Emerson himself whom periodical critics regarded as the outstanding American writer, and he was the one who received the greatest number of notices.[7] These notices began to appear in the late 1830's, just about the time the flow of American books to England gathered force. In 1841 Carlyle observed in the Preface to the English edition of *Essays, First Series,* that Emerson was not entirely unknown in England. Distinguished travelers had brought "tidings

---

[3] Clarence Gohdes, *American Literature in Nineteenth-Century England* (New York, 1944), pp. 16–18.

[4] Ralph L. Rusk, *The Life of Ralph Waldo Emerson* (New York, 1949), pp. 300, 312.

[5] Cooke, p. 101. This piracy was noted by the *Critic,* Dec. 18, 1847, pp. 386–88. Gohdes, *Amer. Lit.,* p. 25, does not estimate the number of pirated editions of American authors, but says that "it was large." Chapman, writes Gohdes (p. 35), brought out cheap editions of Emerson but "rarely" "made payments." Doubtless other publishers did the same. See Rusk, *Life,* p. 285.

[6] Gohdes, *Amer. Lit.,* pp. 20, 46.   [7] *Ibid.,* pp. 138, 139.

of such a man," he wrote, and "fitful hints" of him were to be found in British periodicals.[8] The first of these hints (though Carlyle did not say so) was less than a sentence that appeared in the January 1838 issue of the *London and Westminster Review*. Reviewing Harriet Martineau's *Retrospect of Western Travel,* which had praised Emerson highly, the anonymous critic wrote that the American was "a man who, judging from his address, delivered before a literary society in New England, and which has just reached us, has only to follow the career he has entered upon to . . . rank with the most elevated and eloquent of the expositors of noble truths, of whom his country can boast." [9] The second notice was written by Miss Martineau herself. In it the ardent democrat used the scholar as depicted in "Literary Ethics" (1838) to show her detestation of the literary lion.[10] One of the most important articles about Emerson during the early period appeared in the *London and Westminster Review* in 1840. Written by a devoted friend of America, Richard Monckton Milnes, this study examined in some detail Emerson's literary style, his religion, and his philosophy.[11] It also paid tribute to Emerson the man, mentioned his debt to Carlyle and the Germans, and attempted to refute Emerson's claim in "The American Scholar" that the time had come for America's cultural and intellectual break with the Mother Country.

II

All of these matters were of concern both to Milnes and to many other British critics. They will be dealt with in turn in this chapter. But first, let us see what was said about the difficulties experienced at the outset by nearly everyone who reads Emerson. To a generation brought up on the smooth-flowing and well-organized works of such writers as Macaulay and Newman, the tight, nervous, allusive, and

---

[8] *LWR,* XXXVI (Oct. 1841), 491.   [9] *LWR,* XXVIII (Jan. 1838), 500.

[10] *LWR,* XXXII (April 1839), 280.

[11] *LWR* XXXIII (March 1840), 186–201. This article from the American edition covered everything of importance that Emerson had published up to that time except for a few poems in the *Western Messenger.*

highly elliptical style of Emerson was something of a problem. Reviewers of *Essays, First Series,* noted that the phraseology was "queer," "peculiar—quaint, and rather affected," that the volume embodied "the oddest jumble of bold ideas, rhapsodies and *notions*" that was ever met with "in the same narrow space." The work was, wrote the *Athenaeum,* stylistically "absolutely below criticism." Even this anti-American journal, however, found in the essays "passages of a certain obscure beauty" and at another time commented that Emerson's wide literary reputation was "partly due to the peculiarity (not ineloquent) of his prose style." [12] The latter observation doubtless came after the reviewer had read *Essays, Second Series,* which received better notices than the first—especially with regard to style. The more these early critics read Emerson, it seems, the more his manner grew on them. Although several periodicals found no improvement in Emerson's ability to express himself, others besides the *Athenaeum* maintained that the second work was better stylistically than the first,[13] and *Blackwood's Edinburgh Magazine,* commenting on all of Emerson's works, enjoyed the "terse," "graphic" style, even as it deplored the "obscurity of thought." *Macphail's* observed that Emerson was "exceedingly clear in his style. There are not only the freshness and richness, but also the openness of a summer morning, in his productions." [14]

The most difficult as well as the most characteristic element of this style is the use of ellipses, which one journal amusingly termed "frantic leaps." [15] In explaining the mannerism, *Macphail's* wrote

[12] *MR,* n.s. III (Oct. 1841), 275; *Sp,* Aug. 28, 1841, p. 834; *Tait's,* n.s. VIII (Oct. 1841), 670; *Ath,* Oct. 23, 1841, pp. 803–4; *Ath,* Feb. 6, 1847, p. 144.

[13] George Gilfillan, *Tait's,* n.s. XV (Jan. 1848), 22; *Critic,* Jan. 2, 1847, p. 9; [Charles Wicksteed], *ProsR,* I (May 1845), 252, 257 (Philip Henry Wicksteed, *Memorials of the Rev. Charles Wicksteed* [London, 1886], p. 354, credits this article to his father, who at one time edited the *Review*); *Sp,* Nov. 23, 1844, p. 1122; [McCarthy], *DubR,* XXVI (March 1849), 168 (Professor Houghton credits this article to McCarthy; Cooke, p. 288, credits it to G. Prentice with no further explanation). For the unstable Emerson-Gilfillan relationship, see Rusk, *Life,* p. 337, and Townsend Scudder, *The Lonely Wayfaring Man* (London, 1936), pp. 96–108. When an article was published anonymously but the author's identity is known, the name is given in brackets in the first citation. Subsequent citations are made only by journal.

[14] [William Henry Smith], *Blackwood's,* LXII (Dec. 1847), 648 (Cooke, p. 288, credits this article also to Prentice, with no explanation); *Macphail's,* XV (Feb. 1848), 51.

[15] *BibRev,* I (Feb. 1846), 149.

that Emerson seemed to be "afraid that connexions and transitions would have entailed dulness," and so he dispensed with them.[16] A more perspicacious comment came from *Douglas Jerrold's Shilling Magazine.* The critic—doubtless the redoubtable Jerrold himself—noted that the "logical applicability" of Emerson's "glowing images" "seemed only asserted and not shown" and observed, "The expression of profound ... truths must, to a certain point, be obscure. It is not possible to state long processes of thought in brilliant repartees." "Emerson and other philosophers do not write to save thinking, but to suggest it." "They have solved certain problems, and they show the results; they give enough help to enable the reader to gather data of the theorem, but they do not work it for him." [17]

Even with British readers acquiring a taste for the Emerson manner and with an astute critic or two pointing out its excellencies, the American would have remained neglected much longer as a writer of fine prose if critics had not early seen that he frequently employed the techniques of oratory. In America, Orestes Brownson had suggested that Emerson be read mainly for his "incidental remarks, frequent aphorisms," and Milnes, noting the aphoristic quality of Emerson's literary style, commented that it was better suited for speaking than for writing.[18] Reviewing *Essays, Second Series,* the *Spectator* was unfavorably impressed with "the iterative outpourings," another device of the orator, and *Tait's* declared bluntly that the *First Essays* were "more properly lectures." [19] After praising Emerson's prose for its clarity and freshness, a critic for *Macphail's* used a term often reserved for oratory to make his point perfectly clear: instead of discussing, Emerson "rhapsodizes." [20]

Another characteristic of Emerson's prose which American as well as British critics isolated and one that helped them to understand it better is the poetic quality. In 1838 Brownson, for example, called Emerson a poet rather than a philosopher and maintained that he

---

[16] XV (Feb. 1848), 47.   [17] I (Feb. 1845), 184, 185.

[18] Clarence Gohdes, *The Periodicals of American Transcendentalism* (Durham, N.C., 1931), p. 76; [Milnes], *LWR*, XXXIII, 191.

[19] *Sp*, Nov. 23, 1844, p. 1122; *Tait's*, n.s. VIII (Oct. 1841), 667.

[20] *Macphail's*, XV (Feb. 1848), 47. *Tait's*, n.s. VIII (Oct. 1841), 666, made a like observation.

was to be read not for his "striking philosophical views" but for his "rich and original imagery." [21] English critics evidently made this important discovery only with the publication of *Poems,* a work which came in for much critical abuse. Reviewers apparently glanced through the volume of poetry and then took a hard look at Emerson's prose. Laying *Poems* aside, William Henry Smith, a poet himself, wrote that if one "wished to find instances of the poetry of Emerson," he should seek them in his essays.[22] The poems also seem to have revealed to critics that the essays were rich in "poetical thought" and imagery, pervaded by a "poetic spirit," and "elaborately dyed with poetic hues." Two years after *Poems* had appeared in 1845, the *Critic* wrote that Emerson's "language is always *tinged with poetry,* and occasionally it becomes poetry all over." [23] The *Dublin Review,* which had almost nothing good to say about Emerson, declared that "his diction constantly rises above the literal, and becomes imaginative and brilliant, picturesque and rhythmical," while *Douglas Jerrold's Shilling Magazine,* which had almost nothing bad to say about him, declared that all his works were pure poetry. *Jerrold's* then exhorted Emerson to lay aside further prose works and to devote more time to poetry.[24] This voice was a faint one, as Chapter III will make clear.

III

Nearly all the early Victorians judged Emerson's poetry (and his prose) on other than literary principles, and thus they dwelt upon the faults of his works rather than on the good qualities. One critic deplored the "brain-webs of all sorts and sizes" that Emerson was spinning in his poems and essays, and although *Macphail's* censured those critics who could not separate Emerson the man of letters from the man of thought, the journal observed that the writer's heresies

[21] Gohdes, *Periodicals*, p. 76.   [22] *Blackwood's*, LXII, 656.

[23] *Critic,* Jan. 2, 1847, p. 9; *Ath,* Feb. 6, 1847, p. 145; Gilfillan, *Tait's,* n.s. XV, 20; *Critic,* Dec. 18, 1847, p. 386. Others noting the poetic qualities of Emerson's prose were *Macphail's,* XV (Feb. 1848) , 35–36, and [Parke Godwin], *People's,* Nov. 28 (?) , 1847, p. 306 (Cooke, p. 260, identifies Godwin as the author) .

[24] *DubR,* XXVI, 176; A Student [George Cupples], *Jerrold'sS,* VII (April 1848) , 326, 330 (Cooke, p. 211, identifies the Student as George Cupples) .

marred "the mere literature of his works." [25] Early critics, as these two indicate, treated Emerson's message much more harshly than they treated his style: some of that message they did not understand; some of it they understood all too well.

Almost everything that Emerson had to say during the early years ran counter to the British standard: his religious liberalism, transcendental philosophy, and democratic politics were diametrically opposed to English religious conservatism, empiricism, and monarchy. So outrageous did one reviewer find the *First Series* that he was almost ready to classify it "with Mr. Haughton's Essay on Sex in the World to Come." [26] Probably nothing that Emerson said or wrote in the 1840's caused so much stir as his pronouncements on religion, as one can readily gather by looking through a few church periodicals. The first sect to take notice of Emerson in British journals was, not surprisingly, the Swedenborgians. Emerson showed much interest in the founder of this religious group, and in 1840 the *Intellectual Repository and New Jerusalem Magazine* carried one of the few reviews of *Nature*. The critic observed that the "beautiful" "doctrine of correspondences" was the basis of the anonymous author's thought as well as of Swedenborg's, noted other parallels, and concluded that the writer had doubtless read the works of Swedenborg and was imbued with their truths. [27] Ralph L. Rusk points out correctly that Emerson "never could go more than half way" with the Swedenborgians, [28] a fact which is evident in the lecture he delivered on the religious teacher in 1847 at the Manchester Athenaeum. This address, later published in *Representative Men,* brought to an abrupt end any love that the *Repository* had held for Emerson. The lecturer was wrong, declared the journal, in calling Swedenborg a mystic, in saying that Swedenborg was too narrow in confining the doctrine of correspondences to "the word of God," and in categorizing him as an idealist. [29] In the *Repository* for the same month appeared a letter to the editor that made almost the same points as the article and drew the same conclusions from them. [30]

---

[25] Gilfillan, *Tait's,* n.s. XV, 18; *Macphail's,* XV (Feb. 1848) , 36, 39.
[26] *MR,* n.s. III (Oct. 1841) , 274.   [27] J. B., *IRNJ,* n.s. I (April 1840) , 188–91.
[28] *Life,* p. 204.   [29] *IRNJ,* n.s. VIII (Dec. 1847) , 464, 465, 466.
[30] *Ibid.,* pp. 468–70 *passim.*

Other dissenting sects had even less patience with Emerson than had the Swedenborgians. Convinced that Emerson's theology was "false and flippant," Congregationalists fulminated against the "horrid profanity" resulting from Emerson's belief in a common source of good and evil and his disbelief in divine revelation.[31] Scottish Dissenters also censured Emerson for his heterodoxy. Like the *Eclectic, Tait's* was greatly disturbed by Emerson's optimistic conception of evil, as was even the literary *Spectator.* "Who has anointed his eyes," asked George Gilfillan, so that he can "look complacently" "upon the loathsome shapes of human depravity?" So wary was Gilfillan of Emerson's religious doctrines that he warned the lecturer, who was shortly to speak in Scotland, that his blasphemy would not be tolerated in Auld Caledonia.[32] The same cry of alarm was heard from *Macphail's,* an organ of the Scottish Establishment, which animadverted at length upon Emerson's treating religion as "foolishness" and concluded by calling earnestly on the coming visitor "to turn the whole scrutiny of his genius upon Bible Christianity, and not upon that mock Christianity which is native to, and no higher than, the soul of man." [33]

Even more alarmed than the English and Scottish Dissenters and the Scottish Establishment at Emerson's heresy and its rapid spread was the Establishment in England. One High-Church journal used a review of Emerson's *Poems* to strike both at Gilfillan for his praise of the volume and at the author. After implying that the Scotsman was a detestable freethinker, the critic labeled *Poems* "a directly infidel work" by a man "proudly brooding over mysteries which have already been solved for him." [34] Shortly after Emerson had returned to America, the *English Review,* another organ of the High Church, published "The Emerson Mania," perhaps the most ill-tempered of all the articles appearing on Emerson in the forties. The reviewer called Emerson, among other names, "mighty phrasemonger," "self-idolater," and "narrow-minded fanatic" and declared that his ideas were "treacherous marshlight," "sad twaddle," and "wholesale rub-

---

[31] *BibRev,* I (Feb. 1846), 151; *EcRev,* LXXVI (Dec. 1842), 675, 683, 687.

[32] *Sp,* Aug. 28, 1841, p. 834; Gilfillan, *Tait's,* n.s. XV, 22, 23. Rusk, *Life,* pp. 337–38, gives a good account of the anxiety felt by Scotsmen at Emerson's approach.

[33] XV (Feb. 1848), 34, 42–46 *passim,* 53.   [34] *ChR,* XV (April 1848), 351, 349, 351.

bish." [35] The American was perverting not only the youth of England but adults who should know better. He was, maintained the furious critic, "belauded alike by Tory and Radical organs, by 'Blackwood' and 'the Westminster,' by the friends of order and disorder." Yet these idolaters were not entirely to blame. The "paradox-master," lamented the High-churchman who deplored the wide circulation of Emerson's books, displayed a showy cleverness and external brilliance that were extremely attractive. "Certainly the very dangerous nature of this man's speculations," he warned in conclusion, "are not sufficiently realized, and parents and those in authority are not duly on the watch against them." [36]

Just as the *English Review* had once contended that the Church Establishment would prevent Emerson and his followers from inflicting "serious injury to our national faith," the *Dublin Review* stated that "our faith sets us above his genius." This Catholic journal, as had those of the Protestants, issued a grim warning against "perhaps the most thoroughly *abandonné* writer that ever addressed a great audience": "The atmosphere of his speculation . . . [was] gentle and flower-scented, but a malaria to human life." [37] Several years earlier the literary recluse Smith had put the matter with even more bluntness and in a manner that brought to a focus the whole orthodox view of Emerson's religious doctrines. He asserted that had the American lived in a less tolerant age he would have been burned at the stake. Still, ruefully admitted the writer, Emerson would die a martyr rather than speak less than the truth as he saw it.[38]

Emerson escaped burning, but he suffered from the reviews. He was afraid, for one thing, that the adverse publicity from church journals would scare away his audiences,[39] and as a student and freethinker, George Cupples, reported from Scotland, the lecturer

---

[35] XII (Sept. 1849), 139, 141, 146, 139, 145, 147.   [36] *Ibid.*, pp. 139, 140, 151.

[37] *EngR*, X (Dec. 1848), 379; *DubR*, XXVI, 154, 158, 179.

[38] *Blackwood's*, LXII, 657. Even the liberal Milnes, *LWR*, XXXIII, 200, reproved Emerson's "perilous" religious views. "Take away the control of the conscience and the judgment, or, what is the same thing, override them by an *à priori* conviction of truth, and the Assassins of the East, and the Pazzi of Florence, and the Anabaptists of Munster, and the Fifth-Monarchy men of England, and the Thugs of India . . . are all not only possible but natural."

[39] Rusk, *Life*, p. 333.

displayed considerable tact in avoiding controversial topics.[40] He also suffered from illiberal criticism that found nothing of value in his thought. "If I should believe the Reviews...," he wrote unhappily in his journal while in England, "I have never written anything good." [41] Yet Emerson must have derived some satisfaction from being preached against by the Swedenborgians and the Church of England and from being denounced by newspapers as "a wolf [let] into the English fold." [42] He was, in fact, to declare in 1867 that "the office of America is to liberate, to abolish kingcraft, priest-craft, caste, [and] monopoly." [43] As of 1848 he had perhaps not shaken British foundations, but he had made himself felt, as the dismayed churchmen show. And even though the orthodox condemned him, his message came through to two small but important groups whose names were sometimes associated: the Unitarians and the Secularists.[44]

Smith had alleged in the *Blackwood's* article that Emerson was reputedly a Unitarian but doubted that any Unitarian church would claim him. At the same time, Smith also wrote that Unitarians in America differed more widely from each other and from the standards of orthodoxy than did those in England.[45] The quarrel among American Unitarians, which involved conservatives such as Andrews Norton and Francis Bowen on one side and liberals such as Emerson, Parker, and Alcott on the other, was due to differing concepts of Christ's miracles. Upon this difference, wrote the late Professor Perry Miller, "depended all the other issues between the new school and the old." [46] The conservative Unitarians maintained that a belief in miracles was necessary in order to establish the divine authority of Christ. Wrote Norton: "Nothing is left that can

---

[40] *Jerrold'sS*, VII, 323.

[41] *Journals of Ralph Waldo Emerson*, ed. Edward Waldo Emerson and Waldo Emerson Forbes (Boston, 1909–14), VII, 428 — hereafter cited as *Journals*.

[42] *Letters*, III, 444. *Howitt's*, Dec. 11, 1847, p. 370, also noted Swedenborgian activity against Emerson.

[43] *Journals*, X, 195.

[44] Elie Halévy, *A History of the English People in the Nineteenth Century* (London, 1951), IV, 380, 381, 401; Albert Post, *Popular Freethought in America, 1825–1850* (New York, 1943), p. 197.

[45] LXII, 657.

[46] In *The Transcendentalists*, ed. Miller (Cambridge, Mass., 1950), p. 129.

be called Christianity, if its miraculous character be denied." [47] The new men, on the other hand, argued "that the question of miracles versus nature should never arise because all nature is divine." [48] Emerson summed up the position of the new school in *Nature* (1836) and in "The Divinity School Address," and the arguments were thereafter continued in such works as Alcott's *Orphic Sayings,* Ripley's *Specimens of Foreign Standard Literature,* and Parker's "A Discourse of the Transient and Permanent in Christianity." [49] Norton, the dominant figure in "the theological world of Cambridge," began the counterattack with a letter to the *Boston Daily Advertiser* denouncing the insurgents, several of whom were his former students, and brought the largest guns to bear in "The New School in Literature and Religion," "A Discourse on the Latest Form of Infidelity," and *The Evidence of the Genuineness of the Four Gospels.*[50] Some of the heat generated by the quarrel can be felt in comments made in the British *People's Journal* by the American socialist Parke Godwin. This piece appeared shortly after Emerson began his lecture tour, and from it one can readily place Godwin in the Unitarian controversy. He pointed out that many Americans had underestimated Emerson, whom a few called atheistic, others pantheistic, and all transcendentalist. Rather than taking his ideas seriously, they greeted them with "a kind of moral hoot," and suddenly they found Emerson at "the head of a new and pretty large sect." Godwin warned England not to make this foolish mistake.[51]

The warning fell on deaf ears, so far as English Unitarians were concerned: they regarded Emerson as one of their saints.[52] An article published in the official Unitarian journal, the *Prospective Review,* revealed their veneration and disclosed that English Unitarians were much more liberal than Smith had implied. The author, the Unitarian minister and sometime editor of the *Review* Charles Wicksteed, took mild issue with Emerson's abstract concept of Christ but otherwise praised the American's religious liberalism very highly. Wicksteed declared that he did not condemn others for finding fault with

[47] *Ibid.,* p. 211.   [48] *Ibid.,* p. 220.   [49] *Ibid.,* pp. 107, 192, 303–15, 294–99, 259–83.
[50] *Ibid.,* pp. 159, 158, 193–96, 210–13, 205.
[51] *People's,* Nov. 28 (?) , 1847, p. 306. See Post, p. 185.
[52] Gohdes, *Amer. Lit.,* pp. 146–47.

Emerson's religion, rather he pitied them. "We are sorry," he wrote loftily, "for any human being who has an eye for deformity, who can delve" into a quantity of "grain, and say, that he spies two or three bits of chaff." Every page of the *Second Series* (the volume under review) "has its worth." In conclusion Wicksteed said that America held only two attractions for him—"the Falls of Niagara and Emerson." [53] Emerson was so grateful for this praise that he wrote John Chapman, publisher of the *Review,* a note of appreciation.[54]

Secularists were even more enthusiastic over Emerson's religious ideas than Unitarians: they found no chaff in the grain. Through their official organ the *Reasoner,* edited in its most important years by the professed atheist George Jacob Holyoake, the Secularists extended the hand of fellowship to Emerson on his arrival in England and diligently promoted his ideas (see Chapter IV).

At about the same time that these English freethinkers were proclaiming Emerson nature's priest,[55] Cupples, who, like Chapman, would have eliminated church dogma and tradition while preserving its ethical elements, also defended Emerson's religious views. "If Emerson be not a Christian," asked Cupples begging the question, "what are we?" "Greek though he be, even as Plotinus . . . , Emerson is the *consequence* of Christianity." Cupples wrote that the American did not like to talk about his Christianity, that "he has that love, peculiar to noble spirits, . . . that refrains from its profoundest emotion." Indeed, he was like St. Paul in his stoicism. As for religion, this poet-philosopher was "at one time as much the personal, empirical theist, as at another the percipient of interpenetrating divinity." So strong was his theistical sense that he delighted in giving new names to old divinities, in placing the forms of religion in all possible lights. It was not his fault that formalists could

[53] I, 260, 261, 262. *ProsR* was one of two journals to take note of Emerson's antislavery activity. In I (Feb. 1845), 158–62, it printed an excerpt from Emerson's pamphlet, *An Address . . . on the Anniversary of the Emancipation of the Negro in the West Indies.* The *British and Foreign Anti-slavery Reporter,* Oct. 16, 1844, pp. 197–98, and Oct. 30, 1844, p. 203, also published extracts from the speech. English periodicals were not disposed at this time to make much of Emerson's protests against slavery. In a review of Harriet Martineau's *Society in America,* the *Ath,* May 13, 1837, p. 337, noted the space that Miss Martineau had given to "Dr. Channing's work on Slavery," but the journal did not mention Emerson.

[54] *Letters,* III, 288.   [55] *Reas,* Nov. 24, 1847, p. 639.

not recognize the same spirit in another setting.[56] Cupples' complaint is, of course, that the orthodox refused to follow Emerson's example and to place religion on a philosophical and intellectual foundation rather than on that of blind faith. The orthodox—both Catholic and Protestant—not only rejected vigorously any such basis but declared, as we shall see, that Emerson's erroneous religious doctrine could be traced to his despicable philosophy.

IV

The religious Englishman was not, however, the only one who cried down that philosophy. A nation increasingly under the influence of science and conditioned to empirical, material, and utilitarian doctrines naturally regarded transcendentalism with little favor. Very few British or American critics made any attempt to defend what the *Dublin Review* termed Emerson's "transcendental cant." [57] There were two exceptions. In welcoming him in 1847, the *Critic* declared that "mind, in our generation, has lost . . . its self-reliance, its lofty aspirations"; "enfeebled," it occupies itself with "a material philosophy." The writer did not care, he cried defiantly, if Emerson was "crude, obscure, and visionary" or lost "sight of his land-marks"; we forgive even his "most eccentric dreams . . . for the sake of the [intellectual] agitation they make." Greatly exaggerating, the friendly Jerrold claimed that "the world of readers, wearied with the monotonous cadences" of a "worn-out" empirical school, have "welcomed" transcendentalism.[58]

In the main, however, transcendentalism came in for astringent comment both in the United States and in Great Britain. Convers Francis, John Pierce, Oliver Wendell Holmes, and others in America held transcendentalism to be a synonym for "obscure nonsense," [59] while various British critics described Emerson's philosophy as contradictory, illogical, intuitive, *a priori*, subjective, mystical, and

[56] *Jerrold'sS*, VII, 326, 327.   [57] XXVI, 165.

[58] *Critic*, Dec. 18, 1847, p. 386; *Jerrold'sS*, I (Feb. 1845), 184.

[59] Gohdes, *Periodicals*, pp. 6, 7, 8. *Blackwood's*, LXIV (July 1848), 38, maintained that Emersonians "are laughed at even in Boston."

misty.[60] "The mind which can raise itself to the consideration of abstractions," wrote the *Athenaeum* accusingly, ". . . is very apt to neglect—nay, to deny—the whole universe of realities." The American's "declaration of philosophical ignorance" led to endless speculation and, unforgivably in the eyes of the British, exceeded the boundaries of good taste.[61]

In transcendentalism, according to British critics, could be found the reasons for nearly all of Emerson's erroneous views. Two critics maintained, for instance, that his literary style lacked clarity because his philosophical ideas were vague, and a third observed that Emersonian "hyperbole" was characteristic of Emersonian philosophy.[62] Another equated this philosophy with democracy and implied that both made for political anarchy.[63] Others charged that transcendentalism removed Emerson from the warm world of men into the cold region of ideas. *Macphail's* declared roundly that his "grand and cardinal error [in religion] is an excess of transcendentalism." [64] Although several critics emphasized the practical aspects of Emerson's philosophy, most British and American views were those of the *Examiner:* "Nature meant Mr. Emerson for a straight-forward common-sense man, and he strives . . . to be darkly mystical and preposterously unintelligible." "He thinks nothing of any value in books excepting the transcendental." "We are sorry for it, because if he would make his purpose clearer, and condescend somewhat more

---

[60] *DubR*, XXVI, 158; *Sp*, Aug. 28, 1841, p. 834; *Blackwood's*, LXII, 649; *Ath*, Oct. 23, 1841, p. 804; *Ath*, Dec. 28, 1844, p. 1197; *Blackwood's*, LXII, 650; Goodwyn Barmby, *Howitt's*, Nov. 13, 1847, p. 316. For similar comments, see the *Critic*, Jan. 2, 1847, p. 9; *LWR*, XXXIII, 199; *MR*, n.s. III (Oct. 1841), 276; Gilfillan, *Tait's*, n.s. XV, 20; *Ath*, Feb. 6, 1847, p. 146. The most interesting comment on Emerson's mysticism was made by a critic on the *EdRev*, LXXXIV (July 1846), 208–9, who found parallels between Emerson's comments on miracles in "The Divinity School Address" and "the doctrines of Catholicism; respecting the perpetual supernaturality of the church, the continuance of Divine teaching" (p. 209).

[61] Oct. 23, 1841, p. 803; Dec. 28, 1844, p. 1197; Oct. 23, 1841, p. 803. "'It is in bad taste,' is the most formidable word an Englishman can pronounce," wrote Emerson in the *Journals*, V, 176.

[62] *DubR*, XXVI, 161; *Critic*, Jan. 2, 1847, p. 9; *WR* XLIX (July 1848), 339.

[63] *Blackwood's*, LXII, 644–45.

[64] *People's*, Nov. 28 (?), 1847, p. 306; *Ath*, Oct. 23, 1841, p. 804; *Macphail's*, XV (Feb. 1848), 46.

to the realities of earth, there is no voice in either continent of more musical and manly tone." [65]

The most caustic criticism of Emerson's philosophy centered on the Over-Soul and pantheism. Emerson himself, as Rusk writes, never succeeded in making clear what he meant by the Over-Soul,[66] and therefore this concept was easy to attack and impossible to defend, as Cupples discovered. All that he could say was that Emerson sought "to awake the spark of 'Over-soul' in the popular breast." [67] Churchmen looked askance at such an awakening. They were especially resentful of Emerson's assertion that the Over-Soul was available to all men and that through it man achieved divine status. The Catholic *Dublin Review,* which equated the Over-Soul with "whim," protested that it was "an error in Religion and a blunder in philosophy." [68] The Establishment agreed. According to Emerson, commented the *English Review,* "man himself is God, or at least the purest embodiment of the 'over-soul.' " "Ah, poor Emerson! can *you* believe this sad twaddle?" [69] And the Dissenting *Eclectic* said: Every man "is God, making himself manifest in flesh." "We do not see that it could be far wrong, according to the scheme here laid down, to set up a negro in Maryland or Virginia, and to bow down to the Divinity . . . inasmuch as Sambo is a portion of existence, that is, of God." [70]

British critics were also troubled by Emerson's pantheism. Unfortunately, the essay that would have done much to explain this doctrine was not widely known at the time. Although Emerson denied giving a portrait of himself in "The Transcendentalist," an address delivered in Boston in 1841 and published in the *Dial* in 1843, "his own features were not missing." [71] He was certainly revealing the subjective idealism of his early years [72] when he stated in the address that the idealist's "manner of looking at things transfers every object in nature from an independent and anomalous position" and places

---

[65] *MonM,* n.s. II (Sept. 1839), 351; Gilfillan, *Tait's,* n.s. XV, 21; *Ex,* May 8, 1847, p. 292, and Nov. 30, 1844, p. 757.

[66] *Life,* p. 283.   [67] *Jerrold'sS,* VII, 330.   [68] XXVI, 158, 156.

[69] *EngR,* XII (Sept. 1849), 145.   [70] LXXVI (Dec. 1842), 669.

[71] Rusk, *Life,* p. 287.

[72] Stephen E. Whicher, *Freedom and Fate* (Philadelphia, 1953), p. 141.

it in the "consciousness." [73] Only one or two critics seemed to understand this idealism. It was, wrote Milnes tentatively, "an Idealistic Pantheism," and Smith hesitantly labeled Emerson an idealist, adding that he was "something, too, of a pantheist." [74]

Nearer to the Emersonian concept than either of these gentleman reviewers was Gilfillan, the liberal Presbyterian minister, who cogently argued that "Emerson's object of worship has been by many called nature—it is, in reality, man but man ... exhibited in the reflection of nature." Emerson, Gilfillan continued, "feels that every enigma runs into the great enigma—what is man? and that if he could but unlock his own heart, the key of the universe were found. Perhaps nature, in some benignant ... hour, will tell him where the key was lost!" With good insight but still missing the mark, Gilfillan wrote that to Emerson "creation is a vast symbol of man; that every tree and blade of grass is somehow cognate with his nature. ... It is this which so beautifies nature to his eye." [75] An anonymous critic on *Macphail's* was even more successful than Gilfillan in understanding transcendentalism. Emerson "has been called a Pantheist, worshipping all things as divine, and acknowledging no separate or individual Deity." "Now, Emerson has no such unworthy faith. ... He fills the inanimate world with *man's* soul, but not with God's. The music of nature is from man—not Jehovah." "So far as the inanimate creation is concerned, Emerson is an idealist, but not a Pantheist. ... In Emerson's view, the process of inanimate nature is but the visible outgoing of the human mind. ... The universe is but the 'statue of the intellect.' He represents all the universe, material and spiritual, as *subjective in the human mind.*" [76]

Physical nature was to Emerson, then, a symbol of the mind: the NOT ME. It had no true existence. At the same time, his love of nature

[73] *Works*, I, 331.

[74] *LWR*, XXXIII, 194; *Blackwood's*, LXII, 645, 649, 650, 652, 656.

[75] *Tait's*, n.s. XV, 18, 19.

[76] *Macphail's*, XV (Feb. 1848), 41–42, 46. Without mentioning pantheism, an anonymous critic for the *WR*, XLIX (July 1848), 338, 339, castigated Rufus Griswold for not including philosophy in his *Prose Writers of America* and explained that "in no country where philosophical studies were not somewhat popular ... could such a writer as Mr. Emerson have appeared as the only American philosopher with whose works we are at all familiar." America's widespread interest in idealism is due to the "extreme notions that prevail there concerning personal independence."

was so intense and his evocation of the love so vivid that a reader quickly and easily classifies him as a pantheist. A British critic wrote: "One cannot open" the *First Series* "but he soon finds himself amidst the sweetest fragrance; the finest music of all natural objects —streams, waterfalls, and birds," and another agreed that Emerson's essays "smell of the woods." Only in the nature studies, said a third, can be found a "rational and intelligible" writer.[77] Such studies led the British to conclude—mistakenly but understandably—that Emerson was, in the words of the *Dublin Review,* "a mere Pantheist." [78] Emerson's worship of nature, declared the critics, was the source of many sins, among which were equating nature's energy with God, equating man with God, and attributing to nature all-healing powers.[79] Because of his pantheism, they wrote, he denied free will and confused the individual with the universal.[80] The *English Review* pinpointed irascibly but precisely the general comment on this aspect of Emerson's philosophy: he is speaking "wholesale rubbish" when he says "that God re-appears *with all his parts* in every moss and cobweb." [81]

Cupples loyally defended Emerson's pantheism, but, unhappily, his defense of this was no more effective than was his defense of the Over-Soul. Cupples stated weakly that Emerson could not be called a pantheist because he did not try, as did Hegel or Spinoza, "gravely to propound the doctrine." [82]

V

Throughout this period, Emerson was often linked with other philosophers: his pantheism was like that of Spinoza and Toland, he owed something to Goethe, Fichte, Kant, Carlyle, and Coleridge and much to Rousseau; he borrowed from Schelling and Hegel. In a word, he was the slave not only to his own system but to the system

---

[77] *EcRev,* LXXVI (Dec. 1842) , 685; *DubR,* XXVI, 162; *ChR,* XV (April 1848) , 315.
[78] XXVI, 165.
[79] *EcRev,* LXXVI (Dec. 1842) , 667; *Macphail's,* XV (Feb. 1848) , 42; Gilfillan, *Tait's,* n.s. XV, 19.
[80] *Ath,* Oct. 23, 1841, p. 804; Barmby, *Howitt's,* Nov. 13, 1847, p. 315.
[81] *EngR,* XII (Sept. 1849) , 146, 147.   [82] *Jerrold'sS,* VII, 327.

of others: he had "gone to a feast" of philosophers and "brought away the scraps." [83] Comments on Emerson's lack of originality occurred more frequently during these years than at any other time; critics were determined to nullify his anti-British comments in the "Phi Beta Kappa Oration."

A year after the "Oration" was delivered, the *Monthly Magazine,* "which excited no little attention" among American transcendentalists,[84] reviewed it together with the *Boston Quarterly Review* for October 1838, in which had appeared "The Divinity School Address" and A. Bronson Alcott's *The Doctrine and Discipline of Human Culture.* The anonymous critic, doubtless the editor of the journal, John Heraud, also commented on *Nature* and erroneously assigned it to Alcott. Heraud's purpose in the article was to discuss these works and to propagate transcendentalism, but his chief concern was to see that proper credit for the movement went to the English transcendentalists. "The spirit of Coleridge, Wordsworth, and Thomas Carlyle," he began, "has spread beyond the Atlantic, and we hear the echoes thereof from afar." In *Nature* Heraud found many of these echoes. After quoting the epigraph taken from Plotinus, he then gave excerpts from the text and immediately discovered influences of English transcendental thinking: "Yes—even to this demand the perusal of Coleridge and Wordsworth has excited the American mind: to it, it ["our original relation to the universe"] is a possibility." " 'The Sun,' says Alcott, truly, 'shines today also.' " Heraud next explained Emerson's (Alcott's to him) theory of the composition of the universe and quoted two sentences: " 'The delight that we feel in Nature is not owing to Nature. The delight resides in man, or in the harmony of him and Nature.' We cannot read such passages without recollecting Wordsworth's *Ode on Immortality* and Coleridge's *Ode on Dejection.*" Having established Emerson's debt, the transcendentalist then took up the book chapter by chapter and continued to praise it. Surprisingly, he also had

[83] *EcRev,* LXXVI (Dec. 1842), 667; *IRNJ,* n.s. VIII (Dec. 1847), 455; *BibRev,* I (Feb. 1846), 149; *Tait's,* n.s. VIII (Oct. 1841), 667; *Ath,* Oct. 23, 1841, p. 803; *Ath,* Oct. 23, 1841, pp. 804, 803. (See *Love's Labour's Lost,* V.i.40.) More gently, the *Critic,* Dec. 18, 1847, p. 386, wrote, "He has been an extensive reader, and he gleans largely from the utterances of the loftiest intellects of all ages and countries."

[84] Gohdes, *Periodicals,* p. 92.

something good to say about the "Phi Beta Kappa Oration" and "The Divinity School Address," but in concluding the article he once more pointed out America's intellectual dependence on England. The *Boston Quarterly* had taken issue with transcendentalism, a position not to Heraud's liking. He was highly gratified to find, however, that the Boston critic was forced to use Coleridge's *Aids to Reflection* as the basis for his arguments.[85]

A year after Heraud's long article and two years after the "Phi Beta Kappa Oration," Milnes in the *Westminster* stressed Emerson's debt to European thinkers and entreated Emerson not to try to break cultural and intellectual ties with England: this chain, he asserted, must be "well soldered together." After quoting Emerson's statement that "every man, were life long enough, would write history for himself," Milnes testily made the rejoinder: "Why was not the . . . United States created by the original children of American nature . . . rather than by the alien blood, and vigour, and culture, and religion of that little island of the distant seas?" When Emerson said that America was ready to produce her own philosophers and artists, Milnes hastily pointed out that the country in its present primitive state was too busy with shelter to develop original writers.[86] In making the same point, Gilfillan hedged a bit as he spoke of Emerson the "genuine man," but in the main he found America's cultural dependence upon Britain analogous to "an upstart hanging heavily, yet with an air of insolent carelessness, upon the arm of a superior."[87] Another fault Milnes found in American literature was a paucity of critics. This deficiency, he wrote, made it easy for a writer to plagiarize without (at least for a time) being detected. "Mr. Emerson himself is evidently no exception . . . : much, nay most, of what his countrymen would probably claim exclusively for his own, has been thought of, spoken of, and written of, by Fichte, or Goethe, or Novalis." The American did not confine his borrowing to the Germans; he was also heavily in debt to such Englishmen as Coleridge and Carlyle.[88]

Some critics, on the other hand, found in Emerson great originality. They noted in admiration that his work was "filled with new

[85] *MonM,* n.s. II (Sept. 1839) , 344, 346, 347, 348–51 *passim,* 352.
[86] XXXIII, 201, 195, 196. 187.   [87] *Tait's,* n.s. XV, 17, 21.   [88] *LWR,* XXXIII, 189.

thoughts," praised him for his independent and original mind, and were happily convinced that he called neither Carlyle nor any other man master. With all his faults, wrote Gilfillan, Emerson was "a peculiar and powerful genius." [89] Wicksteed brought to a climax such encomiums: Emerson had "more learning than Hazlitt, more perspicuity than Carlyle, more vigour . . . than Addison, and [he wrote] with as much originality and fascination as any of them." [90] In statements not quite so sweeping two discerning British critics declared that although Emerson was not entirely his own man, he had his own claim to originality. The touchy Milnes wrote that "this voice [that] has come to us over the broad Atlantic" is sufficiently altered by "personality and place to show that the plant is assimilated to climate and soil, although the seed may have been brought from elsewhere." [91] It was *People's*, however, that saw most clearly Emerson's great contribution to world literature. The journal observed astutely: "To the large learning of the European scholar he adds the freedom and independence of the American mind in forming and expressing his opinions." [92]

VI

American mind; freedom; independence; self-reliance. These words indicate the most sensitive area of Emersonian criticism in Great Britain. Many of the early critics, as we have seen, broke with Emerson over religion because (they said) he depended too much on himself and not enough on God; they broke with him over philosophy because (they said) he was too subjective. Because of the transcendental ego, they also rejected his political, economic, and social views. Politically Emerson was an independent; in economics he was a free trader; he was indifferent to organized social reform. His ideal state was one in which final values resided in the individual—not in an aristocracy, the middle class, or a classless

[89] *EcRev*, LXXVI (Dec. 1842), 685; *People's*, Nov. 28 (?), 1847, p. 306; *Blackwood's*, LXII, 644, 647, 648; *Ath*, June 24, 1848, p. 630; *FQR*, XXXII (Jan. 1844), 311; *Tait's*, n.s. VIII (Oct. 1841), 667, 668; Gilfillan, *Tait's*, n.s. XV, 17.

[90] *ProsR*, I, 262   [91] *LWR*, XXXIII, 186.   [92] April 21 (?), 1848, p. 210.

society.[93] Such a show of independence was too much even for Emerson's own countrymen, and American critics deplored his "calm arrogance" and noted that his work revealed too much "pure egotism." [94] English critics linked Emersonian independence with self-conceit, selfishness, and pride.[95] One is not surprised, therefore, that Emerson managed in one way or another to alienate British conservatives, liberals, and radicals. *Blackwood's,* the great Tory journal, castigated his self-reliance as making him "wilful [and] capricious," and the liberal *Westminster* declared that an "indiscriminate self-reliance" would reduce men to the state of animals.[96] The social radicals also opposed self-reliance. Emerson was sympathetic toward labor, encouraged wide suffrage, and advocated more equitable distribution of wealth.[97] All these reforms were promoted by the socialists, but Emerson's means of accomplishing them were not in accord with those of the reformers. Godwin was

[93] *Works,* III, 207, 213, 214, 219, 210; John C. Gerber, "Emerson and the Political Economists," *New England Quarterly,* XXII (Sept. 1949), 336–57, especially 341, 355; *Works,* III, 235; Percy H. Boynton, "Emerson in His Period," *International Journal of Ethics,* XXXIX (Jan. 1929), 187; *Works,* III, 199, 215; A. I. Ladu, "Emerson: Whig or Democrat," *New England Quarterly,* XIII (Sept. 1940), 419–41, especially 423.

[94] Gohdes, *Periodicals,* pp. 123, 75.

[95] *DubR,* XXVI, 166; *EngR,* XII (Sept. 1849), 141.

[96] *Blackwood's,* LXII, 645; *LWR,* XXXIII, 196. An anonymous critic on the *WR,* XLIX (July 1848), 339, 340, was also dubious of Emerson's democratic pretensions. "Mr. Emerson is so great a republican that he would make nature a republican too. He maintains that all men, intellectually and morally, are by nature of equal capacity and altogether alike." "In this doctrine there is no doubt a considerable intermixture of truth.... Still, when all this is allowed for, we cannot but believe that the order of creation, as regards the soul and intellect of man, is an aristocratic order: that, as all the inferior creatures ... occupy a regular ascending scale, so do the natures of men." *MonM,* n.s. II (Sept. 1839), 352, observed deprecatingly that wisdom in a democracy "resides in the multitude, not of councillors, but in the multitude as a multitude," while the *FQR,* XXXII (Jan. 1844), 296, 295, revealed the almost hysterical fear expressed by many of the early Victorians at "the tangled and hideous democracy of America": "The case of America is no longer a safe example of the working of republican institutions, or of the experiment of universal franchise; ... and he who best appreciates the value of true liberty, will be the very last to apprehend the conditions of social anarchy into which America has fallen." America "seems to have literally mistaken outrage and disorder and naked licentiousness for the assertion of personal and political rights."

[97] *Works,* III, 210; Frederic I. Carpenter, "William James and Emerson," *American Literature,* XI (March 1939), 57; Rusk, *Life,* p. 304; Frederic Ives Carpenter, *Emerson Handbook* (New York, 1953), p. 191.

well aware of the chasm when he stated in his rather impudent article that Emerson was intellectually irresponsible and lacking in social awareness. This transcendentalist, asserted Godwin scornfully, offered only "sickly, unreal dreams of escape" with no practical solutions to the problems of life.[98] A more judicious account of Emerson's social apathy was given by the Christian socialist Good-wyn Barmby, who wrote that the main theme of Emerson's teaching was "individual culture—self-improvement. We believe this is the first sign of reform." But, declared Barmby emphatically, individual culture is not good without "social work—societary rectification." "Enter into the sanctum sanctorum of mystic reverie...but do not forget practical policy, and that there are working days in the divine economy." [99]

That critics of such journals as *People's* and *Howitt's* clashed with Emerson over self-reliance was, at least for the period we are studying, more depressing than the adverse criticism of the prestigious journals; for readers of penny magazines were largely responsible for Emerson's first wide recognition in England. This type of journal, which came into prominence with the agitation of 1832, was very popular by the mid-forties. In 1846, for example, twenty-nine cheap weeklies were published in London alone. Many of the readers of these publications doubtless belonged to the four hundred Mechanics Institutes which had been organized to help prepare the intelligent working man for the rapid changes taking place in England. Emerson had made the tour specifically to lecture to these workmen and their lower-middle-class friends, who were also members.[100]

[98] *People's* Nov. 28 (?), 1847, pp. 306, 308.

[99] *Howitt's,* Nov. 13, 1847, p. 315. Several middle-class journals were also interested in Emerson's connection with social reform. The earnest *Ath,* June 24, 1848, p. 630, was pleased that the proceeds from Emerson's lectures at Exeter Hall were "to go in aid of the early-closing movement. This is a movement," wrote the exuberant critic, "peculiarly marked with the character of the times,—one of whose grand distinctions it is to have at length recognized the general and unprerogatived man as something more than a mere machine out of which it is social economy to get all possible working power." *Blackwood's,* LXII, 643, declared that "it is not a great poem that mankind now want or look for; they rather demand a great work...on human society, on the momentous problems which our social progress, as well as our social difficulties, alike give rise to."

[100] L. E. Elliott-Binns, *Religion in the Victorian Era* (London, 1936), pp. 329–30; Henry Richard Tedder, "Periodicals," *Encyclopaedia Britannica,* 11th ed., XXI, 153; Scudder, pp. 53, 75.

It was therefore natural that the first British periodical to show an interest in the lectures was a people's journal. Before Emerson sailed, *Howitt's* had written him for biographical information which he refused to send,[101] but, nothing daunted, the journal brought out an article only two weeks after he had landed. Barmby was deeply impressed with what for lack of a better term one might call "Everyman's Emerson"—the Emerson of inspiration. Leon Howard has written that Emerson's transcendentalism was new, "a transcendentalism with at least one foot on the ground,"[102] or as *Macphail's* expressed it: "He is a transcendentalist distinguished for sound common sense."[103] His transcendentalism reveals, continues Howard, in an inspirational manner "the common thoughts and impulses of ordinary people." Barmby sensed this when he wrote that Emerson taught the practical virtues of temperance and heroism, and a month later *People's Journal* repeated Barmby with "wherever beats a true and brave heart," dedicated to the "faithful discharge of the high duties of love, courage, and uprightness ... there will Emerson find a willing and sympathetic listener."[104] Some three years before these articles appeared, Jerrold had made a like observation in his magazine.[105]

But the penny journals were not the only English periodicals to feel the impact of Emerson's inspiration: Emerson was not a writer, affirmed the middle-class *Monthly Review,* who will allow readers "to yawn over his pages."[106] In reviewing *Essays, First Series,* the middle-class *Spectator* and *Tait's* commented on the inspirational power of Emerson's detached thoughts and excerpted many of them, and in the essays the *Athenaeum* discovered "fine ideas and elevating sentiments."[107] *Macphail's* also quoted at length many passages "of transcendent beauty" to be found in Emerson's works.[108] In a well-turned phrase, the *Examiner* wrote that not hearing Emerson lecture

[101] Rusk, *Life,* p. 325.
[102] "Americanization of the European Heritage," in Denny and Gilman, p. 81.
[103] XV (Feb. 1848), 34.
[104] Barmby, *Howitt's,* Nov. 13, 1847, p. 316; *People's,* April 21 (?), 1848, p. 210.
[105] I (Feb. 1845), 185.   [106] N.s. III (Oct. 1841), 276.
[107] *Sp,* Aug. 28, 1841, p. 834; *Tait's,* n.s. VIII (Oct. 1841), 667–68; *Ath,* Oct. 23, 1841, p. 804.
[108] XV (Feb. 1848), 35, 48–53.

meant losing "an important, informing fact, out of the nineteenth century." [109] The conservative *Blackwood's* itself could not deny Emerson the inspiration of his message. Sounding like its poor relations the penny journals, this venerable war horse prophesied accurately that even though Emerson's works would not be popular a hundred years hence, they would always be read: not for the philosophical or religious ideas that they expressed but "for those genuine confessions of one spirit to another . . . ; for those lofty sentiments to which all hearts respond." [110]

Early enthusiasm for Emerson was a combination of the inspiration of his message and the inspiration of his presence. Several critics pointed out that Emerson was not to be confounded with the loud, blatant, chauvinistic American.[111] Behind the writer and the lecturer, early Victorians found the man for whom Emerson had searched in vain in Goethe.[112] Milnes had felt the weight of Emerson's character when he wrote that "the best security" against the "disastrous effects" of Emerson's precepts is "the tone of his . . . utterances." His "earnest is good earnest"; "he shows no trace in himself of the evils he deprecates in others." [113] The *Monthly Review*, the *Spectator, Tait's*, and the *Examiner* also commented favorably on Emerson's manifest sincerity and earnestness, as did the *Athenaeum*.[114] Even the Swedenborgians, Catholics, Dissenters, and members of the Establishment were impressed with these aspects of Emerson's message.[115] Emerson's popularity during the early years reached its peak while he was in England. Although the acerb *Literary Gazette* sarcastically called Emerson the "American Demosthenes," Jerrold looked at him on the platform and wrote that "there was an eminent *bonhommie*, earnestness, and sincerity which be-

---

[109] June 17, 1848, p. 388.   [110] *Blackwood's*, LXII, 657.

[111] *Macphail's*, XV (Feb. 1848) , 34; *Tait's*, n.s. VIII (Oct. 1841) , 666, 670. The main difference between Emerson and his compatriots seemed to be his solitary habits. For example, *Macphail's*, p. 30, called him "the finest example of literary hermit," while Gilfillan, *Tait's*, n.s. XV, 21, wrote approvingly of Emerson's "real position" as "a recluse" and the *Ath*, Oct. 23, 1841, p. 804, deplored that position.

[112] See *Works*, IV, 284.   [113] *LWR*, XXXIII, 200.

[114] *MR*, n.s. III (Oct. 1841) , 276; *Sp*, Aug. 28, 1841, p. 834; Gilfillan, *Tait's*, n.s. XV, 17; *Ex*, Nov. 30, 1844, p. 757; *Ath*, Feb. 6, 1847, p. 145.

[115] *IRNJ*, n.s. VIII (Dec. 1847) , 459; *DubR*, XXVI, 153, 175; *EcRev*, LXXVI (Dec. 1842) , 676; *Macphail's*, XV (Feb. 1848) , 36.

spoke sympathy and respect—nay, more, secured veneration." [116] The *Critic* saw in the lecturer "a man with a great soul," and *Tait's*, America's "truest and strongest spirit." [117] Declaring that the eminence of Emerson was due to his character, the *Reasoner* recorded that he was "the most 'distinct man' of thought" of his age, while Barmby and Cupples pulled out all stops: Barmby—"I have seen a star in the skies. . . . Like that star is Emerson to me." And Cupples— in his personal character "Emerson is the most mark-worthy, the loftiest and most heroic mere man that ever appeared." [118]

Near the end of Emerson's lecture tour the *Examiner* noted that the "very striking series of lectures" which he had given in the West End of London "attracted numerous audiences, and counted many distinguished people among their listeners." [119] The make-up of Emerson's British lecture audience has always been something of a puzzle to critics,[120] but it is doubtful that he filled the halls with the distinguished. Early in the tour he wrote that he never saw "the proper aristocracy," which was "a stratum of society quite out of sight," [121] and even though he was later to meet members of this

---

[116] *LitG*, June 28, 1845, p. 423; *Jerrold'sW*, June 10, 1848, p. 750. The famous description of Emerson lecturing at the Portman-Square Literary and Scientific Institution, doubtless written by Jerrold, follows: "Precisely at four o'clock the lecturer glided in, and suddenly appeared at the reading desk. Tall, thin—his features aquiline, his eye piercing and fixed; the effect, as he stood quietly before his audience, was at first somewhat startling, and then nobly impressive. Having placed his manuscript on the desk with nervous rapidity, and paused, the lecturer then quickly, and as if it were with a flash of action, turned over the first leaf, whispering at the same time 'Gentlemen, and *ladies.*' The initial sentences were next pronounced in a low tone—a few words at a time, hesitatingly, as if then extemporaneously meditated, and not, as they really were, pre-meditated and fore-written." "Meanwhile the meaning, as it were, was dragged up from under the veil." A critic on *Howitt's*, Dec. 11, 1847, p. 370, was not impressed: "He is thin and spare in figure." "The tones of his voice are nasal and American; but now and then they come out with musical richness and depth." "His delivery is indifferent and careless. . . . What I distasted most was the woodenness of the face."

[117] *Critic*, Dec. 18, 1847, p. 386; Gilfillan, *Tait's*, n.s. XV, 23.

[118] *Reas*, Nov. 24, 1847, p. 639; Barmby, *Howitt's*, Nov. 13, 1847, p. 316; *Jerrold'sS*, VII, 329.

[119] June 24, 1848, p. 405. *Jerrold'sW*, June 10, 1848, p. 750, also commented on the number of distinguished people in Emerson's audiences.

[120] See Gohdes, *Amer. Lit.*, pp. 145, 146, 147; Rusk, *Life*, pp. 343, 344, 352-53, 357; Scudder, p. v.

[121] *Letters*, III, 454.

class, they did not flock to his lectures. In fact, the West End audiences were so skimpy that Emerson had to arrange for another series in order to recoup his financial losses.[122] This time he wisely chose to speak before the unfashionable Metropolitan Early-Closing Association, which was composed mainly of the lower and lower-middle classes. Emerson fondly called this kind of audience *"my public."* [123] "On Friday evening June 30, [1848]," reported the *Reasoner* on the series, "Mr. Emerson gave his last lecture in this country." At the end Monckton Milnes "called on the audience to manifest their gratitude." This was accomplished "by rising *en masse,* hearty cheering and waving of hats, etc." [124] The demonstration was due, no doubt, to the presence of a man of great soul and strong spirit rather than to acceptance of his doctrines.

Emerson had much the same effect upon his own country. When the *Gazette,* the *Repository,* the *Westminster,* and *Jerrold's* maintained that he was widely popular in America, they were doubtless commenting on Emerson the man, and when *Macphail's* and the *Christian Remembrancer* wrote that he was not well appreciated by Americans, the journals were doubtless reporting on the response to his message.[125] Several critics in the United States and a number in Great Britain gave more accurate reports than the foregoing. The gist of these reports is that both in America and in England, Emerson's influence was deep rather than broad. "Nothing would disgust this man more than followers, to have a school," wrote Cupples; "the

---

[122] Rusk, *Life,* pp. 353, 354.

[123] *Ibid.,* p. 354. An example or two will help define further this public: in the beginning of Emerson's tour, observed the *Critic* (Nov. 6, 1847, p. 302) , "the Manchester people are not a little proud that Mr. Emerson has consented to give them the first edition of his 'great thoughts' "; the second lecture filled the auditorium (*ibid.,* Nov. 13, 1847, p. 317) ; and the third was attended "by a very large and respectable audience—probably a thousand people" (*ibid.,* Nov. 27, 1847, p. 348) . Emerson's audience was also composed, suggested *Ex* (June 17, 1848, p. 388) , of "poets, critics, philosophers, historians, scholars, and the other divine paupers of that class."

[124] *Reas,* July 5, 1848, p. 95. Sophia D. Collet signs the article "Panthea" (Conway, p. 324) .

[125] *LitG,* June 28, 1845, p. 423; *IRNJ,* n.s. VIII (Dec. 1847) , 455; *WRFQ,* XLIX (July 1848) , 338; *WRFQ,* XLVII (April 1847) , 250; *Jerrold'sW,* June 10, 1848, p. 750; *Macphail's,* XV (Feb. 1848) , 34; *ChR,* n.s. XV (April 1848) , 352.

whole of men and women can only be Emersonian by being different from him and from each other." [126] In describing these men and women, Brownson asserted that "Emerson's value is to be ascertained only by 'those who would live in the spirit.' " *Tait's, People's,* and the *Dublin Review* also narrowed Emerson's chief impact upon America to "one select and highly intellectual circle," [127] while Gilfillan spoke for England when he accurately observed that Emerson had, in that country, drawn about him a large number of *"exoterick* disciples." [128]

Unlike the general public, who accepted Emerson the man but deplored his doctrines, this coterie revered his person and loudly applauded his message. They were, in England and in America, the radicals, the freethinkers, the intellectuals. Above all they were—as the *Athenaeum,* the *Biblical Review,* the *Eclectic Review,* and the *English Review* attest—the young.[129] Theodore Parker summed up this feeling when he wrote that Emerson's influence on the young was "the greatest ever exerted by any man who wrote in the English language." [130] These "Emersonidae" [131] found in his message not the ravings of a deranged genius but the articulation of their longing to cast off all restrictions—religious, social, and political. They found in Emerson the man, as Cupples wrote, the one "most freely, fully, and longingly open to the Future." [132] Emerson was, in a word, one of them.

Rusk has written that the England of 1847 was "probably" in a more receptive mood" for Emerson's word than ever before.[133] Even so, she still was not ready: except for the young, the word remained largely his. Reformers who should have listened were, during "the hungry forties" as well as during the first four decades of the nineteenth century, interested mainly in such practical matters as better

[126] *Jerrold'sS,* VII, 329.

[127] *Tait's,* n.s. VIII (Oct. 1841) , 667; *People's,* Nov. 28 (?) , 1847, p. 306; *DubR,* XXVI, 154.

[128] Gilfillan, *Tait's,* n.s. XV, 22.

[129] *Ath,* Oct. 23, 1841, p. 804; *BibRev,* I (Feb. 1846) , 151; *EcRev,* LXXVI (Dec. 1842) , 677; *EngR,* XII (Sept. 1849) , 139.

[130] Gohdes, *Periodicals,* p. 189   [131] *Ibid.,* p. 240.   [132] *Jerrold'sS,* VII, 325.

[133] *Life,* p. 329.

wages and housing, poorhouse regulations, public works projects, and the administration of poor relief.[134] They were not concerned with the theoretical democratic principles which underlay nearly all of these reforms. In the fifties and sixties they were to become more aware of such principles, many of which Emerson had been setting forth in his books and lectures.

[134] Janet E. Courtney, *Freethinkers of the Nineteenth Century* (London, 1920), p. 54; Elliott-Binns, p. 138.

❧ II ❧

Among the Philistines

THE treatment of Emerson in British periodicals bears out the statement of Clarence Gohdes that "the reception of American literature among the British during the nineteenth century was conditioned by political and social views." [1] In the 1840's, as has already been indicated, critics judged Emerson's books almost entirely on the propriety of his religious, political, and social doctrines. For the next two decades—those years ruled by the English middle class [2]—his doctrines were also of concern to periodical critics. The later opinions are in one respect much easier to record than the earlier. The bias of each journal in the forties had to be pointed out individually. In the fifties and sixties it is sufficient to know for what class the periodical was written—and most were written for the middle class. Independents like the *Literary Gazette,* the *Saturday Review,* and the *Spectator;* rationalist organs like the *Westminster Review* and *Tait's Magazine;* religious publications like the *Eclectic Review,* the *British Quarterly Review,* and the *Christian Observer;* people's journals like the *Leisure Hour* and *Hogg's Instructor*—all "fingered the pulse," [3] to borrow a phrase, of the great middle class.

[1] *American Literature in Nineteenth-Century England* (New York, 1944), p. 10.
[2] *Social England,* ed. H. D. Traill (London, 1897), VI, 250. See also Canon Charles Smyth, "The Evangelical Discipline," in *Ideas and Beliefs of the Victorians,* foreword by Harman Grisewood (London, 1949), p. 98.
[3] Gohdes, p. 132. For the pervasive influence of the middle class on Mid-Victorian critics, see Walter E. Houghton, *The Victorian Frame of Mind, 1830–1870* (New Haven, 1957), p. 141.

Matthew Arnold, who knew "the back-bone of England," [4] has given the best contemporary account of that class. Arnold divided the English into three classes, two of which—the lower and the upper —he gave relatively little attention. His interest centered in the members of the middle class, "the great representative of trade and Dissent"; these he called Philistines. They were energetic, enterprising, and self-reliant. Their journals tell them "how 'all the world knows that the great middle class of this country supplies the mind, the will, and the power requisite for all the great and good things that have to be done,' and congratulate them on their 'earnest good sense, which . . . gives to conventional illusions their true value.' " Arnold took issue with this self-praise. Philistines were hard and vulgar, they lacked taste, they showed no interest in culture—that relentless "pursuit" of "total perfection by means of getting to know . . . the best which has been thought and said in the world." All their affairs focused on "business, and money-making . . . comfort and tea-meetings." They were the great "enemy of the children of light." [5] Arnold did not stress another, more agreeable quality: here were men who, as Emerson said, stood "firmest" in their "shoes." [6] Granted that they were, as a recent Arnold follower has written, "voluble, smug, . . . suspicious of the arts" and all else which "could reflect no tangible utility," [7] they were also solid, stubborn, and enduring. The children of light had their work cut out for them; in order to withstand the withering attack of this "awesome, uncouth, vociferous public," [8] they had to be even tougher.

Arnold's term for these children was *aliens*. "They have, in general," he wrote, "a rough time of it in their lives; . . . they appear where and when one leasts [*sic*] expects it, they set up a fire which enfilades . . . the class with which they are ranked; and, in general,

[4] *English Prose of the Victorian Era*, ed. Charles F. Harrold and William D. Templeman (New York, 1938), p. lxiii. See also Geoffrey Tillotson, *Criticism and the Nineteenth Century* (London, 1951), p. 62.

[5] Matthew Arnold, *Culture and Anarchy* (New York, 1928), pp. 99, 72, 115, 113, 60, 6, 106, 99.

[6] *The Complete Works of Ralph Waldo Emerson*, ed. Edward Waldo Emerson (Boston, 1903–4), V, 102—hereafter cited as *Works*.

[7] Robert L. Peters in *Victorians on Literature & Art*, ed. Peters (New York, 1961), p. 4.

[8] *Ibid.*, p. 5.

by the extrication of their best self as the self to develop, and by the simplicity of the ends fixed by them as paramount, they hinder the unchecked predominance of that class-life which is the affirmation of our ordinary self, and seasonably disconcert mankind in their worship of machinery." [9] The Emerson of the early addresses, of the *First* and *Second Series,* and of *Poems* can unquestionably be referred to as an *alien:* his aim was steady, he deplored the materialism of his class, he affirmed and reaffirmed the ME over the NOT ME.[10] What Emerson came to be after 1850, however, is another question. If he is still to be classed as an *alien,* certainly his alienation takes a form different from that of the early years. In the words of one of his most ardent disciples, Moncure D. Conway, Emerson "after a full theoretical utterance gradually incline[d] to criticism and the application of abstract principles to men and institutions." After 1848 he came "down from his ivory tower." "Acceptance and success, instead of spurring Emerson on to new achievement, seemed to make him more content, in the latter half of his life, to abandon...[the] lonely tower in order to regain his hold on ... 'humanity.' " [11]

This abandonment made for considerable confusion among Mid-Victorian critics attempting to judge the major works brought out in their time—*Representative Men: Seven Lectures* (1850), *Memoirs of Margaret Fuller Ossoli* (1852), *English Traits* (1856), *The Conduct of Life* (1860), and *May-Day and Other Pieces* (1867). A few of these critics, regardless of the book under review, treated Emerson as if he were writing on the old topics in the old way; others saw in *Traits* and *Conduct* a change in style as well as a reflection of middle-class values and lavishly praised him, while still others treating the same two books found in them no value of any kind. In this chapter will be recorded these differing views as well as contemporary estimates of the change in Emerson himself. The change in attitude toward Emerson of the Mid-Victorian critics will also be documented. Aspects of these changing attitudes, which became in-

[9] Arnold, p. 207.

[10] *Works,* I, 4–5, 19–20, 32, 95, 332–33, 334; II, 274, 296; I, 107, 114, 359; V, 161–65.

[11] [Moncure D. Conway], "Recent Lectures and Writings of Emerson," *Fraser's,* LXXV (May 1867), 587 (*A Bibliography of Ralph Waldo Emerson,* comp. George Willis Cooke [Boston, 1908], p. 249, identifies the anonymous author as Conway); Ralph L. Rusk, *The Life of Ralph Waldo Emerson* (New York, 1949), p. 387.

creasingly apparent as the period progressed, can be found in commentaries on Emerson's philosophy and religion; and since *Representative Men* and the *Memoirs of Margaret Fuller Ossoli* afforded critics opportunities to comment on these two subjects, these books will be used as bench marks during the twenty years under study.

II

In a long article on Emerson in 1862, the *Eclectic Review* maintained that with only *Representative Men* "we might safely predict how . . . [Emerson] would write upon what topics he has written." [12] The point is well taken, for in this book Emerson dealt with several men whose vision was highly transcendental, others whose views were altogether earth-bound. In attempting to understand the baffling dichotomy, critics of the fifties, like those who had struggled with the *First* and *Second Series,* began by looking for the sources from which Emerson had drawn his ideas. His borrowing lighted up "the entire process of his thought and his writing," declared the *Eclectic,* which interposed sarcastically "that the finer the thing he says the surer" his readers may be that "some one has said it before him." [13] According to the critics, these fine things came from, among others, Channing, Coleridge, Sterling, Grotius, Plato, Aristotle, Shakespeare, Milton—and the ever-present Carlyle.[14] Critics quickly pointed out that the *Memoirs of Margaret Fuller Ossoli* resembled Carlyle's *Life of Sterling,*[15] just as they had even more quickly compared *Heroes and Hero Worship* with *Representative Men.*

Although the Secularist Sophia D. Collet favored Emerson's book, a majority of the critics thought that *Heroes* was better. Emerson

---

[12] 8th ser. III (Nov. 1862) , 370.   [13] Pp. 386, 383.

[14] *Ath,* Jan. 19, 1850, p. 69; *BQR,* XI (May 1850) , 304, 306; *LeisH,* Jan. 4, 1855, p. 14. For other comments, pro and con, on Emerson's originality, see *Wes-Meth,* 4th ser. VI (Oct. 1850) , 1078; *Leader,* Sept. 13, 1856, p. 880; *WR,* LXVI (Oct. 1856) , 494; Atticus [William Maccall], *Critic,* Dec. 22, 1860, p. 778; *WR,* LXXV (April 1861) , 588; *EcRev,* 8th ser. III (Nov. 1862) , 385; W. Clark Russell, *BwyA,* Sept. 1867, p. 41; *SatR,* Feb. 23, 1867, p. 247; *LondR,* May 30, 1868, p. 534; *NatM,* I (1857) , 39; *Hogg's,* 3rd ser. IV (Feb. 1855) , 91; *Whit,* Sept. 20, 1851, p. 713; *Sharpe's,* XI (June 1850) , 364.

[15] *Critic,* Feb. 16, 1852, p. 89; *WR,* LVII (April 1852) , 666.

always imitated Carlyle's style, wrote the *Critic,* but in *Representative Men* he went even further: he copied both "his theme and its general treatment" from *Heroes and Hero Worship.* The *Spectator* made the same observation, adding that although hero worship might not be a good thing, at least "Carlyle's heroes were selected with profound judgment or intuitive sagacity. Little of either is exhibited by Mr. Emerson in his 'representative men.' " [16] These comparisons—invidious or otherwise—contributed no more to the understanding of Emerson's volume than did other comments on the author's originality.

Critics who ignored altogether the question of sources also had trouble distinguishing the figure in the carpet. Among them was the distinguished biographer James Anthony Froude. Victorian criticism was generally based upon the belief that works of art were per se didactic. Observed John Morley, one of the foremost periodical editors of the day, literature is "a weapon, an arm, not merely a literary art." [17] Using this criterion, Froude wrote in the *Eclectic Review* that the failure of *Representative Men* lay in its very design: Emerson had tried to teach the young by setting before them men of thought rather than men of action.[18]

Anonymous critics in the *Eclectic* and the *British Quarterly Review* also judged *Representative Men* in terms of a lesson to be learned and declared the lesson to be nonexistent; intended as a restorative for spiritual man, the work was positively unwholesome. Even Miss Collet regretted that Emerson and *Representative Men* so seldom give us "practical inferences," and the *Spectator* wrote the book off as "a series of . . . 'characters.' " [19] A reviewer for *Sharpe's London Journal* came much closer to understanding the work, at least part of it. Emerson's chief message, said the critic, was that "all knowledge and inquiry should minister to the training and development of the individual man." The most virtuous men are those who

[16] Collet, *Reas,* Dec. 25, 1850, p. 230; *Critic,* Feb. 1, 1850, p. 60; *Sp,* Jan. 12, 1850, p. 42. For other comparisons of Carlyle and Emerson and of their books, see pp. 200–202.

[17] L. E. Elliott-Binns, *The Development of English Theology in the Late Nineteenth Century* (London, 1952) , p. 3. See also Richard D. Altick, *The English Common Reader* (Chicago, 1957) , p. 136.

[18] 5th ser. III (May 1852) , 568. Cooke, p. 109, identifies the writer.

[19] *EcRev,* 4th ser. XXVII (Feb. 1850) , 261; *BQR,* XI (May 1850) , 283; Collet, *Reas,* Dec. 25, 1850, p. 232; *Sp,* Jan. 12, 1850, p. 42.

harmonize most closely with "the design of God—the visible manifestation of the sacred laws, which are the vital forces of humanity, and according to which, all life and human action must practically correspond." Napoleon, "an exposition of the whole character and aims of the age in which we live," wrote this shrewd commentator, was an excellent illustration of this doctrine. The critic consequently devoted nearly all of his article to excerpts from the essay.[20]

The most perceptive review of *Representative Men* appeared in the *Athenaeum*. By discarding didacticism, the critic was able to throw considerable light not only upon one or two essays but on the whole book. He also, and more importantly, sensed (without fully understanding) the transitional character of the book. In "Plato," "Swedenborg," and "Goethe," Emerson was as in most of the early essays attempting to interpret life by relating it to the ideal. In "Shakspeare," "Napoleon," and "Montaigne," he was content to chart "the conditions of mortal life."[21] It was this Emerson whom the *Athenaeum's* critic heralded, writing (as did Rusk one hundred years later) that the design of the book was "to expose the course, the varieties, of human life, as exhibited in the world's great men." The subject was, continued the critic, a vast one; thus Emerson narrowed it to "the greatest elements of man, of society, of civilization."[22] These elements—"Philosophy, Mysticism, Doubt, Poetry, Action, Culture"—were inadequate,[23] for they left out faith, love, and religion. Countries, too, were poorly represented. The best essays, maintained this critic as well as others,[24] were "Shakspeare," "Napoleon," "Goethe," and "Montaigne." With these, commented the reviewer, "we are more at home." The worst essays were "The Uses of Great Men," "Plato," and "Swedenborg," all of which "have the appropriate quality of being unintelligible."[25]

[20] XI (June 1850) , 365.

[21] Stephen E. Whicher, *Freedom and Fate* (Philadelphia, 1953) , p. 154, commenting on the later works.

[22] Rusk, *Life*, p. 374; *Ath*, Jan. 19, 1850, p. 68.

[23] [George Gilfillan], *Pm*, I (July 1850) , 46, made a like observation. Cooke, p. 109, identifies Gilfillan.

[24] Collet, *Reas*, Dec. 25, 1850, p. 230; *Critic*, Feb. 1, 1850, p. 60; *Ex*, March 23, 1850, p. 181.

[25] *Ath*, Jan. 19, 1850, p. 68.

Emerson's early style came in for much abuse, but several critics had indicated that, if given a chance, the Emersonian manner grew upon the reader. A few Mid-Victorian critics agreed. In *Representative Men,* they said, Emerson had shown himself to be "a master of language" and his style to be "rugged, isolated, forceful." [26] Others, however, were as derogatory as the *Athenaeum.* In the book they found *"bad-english"* and a "tedious" style.[27] The *Memoirs* of Miss Fuller, they wrote, was "extravagantly worded," disorganized, "abortive." [28] It was not until the publication of *English Traits* that a majority of the Victorian critics found Emerson's style acceptable. This book was stylistically a "pleasure," "every where readable," and more mellow "in style" than the earlier works. These favorable opinions were well summarized by the *Leader:* Those "who object strongly to much both of manner and matter in his former works will find nothing obscure or fantastical in *English Traits."* [29] Much of the obscurity in the former works was due, maintained the critics, to Emerson's transcendentalism. Because of his "cold and cloudy philosophy," his style was marred by "preposterous paradoxes," "contradictory propositions ... , cloudy expressions, disjointed and disconnected sentences." [30]

III

From the beginning Victorian critics had given Emerson low marks on his philosophy, and in the fifties and sixties these marks grew worse. The intellectual climate of the time was directly counter to transcendentalism, perfectly attuned to pragmatism. Commenting on Emerson's loss of prestige in Great Britain, the *New Quarterly*

[26] *Westminster and Foreign Quarterly Review,* LIII (April 1850) , 280; *Ex,* March 23, 1850, p. 181; *LeisH,* Jan. 4, 1855, p. 14.

[27] *Whit,* Sept. 20, 1851, p. 713; *BQR,* XI (May 1850) , 308.

[28] *Chambers's,* May 22, 1852, p. 322; *ProsR,* VIII (May 1852) , 199; *WR,* LVII (April 1852) , 666; *EcRev,* 5th ser. III (June 1852) , 680.

[29] *BritC,* III (June[?]1857) , 279; *WR,* LXVI (Oct. 1856) , 497; *NatRev,* III (Oct. 1856) , 496; *Sp,* Sept. 13, 1856, p. 981; *Leader,* Sept. 13, 1856, p. 880.

[30] *ScR,* V (Jan. 1857) , 17; Atticus [William Maccall], *Critic,* Oct. 9, 1858, p. 653; *ChO,* n.s. no. 149 (May 1850) , 356.

Review asserted that he and his kind had "fallen upon an ungrateful age and a practical time," while the *Athenaeum* in commenting on Emerson's essay "Wealth" wrote, "It is enough to put a practical man beside his patience to see the . . . utterly impractical manner in which Mr. Emerson handles this subject." "To the practical, in these days," proclaimed the *Critic* in 1851, "every man must come at last, however fond of speculation." [31] The rationalist *Westminster Review* characterized the age in which these practical men lived. When Emerson complained that the English do not generalize, the *Review* answered:

The English mind did not, as Mr. Emerson seems to think, degenerate when it embraced the system of Locke; it merely followed the inevitable road on which it had entered. We cannot in these days think grandly, because we wish, above all things, to think clearly. . . . Our anxiety to have practical demonstrable truths at least keeps us from a hundred delusions which, wearing the mask of sublimity, are infinitely more corrupting in their hollowness and imbecility, than a lifelong study of Paley and Bentham. We can, at any rate, say that the English do not cast away their time on vague spiritual analogies, schemes of grandiloquent transcendentalism, and the inanities of spirit-rapping. [32]

A multitude concurred with the *Review;* they termed Emerson's philosophy an "airy nothing," "philosophic moonshine," "moonbeams," "mystical," "mangled platonism," the "old Pantheism," a "system of man-worship," a "system of negations," "the unintelligible mistaken for the profound," and "egregious nonsense." [33] Not all the Mid-Victorian critics, however, were so presumptuous as these, and several attempted to explain transcendentalism rather than use it as an exercise in verbal ingenuity. Conway correctly saw

[31] *NQR,* V (1856) , 450; *Ath,* Dec. 15, 1860, p. 826; Lucian Paul, *Critic,* Aug. 1, 1851, p. 348.

[32] *WR,* LXVI (Oct. 1856) , 514. For other comments on this important aspect of Mid-Victorianism, see [Charles Kingsley], *SatR,* Oct. 4, 1856, p. 510 (M. M. Bevington, *SatR* [New York, 1941], p. 271, identifies Kingsley as the writer) ; *EcRev,* 8th ser. III (Nov. 1862) , 390.

[33] *LeisH,* Jan. 4, 1855, p. 15; *Hogg's,* 3rd ser. IV (Feb. 1855) , 91; *ChO,* n.s. no. 149 (May 1850) , 356; *DubUM,* L (Aug. 1857) , 226; *Critic,* Feb. 1, 1850, p. 60; [George Gilfillan], *Critic,* July 15, 1851, p. 327; *BQR,* XI (May 1850) , 314; *JSL,* VI (Jan. 1858) , 307; *Hogg's,* 3rd ser. IV (Feb. 1855) , 91; *Critic,* Feb. 1, 1850, p. 60; *Critic,* July, 15, 1851, p. 328.

that Emerson was an idealist, as did a sharp anonymous reviewer.[34] They were successful in understanding Emerson's philosophy partly because they knew something of its history, much of their knowledge coming from a book which received very poor notices in England [35] and several rather good ones in America: [36] the *Memoirs of Margaret Fuller Ossoli.*

Before the appearance of this work, on which Emerson, William H. Channing, James F. Clarke, and (for a short time) Samuel Ward collaborated, few Englishmen were aware of the American Transcendental Movement. They had not seen the transcendental journals, and not many of them had read Emerson's "The Transcendentalist" or Alcott's *Orphic Sayings,* any of which would have given them valuable insights into the New School. The *Memoirs* helped fill the void. For the first time, British critics became fully aware that Emerson and the figures around him were not isolated but part of a movement, and they attempted, with varying degrees of success, to record its history and evaluate its importance. Reviewing the *Memoirs,* the *Critic* wrote that a year earlier it had "probably communicated to our readers their first distinct and correct impression of that rather curious phenomenon," New England transcendentalism. Owing to the dearth of information on the subject, this account was brief; therefore, "with unsated curiosity ... we took up these Memoirs of Miss FULLER." Using the book, the reviewer gave details of the movement: its dawn in 1839, the European influences, the publication of the *Dial,* the Brook Farm experiment, the meetings held by the odd members.[37] This article by no means settled the matter, and for ten or twelve years thereafter critics wrangled over the history of the movement as well as its importance.

Transcendentalism, one can piece together from their comments, had come to America from England: with James Marsh's introduction of Coleridge's *The Friend* and *Aids to Reflection* to the United States in 1835–36, the empiricism of John Locke faded, and German philosophy became the rage. Emerson, Ripley, Brownson, and

[34] Conway, *Fraser's,* LXXVIII (July 1868), 6; *BQR,* XI (May 1850), 311.

[35] *ProsR,* VIII (May 1852), 199; *GentM,* n.s. XXXVII (May 1852), 454; *EcRev,* 5th ser. III (June 1852), 679; *Chambers's,* May 22, 1852, p. 322; *Critic,* Feb. 16, 1852, pp. 89–90.

[36] Rusk, *Life,* p. 379.   [37] *Critic,* Feb. 16, 1852, p. 89.

Parker were especially smitten.[38] Such diverse thinkers could be included in one group because transcendentalism "seems to have been a movement on the part of different minds, as spontaneous and independent in each as it was simultaneous in all." [39] Making use of George William Curtis' sketch, Conway gave an account of a meeting of this group. The Monday Club was "a congress of oracles," each self-consciously attempting to "say the finest thing that has ever been said." [40] Another critic repeated Hawthorne's description of the transcendentalists' followers as "hobgoblins." One of the most ludicrous aspects of the transcendentalists, according to the British, was their conversation. After quoting a few of Margaret Fuller's ethereal comments, the *Saturday Review* barked: "Ridicule would have no function in the world if it might not laugh down such nonsense as this." "How any of the set of people managed to live, and eat bread and meat every day, is surprising." [41]

British critics disagreed concerning leadership of the movement. The *Saturday Review* voted on one occasion for Emerson and on another for Miss Fuller. In one article the *Critic* called Emerson the leader but later divided the honors between them, as did Conway, who said that she was "the blood," he "the brain." [42] Whatever the final verdict,[43] both received the dubious honor of appearing as characters in several books of the time. Miss Fuller was identified as a thinly disguised Miranda in "A Fable for Critics" and as Zenobia in *The Blithedale Romance;* [44] Emerson was barely disguised at all as the egregious philosophers Plotinus Plinlimmon and Mark Win-

---

[38] *BFER*, VI (Oct. 1857), 889, 890. Marsh edited *The Friend* in 1831 and *Aids to Reflection* in 1829. For other speculation as to the beginning of the Transcendentalist Movement, see [Moncure D. Conway], *Fraser's*, LXX (Aug. 1864), 247 (Cooke, p. 587, identifies the writer); *WR*, LVII (Jan. 1852), 291, 292.

[39] *WR*, LVII (April 1852), 665.

[40] *Fraser's*, LXX, 250. See George William Curtis, "Ralph W. Emerson," in *Little Journeys to the Homes of American Authors* (New York, 1896), pp. 5–41, esp. 34–36.

[41] Paul, *Critic*, Aug. 1, 1851, p. 347; *SatR*, Aug. 13, 1864, p. 206.

[42] *SatR*, Aug. 13, 1864 p. 205; *SatR*, Dec. 25, 1869, p. 838; Paul, *Critic*, Aug. 1, 1851, p. 348; *Critic*, Feb. 16, 1852, p. 89; *Fraser's*, LXX, 249.

[43] Clarence Gohdes, *The Periodicals of American Transcendentalism* (Durham, N.C., 1931), p. 204, and O. B. Frothingham, *Transcendentalism in New England* (New York, 1959), p. 285, contend that Miss Fuller was not a transcendentalist at all, a view tentatively set forth by *WR*, LVII (April 1852), 665.

[44] *SatR*, Dec. 25, 1869, 838; *Fraser's*, LXX, 251.

some in Melville's *Pierre* and *The Confidence Man,* and as Mr. Windrush in Charles Kingsley's *Alton Locke* and "Phaethon; or, Loose Thoughts for Loose Thinkers," which was reviewed in the *Christian Observer.* The critic praised fully Kingsley's satirical portrait of the American philosopher who hated Catholic creeds, loved "our glorious nineteenth century," and talked of God in terms of "space, time, passibility, motion; setting forth phrenology and mesmerism as the great organs of education, . . . whenever he talked of nature, he showed the most credulous craving after everything which we, the countrymen of Bacon, have been taught to consider unscientific." [45]

The British also had difficulty in estimating the importance of the Transcendental Movement. One of them applauded it as "the first great protest, made in the breast of a society like the mass of middle-class English society, against the spirit and teaching of that society." "If any one is inclined to cast stones" at the transcendentalists, "let him first remember what is the nature of that spirit of commercial Puritanism against which they entered a protest that was honest, and not ineffectual." [46] The *Critic* was so inclined. It maintained that transcendentalism, which the *Saturday Review* called "one of the noisiest and least popular 'mutual admiration societies' that even America has known," could not "be ranked among the great Isms of human history." It had not, "like Mahometanism, conquered and converted mighty kingdoms" or, "like Methodism, embodied itself in a flourishing and populous organization; . . . for aught we know, it may be now reduced to a 'minority of one!' " A year later this journal tempered its comments. Transcendentalism, it reported, seemed to be dying out or at least taking a different tack from the old mystical philosophy. Margaret Fuller was dead, Parker was more practical, and the Peabodys, the Channings, and Thoreau were almost silent.[47] The *Gentleman's Magazine,* using Emerson as authority, declared that the movement had reached its height as early as 1839, but as late as 1867 the *London Review* wrote that Emerson's "transcendental Utopia [was] bourgeoning forth all around him." Conway, the chief periodical historian of transcendentalism, insisted

---

[45] *ChO*, n.s. no. 182 (Feb. 1853) , 92, 93.   [46] *SatR*, Aug. 13, 1864, pp. 205–6.
[47] *SatR*, Dec. 25, 1869, p. 838; *Critic*, Feb. 16, 1852, p. 89; *Critic*, July 15, 1853, p. 379.

that "when Margaret left, it broke to pieces like a cosmical ring." Some went to "Brook Farm, others to form religious societies, others to become anti-slavery leaders." [48]

Emerson, Conway leads us to believe, was one of these leaders. For a number of years Emerson had shown definite antislavery proclivities, but during the fifties he became somewhat doctrinaire and, most surprising, rather peevish. Because *Blackwood's* and the *Saturday Review* refused to take a definite stand for the Union, he crabbedly referred to them as "the tin horns . . . of the varlets of the hour." [49] Mid-Victorians, except for a few radicals like Conway and Miss Collet, made little of Emerson's abolitionism. In the 1840's several radical journals had extracted parts of Emerson's address on the emancipation of Negroes in the British West Indies, and in 1854 the *Reasoner* praised a speech which he gave against the Nebraska Bill. In 1856 the *Saturday Review, Leader,* and *Anti-Slavery Advocate* commended one which he made against Preston Brooks's caning of Charles Sumner, and in 1867 the *London Review* commented favorably on the number of lectures he had delivered against slavery. [50] Conway dated America's wide interest in Emerson from the time of his speech against Webster's Compromise [51] and implied that the Emancipation Proclamation had its genesis in Emerson's lecture "American Civilisation," given before Congress in 1862. [52] Conway exaggerated Emerson's importance to abolition, [53] but he was correct

---

[48] *GentM,* n.s. XXXVII (May 1852) , 457; *LondR,* Aug. 24, 1867, p. 205; *Fraser's,* LXX, 249. Gohdes, *Periodicals,* pp. 196–209, esp. 196, 198, gives a good account of Conway's place in the Transcendentalist Movement. See *The Transcendentalists,* ed. Perry Miller (Cambridge, Mass., 1950) , pp. 13–14, on why the movement broke up.

[49] Philip L. Nicoloff, *Emerson on Race and History* (New York, 1961) , p. 204.

[50] Collet, *Reas,* May 28, 1854, p. 363; *SatR,* Oct. 4, 1856, p. 510; *Leader,* June 28, 1856, p. 605; *Anti-Slavery Advocate,* July 1, 1856, p. 357; *LondR,* Aug. 24, 1867, p. 206.

[51] *Fraser's,* LXX, 258. Perhaps the main reason for Emerson's popularity in America was his successful English tour: "Until the time of the Civil War," writes Gohdes, *Amer. Lit.,* p. 142, "there was a strong tendency in the United States to accord its authors an importance only as the British critics and readers seemed to indicate."

[52] *Fraser's,* LXXV, 593.

[53] Conway, in *Autobiography, Memories, and Experiences* (Boston, 1904) , I, 408, writes, "To the English people the two striking [antislavery] figures in the North were . . . Garrison . . . and Phillips." See Rusk, *Life,* pp. 413–18, esp. 413, and Nicoloff, pp. 120–25, esp. 121–22, for suggestions that Emerson's seeming humanitarianism was ambiguous, his private attitude being one of "philosophical resignation," his public

in considering the Transcendental Movement an important part of the intellectual history of the United States. He was also correct in suggesting, as Miller does, that the movement had lost its major impetus by the early fifties.[54]

The more the British understood Emerson's philosophy, the more they blamed it for his many shortcomings. His "chilled and frost-bit" mind, his "cold and heartless logic," [55] not only helped to spoil his early style but also partly nullified his efforts as lecturer and teacher. Whatever the British Philistine's actual practice, he professed a belief in a warm, openhearted, emotional approach to all human relationships.[56] His image of perfection was Prince Albert, paterfamilias, surrounded by the adoring Queen and their respectful children.[57] Members of lodges, Sunday schools, churches, sewing circles, and literary clubs met together as hearty, friendly neighbors from down the street. In Emerson, wrote his first biographer, George Searle Phillips, they looked for a man much like themselves: one "of your hale fellows, well-met" who could "fall in with their humour of good fellowship." [58] And they showed their disappointment at not finding this fellow. One reason for Emerson's failure as lecturer, they contended, was his cold and severe demeanor.[59] He failed—and for the same reason—as a teacher and as a man. "Love and pity," said the *Athenaeum,* "A Mirror of Victorian Culture," "Love and pity are the first qualities a man needs who sets up for a teacher," [60] and Emerson lacked both. "His eye has a frosty glitter, like that of a cold-bit basilisk. His manner in private is chilly and reserved." [61] David

---

attitude perhaps reflecting the hysteria of the time. As for the British, the upper class defended the South, the radicals and the middle class, the North (Asa Briggs, *Victorian People* [Chicago, 1955], pp. 223–25). The country was, Clough wrote Emerson (Rusk, *Life*, p. 412), " 'brutally ignorant & unfeeling' about the ... war," an opinion substantiated by the small number of Emerson critics who mentioned it: *LondR,* Aug. 24, 1867, p. 206; *SatR,* Feb. 23, 1867, p. 247; E[dward] D[icey], *MM,* VI (Aug. 1862), 297.

[54] Miller, pp. 12, 13. Gohdes, *Periodicals,* pp. 196, 208, sets the decline several years later.

[55] *ScR,* V (Jan. 1857), 17; *BQR,* XI (May 1850), 310.

[56] Houghton, pp. 273–81 *passim.*

[57] Briggs, p. 20; Peters, pp. 4, 5. See also Smyth, in *Ideas and Beliefs,* p. 103.

[58] January Searle, *Reas,* Aug. 6, 1851, p. 175. *Modern English Biography,* ed. Frederick Boase (Truro, 1892), II, 1505, identifies "Searle" as George Searle Phillips.

[59] *Critic,* July 15, 1851, p. 326.   [60] *Ath,* Dec. 15, 1860, p. 825.

[61] *ScR,* V (Jan. 1857), 18.

Scott, who painted Emerson, congealed at the sight of his subject,[62] as did a number of Americans.[63] Emerson, protested several Englishmen, was devoid of heart, and another wrote that he was "a wonderful impersonal being ... [whose words] seem like the floating of an impersonal, inobjective intelligence." [64] The words fell "like a cold, drizzling rain"; they filled "the ear, but not the heart." [65] This insensible writer even scorned the sick: "As to asking or expecting sympathy, that is too contemptible" for Emerson. Rather let mankind "slink out of human sight and die, and at least do their duty as —guano." [66]

Emerson's philosophy was also blamed, as it had been earlier, for his erroneous religious views. The American, reasoned the Nonconformist *Eclectic*, was a follower of Plato rather than of Christ and like his master was "all things to all men." Nowhere did his discipleship "betray him into greater confusion ... than in his Yeas and Nays on theism and pantheism." "Orthodox, advanced and conservative, deist and positivist, mystic and Philistine, ... all find in him some relation of truth." So variable was his position that we can hardly call him "an acosmist, a theist, or a genuine pantheist." The critic could and did call Emerson a worshiper of man.[67] Even though his argument is long and tedious and the conclusion a familiar one,[68] this writer attempted to treat Emerson's religion on an intellectual plane. The *Eclectic* was one of the few Dissenting journals to do so. "Narrowness, onesidedness, and incompleteness," wrote Arnold, are the traits from which Nonconformists suffer the most; they abound

---

[62] *Critic*, July 15, 1851, p. 327. For more on the Emerson-Scott relationship, see *Fraser's*, LXXV, 586; *Critic*, Aug. 15, 1851, p. 393; Townsend Scudder, *The Lonely Wayfaring Man* (London, 1936) , p. 125.

[63] Gohdes, *Periodicals*, p. 202.

[64] Maccall, *Critic*, Dec. 22, 1860, p. 779; *Ath*, Dec. 15, 1860, p. 826; *EcRev*, 8th ser. XIV (March 1868) , 247.

[65] *Ath*, Dec. 15, 1860, p. 824; Maccall, *Critic*, Oct. 9, 1858, p. 653.

[66] *Ath*, Dec. 15, 1860, p. 825. For other comments on Emerson's coldness, see *LQR*, VII (Jan. 1857) , 382; *Hogg's*, 3rd ser. IV (Feb. 1855) , 91; *Pm*, I, 45.

[67] *EcRev*, 8th ser. III (Nov. 1862) , 371, 373, 375, 376. For other comments on Emerson's philosophy as a source of his errors in religion, see *BQR*, XI (May 1850) , 308; *LitG*, Jan. 26, 1850, p. 61; *ChO*, n.s. no. 149 (May 1850) , 356; *JSL*, VI (Jan. 1858) , 307.

[68] *BQR*, XI (May 1850) , 314; *LeisH*, Jan. 4, 1855, p. 15; *Critic*, July 15, 1851, p. 327; *JSL*, VI (Jan. 1858) , 307.

"in what we call *provinciality*." [69] Certainly the Dissenting reviews of Emerson during the fifties and sixties bear out this assertion: their perfervid comments add a special tone to British strictures against Emerson's religious views.

IV

From the outset, wrote a knowledgeable reviewer, "Emerson has been undeservedly misjudged" by those making a rapid and shallow synthesis of his religious beliefs. Writers of theological tendencies "are more concerned to find out what is his real creed before they allow him the possession or perception of any truth whatever." [70] Shoals of these writers during the fifties and sixties published their articles in Dissenting journals, which were "a kind of common denominator of the general reading public." [71] Reviewing *Representative Men* in one of them, Froude asserted that "we have cast out the catholic devil" and suggested morosely that the real enemy of Dissenters was not the Roman church but the Establishment. He should have specified the High Church, for the Evangelicals, who had reached their maturity by 1850, were very close in tone and dogma to many of the Dissenting sects, which, in the second quarter of the century, were establishing their claims to equality with the Establishment. [72] The Mid-Victorian "found himself at every turn controlled, and animated, by the imponderable pressure of the Evangelical discipline and the almost universal faith in progress." Both Dissenters and Evangelicals believed in the verbal inspiration of the Bible and were opposed to the historical study of it. Their ministers preached long, diffuse sermons—"spontaneous utterance[s] of the heart."

[69] Arnold, p. 10.   [70] *EcRev,* 8th ser. III (Nov. 1862) , 367, 368.

[71] Francis E. Mineka, *The Dissidence of Dissent: The Monthly Repository* (Chapel Hill, N.C., 1944) , p. 28.

[72] *EcRev,* 5th ser. III, 572, 574, 582; Elie Halévy, *A History of the English People in the Nineteenth Century* (London, 1951) , IV, 346. See also Houghton, pp. 171–72; Mineka, p. 54; G. M. Young, *Victorian England; Portrait of an Age* (New York, 1954) , p. 101; Halévy, IV, 391–92, 418, 419; Humphry House, "Qualities of George Eliot's Unbelief," in *Ideas and Beliefs,* p. 158.

A favorite text of these ministers, "Depart from me, ye cursed, into everlasting fire, prepared for the devil and his angels," [73] could have been on the minds of several churchmen reviewing *Representative Men*. Emerson was, they fumed, an "unhesitating infidel" obviously suffering from "an unsettled mind." His books were "rank poison" and should be burned. "Does he never ask himself what, on a dying bed, he shall wish to have written?" His attempt to equate Buddhism, Mohammedanism, and Judaism was a "monstrous . . . misrepresentation," declared the Methodist *British Quarterly Review*, which concluded its sermonizing review with the earnest plea:

Finally, we have asked our *heart*, and request each reader to ask his own heart, whether the old Pantheism, which is thus nibbling at the true, the beautiful, and the right, as entertained by Christians, has any power to allay the surges of passion, . . . any consolation to our wearied nature, bowed down by sorrow or remembered sin in the cold passage from life—all its skies and landscapes, its warm homes and loves, its smiles and tears. . . . Am I but the vibration of a chord—a bubble—a passing cloud? And is this soul . . . no more than . . . a particle of the great mass . . . ? Then let us tear out our heart-strings; . . . let us . . . harden our nature against the wail of humanity . . . ; for all these things are vanity and vexation . . . ! Such is the gospel for which we are asked to give up our ancient faith and hope!

No! . . . There is a deeper philosophy than this . . . ; and our readers need not now be told where . . . [it is] to be found.[74]

Unlike the majority of Americans who by the sixties had "decided to forget" Emerson's "heresies," [75] the English Philistines were not so compassionate. Such shrill notes as the foregoing, so typical of evangelical Christianity, were not confined to the "widely circulated" [76] British church journals. In the highly charged language of the spiritually intoxicated, the *Palladium,* a secular journal that rejoiced in its "entire freedom from party or sectarian influence," [77] directed the

[73] Young, p. 12; Halévy, IV, 349, 350; Houghton, pp. 63, 62.

[74] *ChO,* n.s. no. 149 (May 1850), 356; *BQR,* XI (May 1850), 314–15. For another evangelical treatment see *Wes-Meth,* 4th ser. VI (Oct. 1850), 1078 *n.*

[75] Rusk, *Life,* p. 434.   [76] Mineka, p. 27.

[77] Letter to the author from Mr. Michael L. Turner, Assistant to The Keeper of Printed Books, Department of Printed Books, Bodleian Library, Oxford, June 26, 1962.

English to the "deeper philosophy" mentioned by the Methodist *Review:*

Throughout ... [*Representative Men*], Emerson dwells not with sufficient explicitness or expansion upon the grand distinctions of morality, and on the beauties of disinterested love, although he does vaguely refer to the supremacy of the moral sentiment.... He is ... only a "voice," musical, melancholy, sincere, but bodiless, airy, and leading us farther and farther into the wildnerness, and the silence succeeding it seems that of despair.... Above all, [*Representative Men*] ... discovers, we fear, a more deeply-rooted aversion to Christianity; ... although we cannot and dare not denounce its tone as "worldly, sensual, devilish," yet it is not that of a humble and happy disciple of Jesus Christ, who expects from him, and him alone, the complete solution of the great enigma of the world and of man.[78]

Zealously the *Literary Gazette* began a review of Emerson's works: "We have delivered our opinion of Mr. Emerson on larger occasions, and shall leave him 'in little' to the world's taste and judgment. To truth he is mystical—to religion dangerous." He "sets up a bewildered and bewildering Imagination, in enthusiastic tropes and affectations, to be the God for human guidance. When we worship Will-o'-the-wisps, such should be our priests." [79] One expects the congenitally hostile church organs and the soured *Literary Gazette* to inveigh against Emerson's religion; to find the people's journals joining the hue and cry is disappointing.

In the forties a number of cheap periodicals had loyally championed Emerson. They were brought out by William and Mary Howitt, Douglas Jerrold, and other men and women of fine minds and serious intentions, but with the Chartist failure of 1848 these publications went into a rapid decline. Taking their place was a flood of watered-down, popularized journals, many of which were biased in favor of evangelical doctrine. A good illustration is the *Leisure Hour,* purportedly "A Family Journal of Instruction and Recreation" but actually another of the many propagandist organs of the Religious Tract Society. It denounced Emerson's "miserable delusion" that God was everywhere and nowhere. "These dogmas are," concluded the critic with scriptural heat, ". . . sifted into the

[78] *Pm,* I, 53, 54, 55.   [79] *LitG,* Jan. 26, 1850, p. 61.

minds of the young especially." "Pleasing to the natural heart, attractive to those who are naturally of a dreamy, speculative turn, . . . they work their way amongst us, secretly, insidiously." Continuing, he asked whether "all the avenues of popular influence ought not to be much more carefully guarded than they are; whether the teachers of truth are doing all their duty, in guarding their charge from the subtle approaches of such error?" *Hogg's Weekly Instructor* was another of the people's journals which, "though not strictly religious," originated "in religious feelings and motives." Its fulminations against Emerson exemplify that "zeal without knowledge" scorned by Arnold. To the *Instructor* the American was

"Mowis, the bridegroom of snow," who dissolves and melts away in the sunshine. You follow him for a time, as the fair Lilinau, described by the Indian Woman in "Evangeline," followed her phantom-lover into the deep pine-forest in the hush of twilight, but you soon weary of the way, and retrace your footsteps, and thus escape the fate of the hapless maiden, who "never more returned, nor was seen again by her people." In reading Emerson, at first one is inclined to feel that where there is so much . . . apparent earnestness, there must be something positive. . . . But the beauty . . . is only a mirage—dream light shimmering over a place of graves; and the subtlety is that of a serpent winding on into deeper labyrinths of gloom.[80]

In this culture where "Christian values were the central values of society and all deep individual problems were related to Christian morals," [81] such warnings against a writer like Emerson can appear almost anywhere. "Beware of the Flatterer," warned the literary *Critic.* His system "has shaken belief, has injured morality, has poisoned the purest natures, . . . has all but maddened the strongest minds." And the independent *Athenaeum* warned against *The Conduct of Life:* "Imagine the effect of such teaching . . . upon any Young Men's Christian Association." "No father would give . . . [this book] to his son." [82]

[80] Francis Hitchman, "The Penny Press," *MM,* XLIII (March 1881) , 398; *LeisH,* Jan. 4, 1855, p. 15; *Hogg's Weekly Instructor,* March 1, 1845, p. 1; Arnold, p. 89; *Hogg's,* 3rd ser. IV (Feb. 1855) , 91.

[81] Briggs, p. 147.

[82] *Critic,* July 15, 1851, p. 328; *Ath,* Dec. 15, 1860, pp. 825, 826. For other warnings, see the *BQR,* XI (May 1850) , 282, 308; *BQR,* XXXIII (April 1861) , 550; *EcRev,* 8th ser. III (Nov. 1862) , 406.

The *Athenaeum* exaggerated: a few fathers would have, even though condemned as unfit as Emerson himself. The Secularists in the *Reasoner* and the *National Reformer* and rationalists in journals of "an emphatically freethinking sort" supported Emerson's religious views: *Cooper's Journal* printed extracts of them; the *Fortnightly Review* argued that a preacher like Emerson, even though he denied the divinity of Christ, should be allowed the pulpit; and *Fraser's* lauded Emerson as "the religious revolutionist of America." [83]

V

Using notes from his tours in 1833 and 1847, Emerson began a series of lectures on the English in 1850. At the same time he was also lecturing on topics that eventually became *The Conduct of Life*.[84] In *English Traits* and *Conduct* Emerson was no longer concerned, as he had been earlier, with man's attempt to transcend himself but with how man lived or how he should live on this earth. For the first time Victorian critics had found in Emerson a myriad of facts, but in many instances they were as critical of his facts as they had been of his "vague spiritual analogies." They were particularly skeptical of a number of those set forth in *English Traits*.

So well known were Emerson's American lectures on the English that notices of them began to appear almost immediately in British periodicals and continued to appear until *Traits* was published in 1856.[85] The book was as popular in America as the lectures had been,[86] and in England it received more reviews in British periodicals than any other single work by Emerson. The Philistine may

---

[83] J. M. Robertson, *A History of Freethought in the Nineteenth Century* (London, 1929), I, 304; *Cooper's*, March 2, 1850, p. 135; *Cooper's*, March 9, 1850, p. 151; Viscount Amberley, "The Church of England as a Religious Body," *FR*, VII (Feb. 1867), 206; Conway, *Fraser's*, LXXVIII, 1. For detailed comment on the Secularists' reaction to Emerson's religious views, see pp. 107–9.

[84] Rusk, *Life*, pp. 379, 383, 393.

[85] *Critic*, April 1, 1850, p. 177; *Chamber's*, June 29, 1850, p. 415; *Critic*, July 15, 1853, p. 379; *Cook's*, July 1, 1854, p. 158.

[86] Rusk, *Life*, pp. 379, 393.

have been blind to and bored with "schemes of grandiloquent transcendentalism," but his interest seldom lagged when the subject was men, manners, and institutions. Dickens, Thackeray, and Trollope—all the most prominent literary men of Victorian England—were excellent social critics, and Emerson himself was no neophyte. He had begun in the late thirties, notes Willard Thorp, "to think and write about social questions," and Rusk maintains that in *Traits* he had succeeded, as the best social historians do, "in striking a balance between admiration and censure." [87] Commenting on the book as a whole, British reviewers strike the same balance; when, however, they write on Emerson's criticism of English writers and English institutions, their censure outweighs their admiration.

English Traits, affirmed a number of Mid-Victorians, equaled or surpassed any other travel book written by an American on England.[88] Emerson had brought out a careful, thoughtful, and pleasing book, "the matured results of a matured and original mind."[89] A few American [90] and English critics demurred. Emerson, one Englishman pointed out indelicately, was attempting "to get rid of an unusual overflow of bile" and poured it into *English Traits.* Composed of "scattered reminiscences and fragmentary sketches," the unprofitable book was "about one-half . . . reliable." "One would think," growled the *West of Scotland Magazine-Review,* "that instead of having examined the features of England close at hand, he had scanned them from a distance through the mystifying power of a phantasmagoric imagination." [91] A feature of great interest to these critics was, not unnaturally, the Englishman himself.

Reviewers who approved of this portrait, which was essentially the conventional one painted by foreign as well as English social histo-

[87] Thorp, "American Writers as Critics of Nineteenth-Century Society," in *The American Writer and the European Tradition,* ed. Margaret Denny and William H. Gilman (Minneapolis, 1950), p. 96; Rusk, *Life,* p. 394.

[88] [Gerald Massey], *QR,* CXV (Jan. 1864), 48–49; *LQR,* VII (Jan. 1857), 383; *BritC,* III (June[?]1857), 275; *Critic,* Sept. 15, 1856, p. 446; *LitG,* Sept. 6, 1856, p. 658; *Reas,* Sept. 28, 1856, p. 98.

[89] *Critic,* Sept. 15, 1856, p. 446; *NatRev,* III (Oct. 1856), 496; *Ex,* Sept. 20, 1856, p. 599; *BritC,* III (June[?]1857), 279; *Leader,* Sept. 13, 1856, p. 880.

[90] Rusk, *Life,* p. 394.

[91] *NQR,* V (1856), 451; *LitG,* Sept. 6, 1856, p. 657; *Ex,* Sept. 20, 1856, p. 599; *DubUM,* XLVIII (Nov. 1856), 569; *WScM,* n.s. I (Oct. 1856), 80.

rians,[92] were often tempted to seize upon Emerson's flattering comments and ignore completely the derogatory. One critic complimented Emerson on his ability to appreciate English "taciturnity, stolidity, self-sufficiency, and the imperturbable assertion of superiority as often noticed in the English character," while four others praised the cogency of his references to an assortment of English virtues—courage, manliness, logical thinking, unselfishness, truthfulness, and solidarity.[93] Some reviewers were not to be put aside by such encomiums: they were especially incensed by his treatment of British writers.

The roots of this quarrel went back to the early thirties, when Emerson became the patron of Carlyle, whom the British had ignored. In the forties the American's statements favoring the Romantics and his aversion to the Neoclassicists kept the quarrel moving well,[94] but perhaps none of his literary criticism stirred the periodical critics so much as that on Shakespeare and Landor. In *Representative Men* Emerson had referred to Shakespeare as "master of the revels to mankind," an opinion that led "An American Lady" to inquire archly in the *Examiner* whether there were not a "strong protest against causeless jealousy to be drawn from the 'Winter's Tale' " and two Britishers to defend Shakespeare as a great moralist. One declared that Shakespeare was "a moral and social philosopher," while the other maintained that the poet's power "consists in his *inculcation of grand moral principles and the diffusion of humanizing and fraternizing sentiments.* He was 'full o' the milk of human kindness,' and instilled into his auditors and readers the now widespreading doctrine of Universal Brotherhood." [95] Emerson was doubtless looking for morality in Shakespeare, just as he was looking for it in Goethe, but he chose Shakespeare to represent the poet *sui generis.* In one line in the essay "The Uses of Great Men" Emerson reveals the true source of Shakespeare's genius: "He of all men best

---

[92] Nicoloff, pp. 158–59.

[93] *WR,* LXVI (Oct. 1856), 503; *LQR,* VII (Jan. 1857), 386–98 *passim; BritC,* III (June[?]1857), 277; *SatR,* Oct. 4, 1856, p. 510; *QR,* CXV, pp. 45–52 *passim.*

[94] Scudder, pp. 32–37 *passim; Works,* I, 109–12, esp. 112; II, 287.

[95] *Works,* IV, 217; *Ex,* as quoted in *Littell's,* June 1, 1850, p. 430; *Sp,* Jan. 12, 1850, p. 42; *Whit,* Sept. 20, 1851, p. 713.

understands the English language, and can say what he will." [96] In a long letter to the editor of the *Gazette,* an anonymous correspondent defended this view; the letter writer and Emerson were on the side of the angels, as Otto Jespersen, G. Wilson Knight, and other modern critics have shown.[97]

Unfortunately Emerson does not score so well in his comments on Landor. He had met the Englishman in Florence in 1833 and had recorded that meeting in the first chapter of *Traits.* If Conway was correct in saying that by reading Landor Emerson had learned to express himself clearly, the pupil had an odd way of showing his gratitude. He directed his comments to Landor's irascible disposition.[98] This "hurt was not serious ...," wrote the *Athenaeum,* "but a prick rouses the war-horse," who brought out a twenty-two-page shilling pamphlet in reply to Emerson. Reviewing this open letter, the *Athenaeum* noted Landor's aversion to Goethe, Carlyle, and Wordsworth, all of whom Emerson had praised in *English Traits.* "Neither in my youthful days nor in any other," the journal quoted Landor as writing, "have I thrown upon the world such trash as 'Werter' and 'Wilhelm Meister,' nor flavoured my poetry with ... metaphysics." As for Carlyle and Wordsworth, the latter's "bile is less fervid than Carlyle's: it comes with more saliva about it, and with a hoarser expectoration." [99]

Other critics were hardly so vehement as Landor, but they too found Emerson's practical criticism of little value. Although one wrote that Emerson proved himself in the book to be a perceptive literary critic, and another that he was an "original and noteworthy" one,[100] the more discerning reviewers were less charitable. In the chapter "Literature" Emerson had argued that the trait which most noteworthy British authors shared was common sense and that it was not enough. Emerson's own prejudices are, of course, apparent here.

[96] *Works,* IV, 15.

[97] *Whit,* Nov. 1, 1851, p. 762; Otto Jespersen, *Growth and Structure of the English Language* (New York, 1955) , pp. 224–48; G. Wilson Knight, *The Wheel of Fire* (London, 1930) ; Caroline F. E. Spurgeon, *Shakespeare's Imagery and What It Tells Us* (London, 1935) ; R. B. Heilman, *This Great Stage* (Baton Rouge, La., 1948) .

[98] Conway, *Fraser's,* LXXVIII, 9; *Works,* V, 6–10, esp. 7, 9.

[99] *Ath,* Nov. 29, 1856, p. 1460.

[100] *BritC,* III (June[?]1857) , 278; *Press,* Sept. 13, 1856, p. 879.

The often splenetic William Maccall was doubtless correct in pointing out that as a literary critic Emerson eschewed "impartiality"; he
was also perhaps correct in saying that "literature has obviously
been for him [Emerson] a luxury, never a discipline. He is too much
the student, too little of a scholar." Emerson was not, as Maccall
asserted, one of the worst of critics, but he did, as Maccall said, place
too much emphasis on the classical writers—notably Plato—and he
did not like many English writers, especially his contemporaries.
perhaps the *Literary Gazette* best summarized Emerson's rather un-
distinguished chapter when it commented with fine understatement:
"The remarks on literature are not so attractive as might have been
anticipated." [101]

His treatment of the three great interlocking British institutions—
the Establishment, the aristocracy, and the universities—was not
(according to the critics) very attractive, either. Although one of the
more ambitious Dissenting journals and several of the more radical
praised Emerson's comments against the Establishment, listened
gladly to his prophecy that the middle class would soon usurp the
place of the aristocracy, and agreed that the universities were ready
for an injection of new blood, another periodical was so appalled at
the brash remarks on the three institutions that it refused to record
them. Mr. Emerson, sniffily declared the *Literary Gazette,* was "not
well qualified for writing on the subjects." [102] In *Traits* Emerson had
frankly and accurately described the English Church as an excellent
body for the furthering of political and social aims, but the British
did not welcome his frankness. All that Emerson wrote on religion,
stated the Methodist *London Quarterly Review,* was suspect, while
the *West of Scotland Magazine-Review* "unhesitatingly" condemned
his religious views. A third journal suggested unkindly that he leave
English and American churches alone and speak for himself.[103]
Other reviewers found the chapter unduly "caustic," "flippant, vul-

---

[101] *Works,* V, 232–60 *passim;* Maccall, *Critic,* Dec. 22, 1860, p. 778; Maccall, *Critic,* Oct.
9, 1858, p. 653 (see *NQR,* V [1856], 453, for a similar opinion) ; *LitG,* Sept. 6, 1856, p. 658.

[102] *EcRev,* 8th ser. III (Nov. 1862) , 399; *SatR,* Oct. 4, 1856, p. 510; *WR,* LXVI (Oct.
1856) , 507; *Leader,* Sept. 13, 1856, p. 881; *LQR,* VII (Jan. 1857) , 398–400; *Press,* Sept. 13,
1856, p. 879; *LitG,* Sept. 6, 1856, p. 658.

[103] *Works,* V, 214–31, esp. 217–20; *LQR,* VII (Jan. 1857) , 381; *WScM,* n.s. I (Oct. 1856) ,
76; *DubUM,* XLVIII (Nov. 1856) , 573.

gar, and profane," "merely a diatribe," and "treated with Emersonian peculiarities." In all this comment on the church, firmly spoke
the theologian and novelist Kingsley, "Mr. Emerson sees as far as he
can see, and no further." [104]

"Aristocracy" and "Universities" drew the same kind of unfavorable reaction. Emerson, whose major complaint against the nobility
was its cynicism,[105] ignorantly confounded "gentility with titles,"
asserted one critic, while another said that the American regretted
that his country "has no corresponding class." [106] Emerson had criticized the universities as mere "finishing schools for the upper classes"
and Oxford as "a Greek factory," views that led the *Dublin University Magazine* to write snobbishly: Emerson "does not understand
the kind of men who are formed by the English Universities." He
falls into a "vulgar delusion" when he states that "classics are the sole
element of Oxford culture." [107] In an earlier article the *Magazine* had
maintained that Emerson's remarks on British schools were full of
blunders, and the *Press* wrote sarcastically that he discussed the
subject "with as little ignorance . . . as could perhaps be expected." [108]

Another subject which Victorians found Emerson unqualified to
discuss was one very dear to them, the conduct of life. Philistines
were almost obsessed with doing the correct thing. Like members of
all middle-class civilizations, they had developed an insatiable appe-
tite for books, magazines, and pamphlets advising them how to walk,
talk, and act in a becoming manner.[109] So welcome was such literature that critics were ready to forgive Emerson his more venial sins
and eagerly awaited the "new volume" that was "to teach 'The
Conduct of Life.' " [110] To their disappointment it did no such thing.
In this book, complained the periodicals, "we naturally expect some

[104] *WScM,* n.s. I (Oct. 1856) , 80; *DubUM,* L (Aug. 1857) , 234; *Press,* Sept. 13, 1856, p.
879; *BritC,* III (June[?]1857) , 278; *SatR,* Oct. 4, 1856, p. 510.

[105] Nicoloff, pp. 193–94.

[106] *Press,* Sept. 13, 1856, p. 879; *BritC,* III (June[?]1857) , 278.

[107] *Works,* V, 209, 204; *DubUM,* L (Aug. 1857) , 233, 228.

[108] *DubUM,* XLVIII (Nov. 1856) , 571; *Press,* Sept. 13, 1856, p. 879.

[109] Young, p. 30; Briggs, pp. 118–19. See also Jerome Hamilton Buckley, *The Victorian
Temper* (Cambridge, Mass., 1951) , p. 10.

[110] *BritC,* III (Feb.[?]1860) , 144.

guidance," [111] but Emerson gave none. The little counsel which he did give, wrote two reviewers, was "puerile": "be rich, healthy, and wise, . . . loving, humble, and believing"! [112] As with Emerson's other works, at least part of the blame for such obtuse comment lies with the critics themselves. Emerson had gradually recognized that man as "presently constituted" "was incapable of the illimitable spiritual ascents which his early essays had called for," and in *The Conduct of Life,* as Nicoloff writes of *English Traits,* he was giving "a rather detached formulation of the general condition of man." [113] For better or worse, Emerson was saying, people seek power, wealth, and beauty; they are nearly always controlled by fate and are often the victims of illusions. Whether this vision is not considerably narrower than the earlier one and thus indicative of lessening powers is a point that concerned a number of critics. In America, Emerson as early as 1850 was "thought to be past the peak of his performance," and he himself declared unhappily that "the English journals snub my new book [*Representative Men*]; as, indeed, they have all its foregoers. Only now they say that this has less vigor and originality than the others." [114]

The complaint had certainly been made,[115] but with *Conduct* it became a common one. Much in the book "is undeniably excellent and true," wrote one responsive critic, but "there is more self-surrender to the impulses of the time, a narrower view of human life and human capacity, . . . an unmistakable preaching of a positivism that comes ill from one who started with Plato." [116] The *Athenaeum* averred that Emerson "has come to the end of all he had to say, and is repeating himself, but with a colder and more feeble utterance." The *Westminster Review* called for a reassessment of his

[111] Maccall, *Critic,* Dec. 22, 1860, p. 778; *Ath,* Dec. 15, 1860, p. 824; *Sp,* Dec. 22, 1860, p. 1217.

[112] Maccall, *Critic,* Dec. 22, 1860, p. 778; *Sp,* Dec. 22, 1860, p. 1218.

[113] Nicoloff, pp. 62, 241.

[114] Rusk, *Life,* p. 377; *Journals of Ralph Waldo Emerson,* ed. Edward Waldo Emerson and Waldo Emerson Forbes (Boston, 1909–14), VIII, 88.

[115] *Pm,* I, 45.

[116] *EcRev,* 8th ser. III (Nov. 1862), 407. For critics making the same comment, see the *Ath,* Dec. 15, 1860, p. 824; *WR,* LXXV (April 1861), 589. In America, Alcott and Thoreau set forth similar views (Rusk, *Life,* p. 406).

works: its own was unfavorable. The books were "mere desultory musings," "vehement exhortations." Assenting, the *Saturday Review* found *Conduct* to be "an average specimen of the sort of remarks which he has been making for ... years; ... the weakest kind of commonplace elaborately thrown into unintelligible shapes." [117] Other critics wrote that *Conduct* repeated too many of the old ideas, as inferior to his early essays, "sketchy and discursive," "thin, meagre, and unsubstantial"—Emerson's "worst book." [118]

Some of the criticism of the work was more appreciative. One lenient reviewer noted that although it contained "maimed thoughts," Emerson was still a writer of "large cultivation." Another confessed that underlying "the mannerism and affectation" were "grandeur, purity, and sincerity," while a third commended several of the essays for a few interesting "anecdotes" and the volume for "a certain intellectual hardness." [119] The only two journals that bestowed high honors upon the work were antithetical in every way— the hard-bitten, secular *National Reformer* and the fastidious, prudent *Ladies' Companion.* The first, as I have suggested, was struck by Emerson's pronouncements on religion, the second by those on wealth. In its review of *Conduct* the *Companion* quoted the "noble verse with which he prefaces" "Worship" and then turned to the essay on wealth. Unlike the critics who complained that the book offered no guidance, this one affirmed that its pages were "replete with noble axioms and practical suggestions," many of which concerned what the *Athenaeum* called in a telling phrase "the art of 'earning money.' " [120] Another journal praised Emerson's comments on this art, but it lacked the enthusiasm of the *Ladies' Companion.*[121] The *Companion* expressed in its approval of Emerson's essay the very *Zeitgeist* of the Mid-Victorian era:

[117] *Ath,* Dec. 15, 1860, p. 824; *WR,* LXXV (April 1861) , 589; *SatR,* Dec. 15, 1860, p. 762.

[118] *Sp,* Dec. 22, 1860, p. 1218; *Ath,* Dec. 15, 1860, p. 826; *LitG,* Dec. 29, 1860, p. 562; Maccall, *Critic,* Dec. 22, 1860, pp. 778, 779.

[119] *BQR,* XXXIII (April 1861) , 551, 549; *LitG,* Dec. 29, 1860, p. 563; *Sp,* Dec. 22, 1860, p. 1218.

[120] *Ladies',* 2nd ser. XIX (1861) , 108; *Ath,* Dec. 15, 1860, p. 826.

[121] *LitG,* Dec. 29, 1860, p. 563.

At last we have a book written, wherein wealth and the accompanying power, which is its attribute, is justly valued. I look upon the present strife after wealth among the citizens and farmers of our towns and shires as the surest sign of our intellectual and moral advancement and greatness. National wealth is the representative of comfort, art, glory, and all legitimate belongings. . . . Wealth is the key to art culture, love, and religion. . . . moreover work, the first attribute to wealth, is noble and ennobling in itself. . . . We have been called a nation of shopkeepers, and there have not been wanting voices . . . to resent the so-called indignity; but we might let the imputation pass. We are shopmen in the shop, artizans in the workroom . . . but abroad we are part and parcel of God's universe.[122]

Nation of shopkeepers and proud of it, part and parcel of God's universe—the critic strikes notes that echo through these articles on Emerson.

VI

England was never more sure of herself and of her destiny than in the 1850's and 1860's. She had "good trade, steady agriculture, a free constitution, an apparently inviolable security, a loyal people." [123] "Not for a long time," writes G. M. Young ironically, "had the English character seemed so upright, or English thought so formless, as in that happy half generation when the demand for organic change was quiescent, the religious foundations were perishing, and the balance of land and industry was slowly toppling." [124] Other historians have conjectured that the English knew that all was not well: "Beneath the Victorian's air of confidence there was . . . a haunting doubt" that prosperity and peace might not last.[125] A sensitive minority may have been fearful, but the great middle class had no doubt that its good fortune would last forever.[126] In fact, all

---

[122] *Ladies'*, 2nd ser. XIX (1861) , 107.
[123] Halévy, IV, 419. See also Harrold and Templeman, p. xlviii; Briggs, pp. 2, 299.
[124] P. 154.
[125] Harrold and Templeman, p. li; Houghton, pp. 11–13; Elliott-Binns, p. 7.
[126] Briggs, p. 51.

classes—upper, middle, and lower—were well satisfied. "The Barbarians remain in the belief that the great broad-shouldered genial Englishman may be well satisfied with himself; the Philistines remain in the belief that the great middle class of this country, with its earnest commonsense penetrating through sophisms and ignoring commonplaces, may be well satisfied with itself; the Populace, that the working man with his bright powers of sympathy and ready powers of action, may be well satisfied with himself." [127] From such an outlook came a pervasive and easy complacency, "a thing to marvel at." [128] Scholars of the period never tire of giving examples of it,[129] Gilbert and Sullivan have satirized it,[130] and critics of Emerson have revealed it in their comments in periodicals.

Reviewing his works, one middle-class organ exulted: "Much of that peculiarity" which makes an Englishman so "inexplicable" is "his settled conviction that, a better fellow than he is, or a better country than that he lives in, you cannot find on earth." "We believe the Englishman enjoys the best conscience of any man on earth." Modestly wrote another: "Our preeminence amongst races and nations lies chiefly in the fact that bristling and startling individualities . . . can be all turned in one direction when the foe is in front." Perhaps the *National Magazine* articulated best of all what Arnold called the "incomparable self-satisfaction" of the middle class: "Where a foreigner appreciates England, he will in general be found to be tolerably accurate . . . ; where he depreciates, to be largely inaccurate." [131] One of the unappreciative was Hawthorne, who subsumed all Englishmen under the title John Bull. "We never knew John Bull in better health and spirits," tartly replied the complacent *Quarterly*.[132] A favorite way the Englishman over the years has beto-

---

[127] Arnold, p. 114.

[128] L. E. Elliott-Binns, *Religion in the Victorian Era* (London, 1936), p. 499; Briggs, pp. 50, 51.

[129] Harrold and Templeman, p. xlviii; Houghton, p. 48; Briggs, pp. 16, 27; R. Glynn Grylls, "Emancipation of Women," in *Ideas and Beliefs*, p. 254.

[130] Audrey Williamson, *Gilbert & Sullivan Opera: A New Assessment* (London, 1953), pp. 69, 80, 263.

[131] *LQR*, VII (Jan. 1857), 395; *QR*, CXV, 55; Arnold, p. 88; *NatM*, I (1857), 39.

[132] *QR*, CXV, 67. For other examples of British complacency, see *LitG*, Sept. 6, 1856, p. 657; *SatR*, Oct. 4, 1856, p. 510.

kened his superiority is to point to shortcomings in the American. Mid-Victorians were adept: they felt an "inherent superiority to other societies on the continent of Europe or across the Atlantic." [133] Philistines accused Americans of being pretentious, "godless and materialised," self-satisfied, self-complacent, and conceited; their country was devoid of art, tradition, literature, church, university, and aristocracy.[134] Since Emerson was considered by many critics to be the representative American,[135] he naturally came in for much abuse. Critics found in him the same "boundless arrogance," "interminable" gabble, and "laughable Yankee pertness" which they found in his bumptious countrymen.[136]

Emerson had a superb ability to infuriate the English; he showed more talent in this area than any other American of his time, perhaps of all time. "He first gives you a little honey," wailed one victim, "and then stings you." [137] Mid-Victorians detested Whitman, but they easily wrote him off as a boor. Like Emerson, both Bryant and Longfellow had protested America's intellectual dependence upon England; yet critics cheerfully conceded Bryant to be America's best nature poet and affectionately embraced Longfellow as another English writer publishing in America.[138] Some twelve years after Emerson had made the same protest, the British were still sarcastically referring to him as "the American Scholar." [139] With wonderful seriousness, the scholar could announce that England, then rising to the height of her commercial and industrial great-

[133] Briggs, p. 12.

[134] *QR*, CXV, 47, 48; *Sharpe's*, XV (April 1852), 201; *NQR*, V (1856), 451; *Press*, Sept. 13, 1856, p. 880; *SatR*, Feb. 23, 1867, p. 247; *SatR*, Aug. 13, 1864, p. 205. For other anti-American commentary, see *LQR*, VII (Jan. 1857), 396; *Ath*, Sept. 6, 1856, p. 1109; *BritC*, II (Oct.[?]1856), 192; *SatR*, Dec. 15, 1860, p. 762; *WScM*, n.s. I (Oct. 1856), 79; *WR*, LXVI (Oct. 1856), 501.

[135] *Fraser's*, LXXV, 587; *EcRev*, 8th ser. III (Nov. 1862), 367; *LondR*, Aug. 24, 1867, p. 206; *NatM*, I (1857), 39; *Museum*, II (Oct. 1862), 275.

[136] Maccall, *Critic*, Oct. 9, 1858, p. 653; Maccall, *Critic*, Dec. 22, 1860, p. 778; *Press*, Sept. 13, 1856, p. 879.

[137] Maccall, *Critic*, Oct. 9, 1858, p. 653.

[138] Russell, *BwyA*, Sept. 1867, p. 45; *WR*, LVII (Jan. 1852), 304; *Museum*, II (Oct. 1862), 276, 270; Russell, *BwyA*, Sept. 1867, p. 41; *SatR*, Feb. 23, 1867, p. 247. See also Gohdes, *Amer. Lit.*, pp. 110–26.

[139] *BQR*, XI (May 1850), 309. For other comments on the continuing efforts of the English to downgrade American literature, especially poetry, see p. 96.

ness,[140] was "already declining" and imply that one could expect little else from a nation which allowed a husband to sell his wife. The Englishman was frank, artless, truthful; and the reason: "His choler and conceit force every thing out." [141] In attempting to laugh off the sting, critics often sounded somewhat hollow. The *Westminster,* for instance, began a review of *English Traits* with the light-hearted observations that Englishmen were "perfectly impervious to the shafts of ridicule," that they could "enjoy a joke at their own expense," but in a short time blurted out that reading the book was "like eating potted meat; . . . a little of it goes a long way." The *Athenaeum* boasted that "the faults which he finds with us [in *Traits*] we read of with perfect good humour" and then in the remainder of the article proved exactly the opposite: to read the book was to tear "through a copse that leads no-whither"; the work "will be remembered—if remembered at all" as "wanting in substance and genuineness." The *Press* lightly wrote that it did not share the dissatisfaction of other critics with *Traits,* only to pick testily at the "hash-up of old notes," in which Emerson describes not England and her institutions but "his own small, cold nature." [142] Many other critics attacked Emerson's works directly, with no attempt to conceal resentment under a cover of good humor. Their weapon was undisguised ridicule.

In the forties critics had denounced Emerson's books, but they seldom ridiculed them. Early Victorians took Emerson seriously, an attitude that makes reviews of his later works different in tone from reviews of, for example, "The American Scholar." The British had discovered in the address not only an unwarranted attempt to cut loose from the Mother Country but a manifesto furthering the aims of political anarchists. With the victory of the middle class in 1848, these aims had been defeated,[143] and by 1856 memories of the incipient revolution lay far behind. For the first time since 1832, when

[140] John R. H. Moorman, *A History of the Church in England* (New York, 1954), pp. 380–81; Briggs, p. 15. See also Buckley, p. 112.

[141] *Works,* V, 37, 64, 116–26, 236–37, 261. Several critics noted Emerson's humor: *Fraser's,* LXXV, 587; Paul, *Critic,* Aug. 1, 1851, p. 347; SatR, Oct. 4, 1856, p. 510.

[142] WR, LXVI (Oct. 1856), 494, 495, 496; *Ath,* Sept. 6, 1856, pp. 1109, 1111; *Press,* Sept. 13, 1856, pp. 880, 879.

[143] Traill, VI, 251; Halévy, IV, 337.

the meaning of radical democracy had first become manifest, the once "terrified" Englishman could now relax.[144] Evidence that Emerson and his inflammatory political and social ideas were no longer frightening is found in the relatively small number of critics taking note of his comments on democracy [145] and in the very large number who greeted his comments in many areas with unmitigated sarcasm, a luxury befitting only the safe and satisfied. This studied insolence, indulged in even by the friendly critics, indicates that W. D. Templeman's remark on John Ruskin is also true of Emerson: "He had not really touched their way of life." [146] One Philistine laid aside *English Traits* and snapped: "If you don't like the country—d——n you—you can leave it!" [147]

Mid-Victorians treated Emerson's other works as well as his lectures with little respect. In reviewing *Representative Men,* a critic suggested wittily that Emerson himself had never learned "that *one* use of great men is to teach little men to be modest," while another declared that Emerson seemed to dread above all else "the well-worn highways of common sense." A third wrote sarcastically that he would have done better to "tell us something of the backwoodsmen in Kentucky and Ohio"—types which he knew well—rather than going "exclusively to Europe for his heroes." [148] With the *Memoirs* of Miss Fuller, sardonically noted the *Westminster,* "the rich harvest of American biography that is now ripening finds a beautiful fulfilment." Another journal quoted Miss Fuller's assertion that Carlyle was worth a thousand Emersons, and then scolded: "Put that, Mr. Emerson, in your pipe and smoke it!" One listener scoffed at Emerson's lecture style as being "like that of a spasmodic writing-master crying over his own copy slips," and another disparaged it by quoting one of Emerson's early disciples: "It's quite out of character to say that Mr. Emerson lectures; . . . he drops nectar, . . . he exhales odours, he lets off mental sky-rockets." [149]

---

[144] Halévy, IV, 398; Young, p. 63; Briggs, p. 298.

[145] *QR,* CXV, 44, 45; *Fraser's,* LXXV, 586, 592; *LondR,* Aug. 24, 1867, pp. 205, 206; Robert Buchanan, *Broadway,* n.s. II (May 1869) , 223, 224.

[146] Harrold and Templeman, p. lxiii.   [147] *NQR,* V (n.m. 1856) , 455.

[148] *BQR,* XI (May 1850) , 282; *LeisH,* Jan. 4, 1855, p. 14; *EcRev,* 5th ser. III, p. 568.

[149] *WR,* LVII (April 1852) , 664–65; *Critic,* Feb. 16, 1852, p. 90; *SatR,* Dec. 15, 1860, p. 762; *LQR,* III (Oct. 1854) , 22 *n.*

The Philistines were as derisive of Emerson the man as they were of Emerson the author and lecturer. When, as in *Representative Men*, he expressed admiration for Shakespeare, or, as in *English Traits*, he flattered the English people, or, as in *The Conduct of Life*, he showed a certain admiration for the Goddess-of-Getting-On —when, that is, Emerson had "something definite and fixed to keep his mind within practical limits" [150]—he was handsomely praised as being "generous," "eloquent," "gifted," truthful, a "thinker," and a "genius." [151] Often Emerson did not keep within practical limits, and the genius suddenly turned into a merciless, cold-faced, serpentlike Yankee, who was unable to distinguish among fancifulness, exaggeration, and prevarication.[152] More damaging to Emerson's personal reputation than such malediction was the overspreading sarcasm. When critics—any one of whom could perhaps have been Arnold's "typical middle-class man" [153]—called Emerson "the Sage of Concord," "the American Sage," "the king and pontiff" of transcendentalism, "an American philosopher," "a great original Thinker," "this profound lecturer," "our American," "good Mr. Emerson," an "American 'new-light,'" "brother in letters," "our learned brother," "new mystic," "the quondam Unitarian preacher," "that most unphilosophic of all philosophers, and credulous of all incredulous writers," they meant to be bitingly sarcastic.[154] He was to these

[150] *Ex*, March 23, 1850, p. 181. *Critic*, Feb. 1, 1850, p. 60, expressed a similar opinion.

[151] *BritC*, III (June[?]1857), 279; *Reas*, Sept. 28, 1856, p. 98; *OCM*, I (Oct. 1856), 613; *Sharpe's*, XV (April 1852), 204; *Ex*, March 23, 1850, p. 181; *Pm*, I, 54; *Sharpe's*, XV (April 1852), 201; *Leader*, Sept. 13, 1856, p. 880; *Critic*, Sept. 15, 1856, p. 446; *WR*, LXVI (Oct. 1856), 497; Buchanan, *Bwy*, n.s. II, p. 223; *EcRev*, 8th ser. III (Nov. 1862), 369; *LQR*, VII (Jan. 1857), 382; *Critic*, Feb. 1, 1850, p. 60; *Museum*, II (Oct. 1862), 275; *WScM*, n.s. I (Oct. 1856), 76; *BritC*, III (June[?]1857), 279; *Sharpe's*, XI (June 1850), 364; *Press* in *Littell's*, Oct. 13, 1866, p. 86; *LitG*, Dec. 29, 1860, p. 562; *WR*, LVII (Jan. 1852), 292. "Genius" was as overworked in Victorian times as it is today. "The man of letters," writes Houghton, p. 152, "was generally considered . . . no mere artist or craftsman. He was a *genius.*"

[152] *Critic*, July 15, 1851, p. 326; *WScM*, n.s. I (Oct. 1856), 76; *DubUM*, XLVIII (Nov. 1856), 569, 570; *BritC*, II (Oct.[?]1856), 192; *Sp*, Sept. 13, 1856, p. 981; *Press*, Sept. 13, 1856, p. 879.

[153] Arnold, p. 87.

[154] *Critic*, Feb. 16, 1852, p. 89; *NatM*, I (1857), 39; *Critic*, Feb. 16, 1852, p. 89; *SatR*, Oct. 4, 1856, p. 510; Paul, *Critic*, Aug. 1, 1851, p. 347; *BQR*, XI (May 1850), 285; *Ath*, Sept. 6, 1856, p. 1111; Maccall, *Critic*, Dec. 22, 1860, p. 778; *Whit*, Sept. 20, 1851, p.

Philistines "a transatlantic offender," "the Yankee sceptic," "a small Yankee Montaigne," "that pantheistic rhapsodist," "the Wise Man coming from the West," "the Confucius of the west," "the great Occidental star," "a moral dilettante," "transcendental madman," "a scarecrow likeness of Mr. Carlyle," a writer like "our own weird Carlyle," "a self-bibulous fanatic," and "the prevalent epidemic." [155] No reputation could have remained unaffected by the assault of this powerful class. Emerson's was no exception. What makes his predicament especially interesting in the land "where Mrs. Grundy had become a tyrant" [156] was the reaction of the younger generation, whose members had vociferously championed the American in the forties.

VII

Although one journal maintained that Emerson's reputation in England was not so high in 1850 as it had been three or four years earlier, Bohn had chosen *Representative Men* to begin his celebrated shilling series,[157] and in 1857 a reviewer commented that Emerson was "too well known, even in this country now, to require particular mention here." Another critic asserted that *Representa-*

712; *BQR*, XI (May 1850) , 282, 285; *EcRev*, 8th ser. III (Nov. 1862) , 382; *JSL*, VI (Jan. 1858) , 307; *ChO*, n.s. no. 182 (Feb. 1853) , 92.

[155] *Wes-Meth*, 4th ser. VI (Oct. 1850) , 1078 *n; Hogg's*, 3rd ser. IV (Feb. 1855) , 91; Maccall, *Critic*, Dec. 22, 1860, p. 778; *JSL*, VI (Jan. 1858) , 310; *Sp*, Dec. 22, 1860, p. 1217; *NQR*, V (n.m. 1856) , 449; *Sp*, Dec. 22, 1860, p. 1217; *WR*, LXXV (April 1861) , 590; *EcRev*, 8th ser. III (Nov. 1862) , 400; *Ath*, Dec. 15, 1860, p. 824; *EcRev*, 8th ser. III (Nov. 1862) , 387, 400; *NQR*, V (n.m. 1856) , 449.

[156] Houghton, p. 128.

[157] *Critic*, July 15, 1851, p. 326. *Ex*, March 23, 1850, p. 181, speculated that John Chapman's legitimate English edition of *Representative Men* would "be wrecked" by Bohn's pirated shilling edition. Bohn excused himself "in a brief advertisement, which informs us that having had his most popular volumes printed in America, and his occasional attempts to secure American copyright in England set at nought by competitors, he is now determined, in self-defense, [t]o adopt measures of reprisal." For other comments on Emerson and cheap and/or pirated editions, see *ChO*, n.s. no. 149 (May 1850) , 355; *WFQR*, LIII (April 1850) , 280; *BQR*, XI (May 1850) , 281; *Critic*, March 1, 1850, p. 119; Paul, *Critic*, Aug. 1, 1851, p. 348; *Sp*, Sept. 13, 1856, p. 981; *Critic*, Feb. 2, 1857, p. 61; *NatRef*, March 16, 1861, p. 8; *SatR*, Feb. 23, 1867, p. 247.

tive Men and *English Traits* had given Emerson "a popular reputation," while a third reported in 1860 that "numerous persons" read Emerson. Seven years later, still another Britisher observed that "few authors seem to be more frequently quoted." [158] Other critics were not so sure that Emerson was as popular in the 1860's as he had been in the late forties and the fifties. In 1860 one declared that the American's reputation had "declined to some extent," and a second announced two years later that "rarely we can meet with any one who dares to avow an honest admiration" for Emerson. In 1869 another wrote that "the public, grown familiar with his meaning, accuse . . . [him] of being stale and tiresome. They hunger for a new utterance." [159]

Two other critics — one in 1856 and one ten years later — were not so much interested in how many Englishmen bought Emerson's books or how many read them as upon whom they had a lasting influence. The number was not great; he has "taken his place," wrote the *Press,* "among those American authors whom the best class of English readers honour," and the *West of Scotland Magazine-Review* said that "to admire Emerson we must be admitted into the number of the initiated." [160]

These initiates came mainly from the young intelligentsia: they bestowed upon Emerson his real and lasting acclaim. Speculating as to the reputation Emerson had established in Great Britain by the end of the forties and early fifties, the *Critic* declared that "he has more powerfully contributed to [the] . . . intellectual movement of his generation than any man of his time, CARLYLE excepted." Other than the works of Carlyle and Goethe, proclaimed another journal, *Representative Men* had "attracted more attention among thinkers than almost any book of the present day." The books of "a certain class of modern writers" like Emerson, lamented the *Wesleyan-Methodist Magazine* in 1850, are so "popular" in England "among our intellectual youth" "that the exaltation of literature

---

[158] *BFER,* VI (Oct. 1857), 890; *SatR,* Dec. 25, 1869, p. 837; Maccall, *Critic,* Dec. 22, 1860, p. 778; *BritC* (July[?]1867), 152.

[159] *SatR,* Dec. 15, 1860, p. 762; *EcRev,* 8th ser. III (Nov. 1862), 368; Buchanan, *Bwy,* n.s. II, 223.

[160] *Press* in *Littell's,* Oct. 13, 1866, p. 86; *WScM,* n.s. I (Oct. 1856), 75.

from its proper sphere" is a growing "evil." And another distressed churchman said: "In the present day [1851], thousands of our young, rising, and gifted minds are forsaking the free atmosphere" of Christianity, for Emerson's "dismal . . . and underground abyss." Wrote one of the gifted minds: "He spoke to the young men around him with an emphasis that deprived them of sleep." [161]

These young men of the early Victorian period were a new type "somewhat arrogant and somewhat shy, very conscious of their standing as gentlemen but very conscious of their duties, too"; they were men who were "passionate" for "co-operative societies, disposed to bring everything in . . . England to the test of Isaiah and Thucydides." [162] They were the Arnolds, the Sterlings, the Cloughs, the Barmbys, the Cuppleses, and the Howittses. These *aliens* had made use of the *First* and *Second Series* in their contribution to the political, social, and intellectual ferment that stirred the forties. By the mid-fifties this ferment was no longer manifest. "The fire of the forties . . . ," writes Asa Briggs, "burned out," [163] and with it seems also to have died the fire in Emerson's early disciples. The fire seems also to have died in the master. *Representative Men, English Traits,* and *The Conduct of Life* afforded little of an incendiary nature: they lacked what the *Eclectic* in a fine phrase called "the younger, nimbler spirit." [164] Even if the works had been more nimble, there is no reason to believe that the early champions of Emerson would have been impressed. "As they grew older," observes Scudder of such young men, "they were shouted down from the heights by their prudent Anglo-Saxon temperaments. They analysed the crystal talisman that had held them aloft, and lo, it evaporated under their steady gaze. They felt like men coming out of ether: dazed at first, then—some of them—even slightly angry. Most no longer needed Emerson, for time had brought them their pittance of success." [165]

[161] *Critic,* Feb. 1, 1850, p. 60; *People's and Howitt's Journal,* n.s. II (June 1850), 361; *Wes-Meth,* 4th ser. VI (Oct. 1850), 1078 *n; Critic,* July 15, 1851, p. 327; *Fraser's,* LXX, 246.

[162] Young, p. 110. Alexander Ireland describes them as "ardent, hopeful, enthusiastic moral and religious reformers and visionaries" (*In Memoriam, Ralph Waldo Emerson: Recollections of His Visits to England in 1833, 1847–8, 1872–3, and Extracts from Unpublished Letters* [London, 1882], p. 60).

[163] P. 88.   [164] 8th ser. III (Nov. 1862), 407.   [165] P. 73.

In the fifties and sixties the once fiery Cupples busied himself turning out sea stories. Goodwyn Barmby directed his efforts to the ministry. The transcendentalist John Heraud had become a drama critic on the anti-Emerson *Athenaeum*.[166] The "adventurous" William Howitt turned his attention to Australia, where he traveled and about which he wrote, and Mary Howitt devoted her time to translating the novels of the Emersonian Fredrika Bremer.[167] George Holyoake was eclipsed by Charles Bradlaugh as the leader of Secularism. Jerrold, the great defender of the downtrodden, died in 1857.[168] Only two of the young men who had written about Emerson in the periodicals of the forties continued to publish articles on him in the Mid-Victorian era, and one of these—George Gilfillan, "a masterful critic of wide influence" [169]—retracted his previously favorable opinion.

The Emerson-Gilfillan relationship has been so well rehearsed that only two points need be noted here.[170] First, Gilfillan always took Emerson seriously, an honor not accorded him by many other critics of the fifties, and, second, his overheated emotions led him to pen the ugliest lines on Emerson in British periodicals. In an agony of denial the "Scottish Seceder minister" damned Emerson as *"one* of the *few sceptics* who has [*sic*] *personally,* and by *name,* insulted the LORD JESUS CHRIST." " We have heard a dog baying at the moon— we have heard of a maniac spitting foam at the stars . . . and we have understood, excused, pitied" them. "But how one calling himself a man . . . could, in his most unhappy hour, have uttered a word against our Brother-God—the Eternal Child . . . passes our conceptions." [171] The young Secularist Phillips found Gilfillan's article "so offensive to good taste, and so gross a slander upon Emerson's character" that he made a reply. Gilfillan's remarks were, he

---

[166] Boase, IV, 826; Conway, *Autobiography,* II, 395; *British Authors of the Nineteenth Century,* ed. Stanley J. Kunitz and Howard Haycraft (New York, 1936), p. 295.
[167] Kunitz and Haycraft, pp. 313, 311.
[168] Robertson, I, 297; *WR,* LXVII (Jan. 1862), 87; Kunitz and Haycraft, p. 331.
[169] Scudder, p. viii. For a somewhat different opinion of Gilfillan as critic, see p. 86.
[170] Rusk, *Life,* p. 337; Scudder, pp. 96–108. See also pp. 4, 6, 8, 16.
[171] *Hogg's,* 3rd ser. IV (Feb. 1855), 89; *Critic,* July 15, 1851, p. 327. An anonymous writer in *Sp,* Dec. 22, 1860, p. 1217, also regretted, less noisily, the "loving admiration" he had shown Emerson in the thirties and forties.

wrote heatedly, "crude and puerile," an odious "libel." Emerson was not "cold," as the minister had sneered, but "tall, fair, calm, and self-possessed." "His private manners are simple, winning, and fascinating." [172]

Gilfillan and Phillips knew Emerson personally, they had heard him lecture, and they expressed their opinions in pungent, highly emotional prose. The young critics of the late 1850's and the 1860's were much less emotional and much more skeptical and timid. "Mid-Victorian intellectuals could forgive anything except unbounded self-confidence; they liked doubt, for doubt was the evidence of subtlety." [173] This approach gave these young men, on the one hand, an "open mind" but led, on the other, to what Morley termed an " 'elegant Pyrrhonism' and 'light-hearted neutrality'; . . . he charged the younger generation with making intellectual sport of the most serious problems of human existence." [174] Rather than "feeling 'overwhelmed by the presence of the sublime,' " observed *Fraser's* in 1863, "the younger generation 'judge, compare, and criticise.' " [175]

An anonymous critic on the *Saturday Review* wrote about Emerson in the new way. Speaking of transcendentalism, he reasoned that "an Englishman would be a very poor and narrow critic who was satisfied with merely laughing at [the philosophy]," nevertheless "there is scarcely anything in it of any great value to Englishmen." The movement "wins the affectionate admiration of ardent and generous minds, and persuades . . . a powerful minority to assert itself in the face of a compact tyrannous majority"—yet how are its devotees "to connect themselves with practical life, and to say something that will instruct and please the outer world?" "To say a neat thing about life seemed to . . . [the transcendentalists] the most wise, practical, and philosophical thing they could do." These "sentences which sound neat . . . would probably be found by any one who would take the trouble to unravel them to do nothing worse than wrap up a platitude in obscurity." [176] Lucian Paul was more appreciative of Emerson than was the anonymous critic, but he too was expert at this elegant kind of Pyrrhonism. The Emerson circle,

[172] *Reas*, pp. 173, 174.   [173] Briggs, pp. 198–99. See also Buckley, p. 11.
[174] Houghton, pp. 178, 179.   [175] Quoted *ibid.*, p. 301.
[176] Aug. 13, 1864, pp. 205, 206.

he wrote, was eminent—but small, select, and strange; the works were widely discussed—especially "at advanced tea-parties"; the English lectures were well received by everyone—except by the Mechanics Institutes for which they were intended.[177]

More discerning in his treatment of Emerson and certainly less supercilious than these two critics was Robert Buchanan. Had this young Celt written twenty years earlier, he might have displayed the same enthusiasm as Cupples, Barmby, and Jerrold; instead, he kept his feelings well under control: his was a balanced—and pallid— judgment. Emerson's influence, Buchanan wrote in 1869, had gradually increased until he was now given "the true title of the Seer." The weakness of Emerson's message lay in its mysticism, which had enlarged his horizon so hopelessly that he had no religious convictions. The strength of the message lay in Emerson's ability to treat all subjects disinterestedly. "His business was to be recognized as the student of eternal, as distinguished from contemporary, truth." As a poet, Buchanan continued coolly, Emerson "is to be credited with most of the little actual poetry that America has produced." [178] Yet Emerson's importance lay not in his message or in his poetic ability. Like young Cupples and Barmby in the 1840's, Buchanan discovered Emerson the man. Unlike these young Englishmen, he did not declare this man to be the greatest "mere mortal who had ever lived," or that this man was to him a "star." Rather, he editorialized calmly and judiciously: It is "as a living influence, that Emerson is to be rated. We do him no justice if we criticise his essays or his verses with reference to great literary standards. He is emphatically great because he occupies the place he does, and is the calm referee to the eternal, in the midst of a big and boisterous people." [179]

Such criticism as Buchanan's was certainly several cuts above the dogmatizing typical of the Mid-Victorian era, but it still was not first rate, even by nineteenth-century standards. What we want from these critics, writes Houghton, "is precisely the type of mind which Mill conceived of: one that will combine earnestness with tolerance, 'the strength of an ordered set of convictions, with that pliability

[177] Paul, *Critic*, Aug. 1, 1851, pp. 347, 348. For isolated examples of this kind of criticism, see *DubUM*, LXVIII (Nov. 1856), 576; *NatRev*, XII (Jan. 1861), 272.
[178] *Bwy*, n.s. II, 223, 225, 224, 226.   [179] P. 226.

and that receptiveness in face of new truth, which are indispensable to these very convictions being held intelligently and in their best attainable form.' " [180] What Houghton wanted was, in short, academic criticism at its best, and in 1867 in the *North British Review* he could have found a good example of this criticism in an article on Emerson. The author was John Nichol, the brilliant professor of English language and literature at the University of Glasgow.[181]

Emerson had always interested the academic mind. In the forties his works were read at Oxford; [182] in the mid-fifties the halls of the University "resounded with his name." At Cambridge he served as one of the heroes of A. C. Benson, and "in 1874 the students of Glasgow invited . . . [him] to be a candidate for the office of Lord Rector of their University." [183] Arnold, Sterling, Clough—all professors or closely connected with universities—were inspired by Emerson. Froude and Kingsley were both university oriented.[184] Emerson had, of course, gained the attention of the American academic world also. He was castigated by Professors Norton and Bowen and championed by Professor Hedge.[185] By 1870, when Emerson taught for a few months at Harvard,[186] one could "see a certain change in his audience, above all in the Boston audience for whom he lectured most often, from a preponderance of the 'very quiet, plain, even obscure class, . . . young, or else mystical' who, . . . in 1844, were the readers who belonged to him, to an increasing number of 'the great literary and fashionable army' who began in the next ten years to take him up." [187] Members of the literary army, like Charles Woodbury, were often young, and a number of them, like Franklin B. Sanborn, James E. Cabot, and George E. Woodberry, were closely connected with the academic world.[188]

---

[180] P. 180.

[181] XLVII (Dec. 1867) , 319–58. This essay was rearranged and published in Nichol's *American Literature: An Historical Sketch, 1620–1880* (Edinburgh, 1882) , pp. 287–321, which received fine reviews: *Ac*, Dec. 30, 1882, p. 464; *Ath*, Jan. 20, 1883, p. 80; *BQR*, LXXVIII (Oct. 1883) , 493.

[182] Scudder, pp. 68–69.

[183] Clarence Gohdes, "The Reception of Some Nineteenth-Century American Authors in Europe," in Denny and Gilman, p. 117; Gohdes, *Amer. Lit.*, pp. 145, 146.

[184] Houghton, p. 64; Scudder, pp. 61–63, 155–56, 68.   [185] Miller, pp. 193, 173, 67.

[186] Rusk, *Life*, pp. 442–43.   [187] Whicher, p. 164.

[188] Carpenter, pp. 46, 48; Rusk, *Life*, pp. 430, 387, 390, 306, 442, 443.

Literary ranks were also forming around Emerson in Great Britain, and, as in America, young professors led the movement. After his death in 1882 some of England's finest scholar-critics published articles on him, delivering him almost completely from the hands of the Philistines and the light-hearted neutrals. They will be treated in Chapter V.

⊲ⱥ III ⱦⱦ

The Poet

ARLY Victorians had been disappointed that *Poems* was not a mellifluous, traditional collection after the manner of Longfellow, just as Mid-Victorians, brought up on the more sentimental verse of Tennyson and the warm effusions of Martin Tupper, a poet of "vast and steady popularity," [1] were chilled by the poems in *May-Day and Other Pieces.* That Emerson's poetry received so many notices in Great Britain was due mainly to the fact that the classical tradition, to which the nineteenth century still adhered, viewed a national literature "in terms of its poetry." [2] Although several British reviewers lauded *Poems* and a few American devotees of Emerson liked much of his early poetry, critics were generally derogatory.[3] Out of deference to the tradition and to Emerson's presence in Great Britain shortly after *Poems* went on sale there, three bored reviewers pointed out that some of the volume disclosed "much beauty," that even though the work revealed some atrocious rhymes and imagery it was distinguished by a sense of the beautiful and good, and that of all the poets in Griswold's anthology Emerson was one of the few to rise above an "elegant mediocrity." [4]

[1] *Social England,* ed. H. D. Traill (London, 1897), VI, 515; *Victorians on Literature & Art,* ed. Robert L. Peters (New York, 1961), p. 4.

[2] Clarence Gohdes, *American Literature in Nineteenth-Century England* (New York, 1944), p. 129.

[3] George Gilfillan, *Tait's,* n.s. XV (Jan. 1848), 17; [Parke Godwin], *People's,* Nov. 28 (?), 1847, p. 307; Ralph L. Rusk, *The Life of Ralph Waldo Emerson* (New York, 1949), pp. 322, 323; Clarence Gohdes, *The Periodicals of American Transcendentalism* (Durham, N.C., 1931), p. 184.

[4] *WFQR,* XLVII (April 1847), 250; *Ex,* May 8, 1847, p. 292; *FQR,* XXXII (Jan. 1844), 311.

Other critics were more caustic. They termed the poems "turgid and extravagant," cold and inartistic. To George Gilfillan's comment that in "Wood-Notes" Emerson seems "an inspired tree," a furious reviewer answered, "We cannot here agree with Mr. Gilfillan; to us, the fir-tree is very like Mr. Emerson, and not at all like a tree." [5] In the fifties one critic declared that Emerson's "verses fall upon us with the cold and heavy rumble of mere corpses," another that "his proudest passages resemble the nodding plumes of a hearse." [6] Even the critics who found adequate warmth in his verses were not enthusiastic about them. Mid-Victorians grumbled that many of his poems were "riddles which would have baffled Oedipus"; one half of the stanzas introducing chapters in *The Conduct of Life* were "not worth the trouble of reading, and the other not worth the trouble of understanding." [7] *May-Day and Other Pieces*, they said, "displays all those peculiarities which make the author's poems so attractive to his disciples, and so unreadable to the outer world"; in the book he wrote too much of man and not enough of men; some of the work was "doggrel." [8]

Not all comments of Mid-Victorians on Emerson the poet were quite so derogatory. Charles Kingsley suggested that Emerson "has a faculty for rapidly seizing remote analogies, which is rather poetic than philosophic," [9] but it was the *Eclectic Review,* "ablest" of the orthodox Dissenting journals,[10] that gave the most appreciative account of Emerson's poetry. "Above all," wrote the excellent critic and clergyman, "he is a poet, although a peculiar one.... He does not dazzle by solitary images and single verses, but pleases most by a playful, coaxing, half-tantalizing beauty. His verse is rarely polished, often faulty, seldom mellifluous, but never spasmodic. Gentle, serene, meditative, it runs and hops along in defiance of Horace, Boileau, and all the vicegerents of Parnassus. For many reasons it

[5] *DubR,* XXVI (March 1849) , 177; *Critic,* Jan. 2, 1847, pp. 9, 10; *ChR,* XV (April 1848) , 349.

[6] *BQR,* XI (May 1850) , 313; *ScR,* V (Jan. 1857) , 17.

[7] *Museum,* II (Oct. 1862) , 276; *SatR,* Dec. 15, 1860, p. 762.

[8] *SatR,* Aug. 24, 1867, p. 268; *LondR,* June 1, 1867, p. 629; *Ath,* May 2, 1868, p. 626.

[9] *SatR,* Oct. 4, 1856, p. 510.

[10] Francis E. Mineka, *The Dissidence of Dissent: The Monthly Repository* (Chapel Hill, N.C., 1944) , p. 67.

might almost as well have been in prose, but then one would have been as much inclined to recommend [that] it should be at once turned into verse, so delicately indefinite are most of his poetic graces." [11] One would like to have heard more from this churchman on Emerson's poetry, but, unfortunately, he devoted only several paragraphs to the subject.

In fact, the first long article in English journals devoted exclusively to the poetry of Emerson appeared in 1884, some forty-five years after the *Westminster Review* had brought him to the attention of British periodical readers and almost twenty years after *May-Day and Other Pieces* had appeared. In this article C. E. Tyrer commented on several themes running through Emerson's poetry, mentioned the influence of other poets on Emerson, and compared his poetry with that of other American poets. He also examined Emerson's unorthodox prosody and tried to account for it by referring to Emerson's poetical theories.[12] The rest of this chapter will treat each of these topics. This treatment will reveal that as the century progressed Victorians never wavered in their appreciation of some of Emerson's poetry, that they never changed in their aversion to some of it, and that in several instances late Victorians accepted poetry that the earlier had derided. Most interestingly, the comments of these critics gave a clear view of the struggle that takes place when the critical *status quo* is confronted with a new art form.

II

Keepers of the critical seal sensibly began their inspection of the brash Emerson with a search for his themes, one of which was patriotism. "There have yet been few better citizens or truer patriots than he," wrote Tyrer, who maintained that the American's patriotism was especially manifest in his antislavery activities. Emerson "caught the glow [of the movement], and coming out of his scholarly retreat gave lectures and addresses on the burning topics of the hour." In addition, said Tyrer, he wrote an excellent poem

---

[11] 8th ser. III (Nov. 1862), 400, 402.   [12] *ManQ*, III (April 1884), 105–28.

entitled "Boston Hymn." Tyrer also praised "Concord Hymn," as did John Nichol. A trumpet call of liberty, wrote the Scottish professor, "the hymn sung at the completion of the Concord Monument is thoroughly patriotic and at the same time strong and dignified." An anonymous reviewer praised both the Boston and Concord hymns, while another said that the latter poem was among Emerson's best. Matthew Arnold also lauded "the noble lines graven on the Concord Monument," and Coulson Kernahan, a poet in his own right, asserted that "the most faultless of . . . [Emerson's] poems is the one on 'Concord Fight.'" Writing in a British journal in 1887, an American, F. H. Underwood, who claimed "to have been the projector of the *Atlantic Monthly*," maintained that the poem was "an almost perfect specimen of art, and one stanza [the first] is surely immortal." [13]

A second theme that the Victorians were able to isolate falls within a category which Professor Nichol termed the "home affections" and which the editor R. E. Prothero called poems of "self-revelation." [14] In these pieces, Nichol wrote admiringly, Emerson spoke "of a love that is neither 'initial,' 'demonic,' nor 'celestial,' but human, and the consciousness of a common share in common joys and griefs." The best examples, according to the professor, were "In Memoriam," "The Farewell," "To J. W.," and "To Ellen." Other critics also praised Emerson's poems celebrating the affections. "No one," declared one reviewer, "has written more beautifully of those twin-sweeteners of life, love and friendship, than he has," and another commended "Good-bye" and "Give All to Love" for their "extreme sincerity and simplicity." Emerson's son wrote in the *Bookman* that "the poem 'Good-bye, proud world . . . ,' bears witness to the delight and relief with which a shy boy, teaching bright and pretty Boston girls of nearly his own age all day, plunged into the safe and picturesque thickets on the rocky hillsides of Roxbury." "Most ex-

[13] *ManQ*, III, 125, 126; *NBrR*, XLVII (Dec. 1867), 331; *LondR*, June 1, 1867, p. 630; *Museum*, II (Oct. 1862), 276; Arnold, *MM*, L (May 1884), 4; *LQR*, LXXIII (Oct. 1889), 32 (internal evidence strongly suggests that this article was written by the author of "Is Emerson a Poet?" *NatRev*, XXXVI [Dec. 1900], 523–36, which was signed by Coulson Kernahan); *LitW*, June 23, 1882, p. 387; F. H. Underwood, *Good Words*, XXVIII (Dec. 1887), 810.

[14] *NBrR*, XLVII, 329; *QR*, CLXIII (Oct. 1886), 378.

quisite of all [Emerson's lyrics]," declared Tyrer, "perhaps are three little love poems, all probably addressed to the lady who became his first wife. . . . These are 'To Ellen at the South,' 'Thine eyes still shined for me,' and 'To Eva.' " [15]

Another subject, which Nichol put under the home affections, was that of death. Although Coulson Kernahan and John Morley commented on the "absence of all that is doleful" in Emerson's poems and Nichol himself said that "the prevailing tone of the most intelligible [poems] . . . is cheerful," the Scotsman also praised "Dirge" and "Threnody." So did many other Victorian critics, among whom was Leslie Stephen. "Few poems are more touching," he said, and an anonymous reviewer wrote that "in the DIRGE and again in the beautiful THRENODY, . . . we see the suppressed grief of a truly noble nature teaching how a great sorrow should be nobly borne." Tyrer declared that "there are few sweeter lamentations than the 'Dirge,' " a view shared by a critic on the *Museum*.[16] Perhaps the more popular of the lamentations was that on the dead son. Among Emerson's pieces, wrote Kernahan, none is "so full of noble pathos, so touching in the tenderness and yet the manliness of its sorrow, as his 'Threnody.' " The *Dublin Review* found the poem an exception to his "enigmatical inversions," and other periodical critics described it as "exquisite," "a sob of passionate grief," and "beautiful." It was, said the *London Review*, "one of the noblest poems ever written." In "Terminus," another poem of the home affections, a journal noted that "Emerson strikes the first note of his advancing years, and [that] it is fitting to take leave of this simple and sincere soul, . . . in the concluding lines of what there is every reason to believe was his last poem." [17]

A third theme which critics fixed upon in Emerson's poetry was the religio-philosophical. Unlike the "home affections," it received

[15] *NBrR*, XLVII, 330; *MM*, LXXXVIII (May 1903) , 44; *Sp*, Feb. 10, 1906, p. 220; *Bookman*, XXIV (June 1903) , 94; *ManQ*, III, 122.

[16] *LQR*, LXXIII, 26; Walter Lewin, *Ac*, Aug. 16, 1884, p. 101; *NBrR*, XLVII, 330; Stephen, *NatRev*, XXXVI (Feb. 1901) , 896; *MM*, LXXXVIII (May 1903) , 45; Tyrer, *ManQ*, III, 122; *Museum*, II (Oct. 1862) , 276.

[17] *LQR*, LXXIII, 33, and *NatRev*, XXXVI, 531; *DubR*, XXVI, 177; *ModR*, IV (Oct. 1883) , 856; *QR*, CLXIII, 378; *MM*, LXXXVIII (May 1903) , 45; *LondR*, June 1, 1867, p. 630; *MM*, LXXXVIII (May 1903) , 45.

little praise. Early critics especially were affronted at Emerson's treatment of this theme, one of them painfully asserting that *Poems* was "distinct pantheism." Emerson's "universe without a God," darkly proclaimed the *British Quarterly Review* in 1850, extinguished "the fires of eloquence and poetry. . . . Whether he sings of riddles, problems, fate, love, . . . it is still the dull chatter of mummies." A third journal complained that "The World-Soul," "Fate," "Uriel," and "Each and All" were merely "philosophical memoranda," and another early critic declared that "The Sphynx" "shews him at his worst in matter and in manner," while the *Remembrancer* called poems like "Uriel," "Mithridates," and "The Sphynx" "nonsense." [18] Some ten or twelve years later critics were still animadverting against Emerson's religio-philosophical verse. The *Scottish Review* asserted in 1857 that he customarily dwells "in an element of joy; but it is a dreary joy, scarce equal to a Christian's melancholy." In 1862 the *Museum* sarcastically noted Emerson's "speculations about the 'world soul,' " and eight years later the *Westminster* complained that Emerson's poetry was highly "Germanized." "There is a mystic abstruseness about his poems, marring their harmony; for the interblending of philosophy and poetry is far from successfully managed." Nichol wrote in 1867 that "most readers of our author's earlier volume of verse have puzzled over 'The Sphinx.' Let them endeavour to unravel . . . 'Brahma.' " [19]

Later critics found more of value in this poem and in Emerson's other philosophical memoranda than did Nichol and the early critics. They were unable to shed light on many of Emerson's "transcendental enigmas," but a few had heard what Prothero called Emerson's "bugle-call . . . against utilitarianism." Egan Mew wrote approvingly that the American's poetry often rose to "flights of transcendental beauty," and Tyrer expressed admiration for that philosophy which offered Emerson "infinite consolation amid all the perplexities and basenesses of the times." In "Xenophanes," he had effectively set forth "the unity that underlies and binds together the

[18] *ChR*, XV (April 1848), 349; *BQR*, XI (May 1850), 313; *Ath*, Feb. 6, 1847, p. 145; *Critic*, Jan. 2, 1847, p. 10; *ChR*, XV (April 1848), 348, 349.

[19] *ScR*, V (Jan. 1857), 17; *Museum*, II (Oct. 1862), 276; *WR*, XCIV (Oct. 1870), 268; *NBrR*, XLVII, 331.

variety and multiplicity of things."[20] Several late Victorians even praised the poem which had unnerved Nichol. Writing of "Brahma," the editor and essayist George Stewart found the poem "fantastic, but very pretty," and another critic could not "help feeling a haunting quality about these lines, a kind of individual charm which belongs to Emerson alone. There is something in their mystic dryness, in their uncoloured nudity, which stamps them in the mind, and may perhaps preserve them. It will not surprise us . . . to find Emerson better remembered by this fragment than by all the volumes of his collected works." And in 1906 a perceptive reviewer observed that "poems like 'Merlin' and 'Brahma' owe their merit to their sheer imaginative force."[21]

Later Victorians were also more sympathetic to Emerson's pantheism than the earlier had been. Nichol maintained that "Mr. Emerson's allegorical poetry is mainly employed in giving a body, at times somewhat nebulous, to what we may term his physical idealism. The nature we see around us . . . is, he maintains, the key to the nature which is unseen." "In his temple, man as he is is the worshipper, and man as he ought to be and may be is the chief object of worship. In this spirit his recent 'Song of Nature' anticipates the development yet awaiting the race." A church journal observed in 1899 that "one of the first things to notice in Emerson's poems is his intense love of Nature." "Emerson describes how Nature manifests Deity." It was, wrote the churchman, "impossible . . . for Emerson to . . . write about Nature and forget God."[22] Unlike these two critics, most other Victorians made no attempt to link pantheism with Emerson's poetry. This was fortunate, for with the veils of philosophy removed from Emerson's nature poems, Victorians could enjoy the pieces for themselves. Many did.

"Emerson's love for nature," wrote a critic in 1849, "is one of the most remarkable of his characteristics as a writer. . . . And in many

[20] *NBrR*, XLVII, 331; *QR*, CLXIII, 377; Mew, *Lit*, Sept. 21, 1901, p. 272; Tyrer, *ManQ*, III, 117, 118.

[21] George Stewart, Jr., *Belford's*, I (Jan. 1877) , 226; *Ath*, March 8, 1884, p. 307; *Sp*, Feb. 10, 1906, p. 220.

[22] *NBrR*, XLVII, 338, 339; Henry J. Foster, *PMQR*, n.s. XXI (April 1899) , 295, 296, 297.

respects, it is a true, modest, and poetic love." "Breathing through all his poetry and most of his prose, it furnishes his most beautiful illustrations. . . . In the fields under the woods, among the mountains, he loses himself, and becomes a poet—a POET full of eloquence, gladness, and love." Among Emerson's works are to be found poems, said the *Museum* in 1862, "clear and strong as a torrent from his native hills, fresh with 'odours of brine from the ocean,' or clover from the fields." Nichol wrote in 1867 that "the rippling of rivers, the sough of the pine . . . give life to his descriptions. A morning light is thrown over his happiest pages." [23]

A multitude of critics snipped excerpts from the nature poems and held them up for approval. After quoting a passage from "May-Day," the *London Review* observed that the poem was "an exquisite spring cantata." It "brings together," said the poet-priest John Charles Earle, "more lovely images of Spring than were probably ever before collected into so small a compass," while George Saintsbury referred to the poem as "charming." It was, asserted Underwood, "a New England spring," and " 'Each and All,' 'The Problem,' 'Woodnotes,' and other poems, . . . many persons maintain[, are] . . . the most strikingly original and imaginative of the century." [24] Tyrer wrote that in "May-Day," "My Garden," "Woodnotes," and "Waldeinsamkeit," "we seem transported into the solemn avenues of the forest, roofed and carpeted with green, and the fragrance of pinecones fills the air." "The Adirondacs," said the *London Review,* was "very charming." "The Rhodora" was another poem highly praised by the British. It was "exquisite," "a perfect gem." When someone asked Emerson, wrote W. J. Gallagher, " 'Whence is the flower?' he gave in answer ['The Rhodora,'] one of the noblest sonnets, . . . in this or any other language." The "grand words" of "The Snow-Storm" rang into the ears of Stewart "like the sound of silver bells." [25]

A random sampling follows: "Many of his descriptions of field and

---

[23] *DubR*, XXVI, 162; *Museum*, II (Oct. 1862) , 276; *NBrR*, XLVII, 329.

[24] *LondR*, June 1, 1867, p. 629; [Earle], *DubR*, n.s. XXIII (July 1874) , 74; Saintsbury, *Ac*, May 6, 1882, p. 320; Underwood, *Good Words*, XXVIII, 813, 810.

[25] Tyrer, *ManQ*, III, 111, 112, 114, 112; *LondR*, June 1, 1867, p. 630; Tyrer, *ManQ*, III, 124; *MM*, LXXXVIII (May 1903) , 45; Gallagher, *Great Thoughts*, 4th ser. VIII (July 1901) , 180; Stewart, *Belford's*, I, 225.

forest are wonderfully truthful"; "Emerson is generally at his best when he is describing nature"; "here and there" in such poetry "he touches the soul with something like an inspiration." His poems have "a wild music" allied "to the spontaneous outbursts of Nature"; "the lilt of them seems borrowed unconsciously from nature's music." Gallagher declared rapturously, "I read homely wisdom in Burns; scenery and nobility in Scott; strength of wild imagery in Byron. . . . But, on another day, I wanted to find out this: who amongst them all shall teach me the combined lore of soul, and heart, and exertion; the whole lore of woodland, valley, and river in one? And I opened Emerson. . . . All the mildness of Thoreau; and all the simplicity of Wordsworth centre in this strong-minded man." [26]

III

Very few critics set Emerson's poetry beside that of Thoreau, and only two compared it with Swinburne's and Carlyle's,[27] but several did compare and contrast Emerson's poetry with Wordsworth's as well as with that of Blake and the metaphysicals. The American's message, said the critics, was like that of the Cumbrian, his manner akin to that of Blake, Marvell, and Herbert.

Wordsworth, wrote the *London Review*, was the modern poet whom Emerson admired above all others, and both poets, observed another journal, had their "working-room" outdoors. The Englishman, according to most of these journals, was more at home in this room than the American. Emerson's themes, wrote the *Review*, "take on less various forms . . . and have also less colour" than those of Wordsworth, and Nichol said that "the delicate touches in some of his quieter reflective pictures are not unworthy of the author of 'The Excursion.' " [28] Several other commentators extended the compari-

[26] *LQR*, LXXIII, 31; W. L. Courtney, *FR*, n.s. XXXVIII (Sept. 1885), 330; Tyrer, *ManQ*, III, 107; Gallagher, *GT*, 4th ser. VIII, 179, 180.

[27] Stewart, *Belford's*, I, 223: [Richard Holt Hutton], *Sp*, May 6, 1882, p. 590. One of the wittiest comments on Emerson the poet was made by De Quincey, who described him "as the palimpsest of a small Thomas Carlyle upon the Yankee copy of a Martin Tupper" (P. L[andreth], *Blackwood's*, CLV [April 1894], 481).

[28] *LondR*, June 1, 1867, p. 629; Hamilton Wright Mabie, *MMR*, LVIII (July 1903), 18 (condensed from the *New Outlook*); *LondR*, June 1, 1867, p. 629; *NBrR*, XLVII, 329.

son between the two. Both poets, wrote Kernahan, expressed a "lordly contempt for the mere rhyme-maker" and "for the man who cannot forget 'copy' even in his secret communings with Nature." Both worship "the great Mother"; "the poems of the one are as passionless as those of the other. Like Wordsworth it is Nature to whom Emerson turns for consolation in all his woes." "Each and All" is Wordsworthian in "form" as well as in "spirit." The widely known classicist, Richard Garnett, asserted in *Literature* that both poets lack humour, yet "Emerson never appears absurd from insensibility to the humourous, as frequently happens to Wordsworth." Both are "children of nature." The main difference between the two children, Garnett said, lay in their sense of mission. "Wordsworth is conscious and overconscious of a mission, while Emerson can hardly be said to have proposed any object to himself except that of speaking as it might be given to him to speak." Emerson is, maintained Garnett cogently, "the ideal which Wordsworth frequently embodies in his personages, but rarely realizes in himself." [29]

Of these critics who found an affinity between Emerson and Wordsworth, three made very astute comments, for they found in the poetry a new message. Emerson "caught the luminous glow, the chastened passion, the serene outlook on life, of the great Cumbrian's noblest verse," wrote James Bell. "To him Wordsworth was a revealer of realities behind the passing shows of sense and time: a voice speaking to a perplexed generation a message of ideal power and peace." At the center of this reality was a love of nature. The American, continued Bell, "assimilated the real message of Wordsworth to the age —his new attitude towards nature, his intuition of the essential dignity and worth of man as man." Underwood concurred with Bell: "Every one knows that the passion for natural scenery is modern, hardly more remote than the time of Wordsworth; ... to Emerson, perhaps more than any American writer, is due the revolution in taste and in the judgment of poetry.... [It was a] victory won by Wordsworth, aided so powerfully in America by Emerson." This victory, Milnes had suggested, constituted a part of the very heart of the American's philosophy: "the Poetry of daily life," "the recogni-

---

[29] Kernahan, *NatRev*, XXXVI, 528, 529; *Lit*, Sept. 21, 1901, pp. 276, 275.

tion of the elements of Poetry in the circumstances of the most humble and usual life." [30]

Emerson would have been still more effective, these critics pointed out, if his prosody had been acceptable. In comparing Wordsworth and Emerson, Garnett had written that the American's "feeling for artistic form, except in isolated sayings," makes the "generally amorphous character of his poetry almost incomprehensible." [31] Emerson's prosody is, indeed, much different from Wordsworth's: it is closer to that of Blake and the metaphysical poets, as several critics make clear. "Resemblances to Emerson," commented a perspicacious critic, "are not easy to find in modern poetry," but "there is one . . . later poet of whom Emerson reminds us, at times very strongly"—Blake. Appreciation of one, wrote this critic, implied appreciation of the other. "The poet of 'The Sphinx' and 'Uriel' has much in common, and deeper than any trick of form, with the poet of the 'Songs of Experience.' " The critic discovered "something very Blakish in the tone of the 'Boston Hymn.' " Other critics saw something Blakish in Emerson's poems, too. Leslie Stephen observed that a true poetic inspiration came to Emerson "as it came to Blake in the midst of much incoherence and stammering utterance." "The Romany Girl," declared an anonymous reviewer, "might be William Blake's," and Garnett asserted that Emerson's poems breathed the spirit of Blake. Like the English poet, Emerson was "more fitly classed with the seers, whose insight comes to them by simple intuition, than with the poets and prophets, who require to be taken out of themselves." At the same time, Emerson's "supernatural pretentions" were not so offensive as Blake's. [32]

Closer to Emerson than either Wordsworth or Blake were the poets of the seventeenth century, a discovery that only a few Victo-

---

[30] Bell, *Quarto*, I (1897), 22; Underwood, *Good Words*, XXVIII, 809; R[ichard] M. M[ilnes], *LWR*, XXXIII (March 1840), 193, 194. For other comments on the Emerson-Wordsworth relationship, see *MonM*, n.s. II (Sept. 1839), 344, 347; [George Cupples], *Jerrold'sS*, VII (April 1848), 326; *NBrR*, XLVII, 322, 338; *Ac*, Feb. 28, 1885, p. 143; Tyrer, *ManQ*, III, 110; Walter Lewin, *Ac*, July 12, 1890, p. 26; Courtney, *FR*, n.s. XXXVIII, 331.

[31] *Lit*, Sept. 21, 1901, p. 275.

[32] *SatR*, April 18, 1885, p. 513; Stephen, *NatRev*, XXXVI, 896; *ModR*, IV (Oct. 1883), 856; Garnett, *Lit*, Sept. 21, 1901, p. 275.

rians made. Emerson's poetical work, wrote a sympathetic reviewer, abounds in a "rough-hewn simplicity," which is characteristic of the poetry of that period. Although Emerson's poems were like those of the early Milton, continued the critic, they were even more akin to those of Marvell. Nichol expressed something of the same opinion when he wrote that "Good-bye" "breathes the spirit of Quarles or Andrew Marvell." According to Underwood, "Emerson's debt to Wordsworth was a matter of sentiment only." "If he imitated any poet, it was ... Herbert." [33] An army of critics defied such poets: their works lacked the first requirements of good poetry—melody and structure.

IV

Doting on the ringing passages of what one critic called the "elaborate verse-makers," the nineteenth century was ill prepared for Emerson's cacophony. In 1847 William Henry Smith wrote that *Poems* revealed "an inaptitude to employ the forms of verse, so that the style, instead of being invigorated, and polished, and concentrated by the necessary attention to line and metre, becomes denaturalised, constrained, crude, and unequal." In the same year the *Examiner* complained that "the structure of his stanzas often suggests a doubt as to the accuracy of his ear for rhythmical melody." Two years later the *Dublin Review* asserted that "trammelled by rhyme, he twists old English into the oddest paroxysms and the most enigmatical inversions." [34] This dissatisfaction was heard throughout the century. Critics castigated Emerson's "laborious," "harsh, clumsy, depressing," "lame, unscannable lines." His verse, others said, occasionally "hobbles ... and stumbles," it was "sometimes crabbed," it was "somewhat rugged and unmatured." The poems were "wanting in melody"; they "limp, and halt, and start, and leap, and fairly tumble." [35] Emerson had no ability "to rhyme correctly";

[33] *SatR*, April 18, 1885, p. 513; *NBrR*, XLVII, 330; Underwood, *Good Words*, XXVIII, 814. Tyrer, *ManQ*, III, 110, agrees with Underwood.

[34] Tyrer, *ManQ*, III, 107; *Blackwood's*, LXII (Dec. 1847), 656; *Ex*, May 8, 1847, p. 292; *DubR*, XXVI (March 1849), 177.

[35] [Richard Holt Hutton], *Sp*, Feb. 2, 1884, p. 155; Mew, *Lit*, Sept. 21, 1901, p. 272; Foster, *PMQR*, n.s. XXI, 294; *QR*, CLXIII, 378; *Notes*, Aug. 26, 1905, p. 160; E. Forster, *Ac*, Dec. 11, 1897, p. 533; *NBrR*, XLVII, 329; *DubR*, n.s. XXIII, 74.

"his deep thoughts are linked to club-foot rhymes"; "his entire lack of ear for music rendered poetical success impossible to him, although many pieces in his two volumes of poems ... are much valued by thoughtful readers." W. L. Courtney, philosopher and editor, gave the heart of the matter when he wrote, "The natural tendency to obey laws of metre and rhythm—seems entirely wanting." [36]

Victorian critics also showed their aversion to the structure of Emerson's poems. "There is no art prescribing the mould into which such materials would be best cast," wrote the *Athenaeum* in 1847, "—no aim ... at composition." Emerson showed "a careless and wilful indifference to form." "Only now and then," said the *Museum* in 1862, does he display "the artistic skill of a poet." Another complained that *May-Day and Other Pieces* displayed everywhere "both slovenliness and indelicacy of workmanship," and other journals maintained that Emerson lacked "an instinct for formative art." "We are perplexed," they said, "by the sudden transition from one idea to another without any 'flowing speech' to carry us across. This is not poetical." [37] Emerson's poems were too fragmentary; "formless, without end, beginning, or middle"; lacking in "an adequate design." Wrote Arnold: "In general, his poems have no evolution." [38]

A great weakness in nineteenth-century critical theory was, according to Emerson, the emphasis it placed upon the whole. "Wonderful is the inconsecutiveness of the Persian poets," he wrote in praise of Saadi. "European criticism finds that the unity of a beautiful whole is everywhere wanting. Not only the story is short," he continued in admiration and as though describing his own poetry, "but no two sentences are joined." [39] Fortunately, a few critics besides Emerson

[36] *MM,* LXXXVIII (May 1903), 44; *CQR,* XXVII (Oct. 1888), 57; *Ath,* May 6, 1882, p. 570; Courtney, *FR,* n.s. XXXVIII, 329.

[37] *Ath,* Feb. 6, 1847, p. 145; Saintsbury, *Ac,* May 6, 1882, p. 320; *Museum,* II (Oct. 1862), 275; *Ath,* May 2, 1868, p. 626; Garnett, *Lit,* Sept. 21, 1901, p. 275; Forster, *Ac,* Dec. 11, 1897, p. 533.

[38] *DubR,* n.s. XXIII, 75; Courtney, *FR,* n.s. XXXVIII, 329; *DubR,* n.s. XXIII, 75; Arnold, *MM,* L, 4. For more comments on Emerson's deficiency in "architectonics," see Garnett, *Lit,* Sept. 21, 1901, p. 275; Stephen, *NatRev,* XXXVI, 896; *SatR,* March 6, 1886, p. 342; G. W. Foote, *Freethinker,* May 24, 1903, p. 321.

[39] Pref. to *The Gulistan; or, Rose Garden,* by Musle-Huddeen Sheik Saadi, trans. Francis Gladwin (Boston, 1865), p. xi. See also Jerome Hamilton Buckley, *The Victorian Temper* (Cambridge, Mass., 1951), p. 25.

understood that such poetry could not be satisfactorily judged by traditional standards, and, even more fortunately, one or two discovered standards that were fairly satisfactory for judging it. One reviewer commented in 1862 that "so peculiar an admixture of shrewd practical insight, ethical by-play, transcendental wit, and original rhyme" as that in Emerson's poetry, is not "likely to be fairly estimated, by those who judge of poetry as professors do of prize-poems, awarding the palm to what is most graceful, rhythmical, and accurately developed." The American Joel Benton, who in 1883 brought out the first book devoted exclusively to Emerson's poetry, suggested in it (wrote Hutton), "There is no delinquency of perception so unhelpable as that which discerns but one literary fashion." And said Tyrer: "That he is truly a poet cannot . . . be denied by any genuine lover of poetry who does not stumble at the unusual, or refuse to acknowledge beauty when it appears in other than the recognized forms." [40]

One critic who did not stumble declared that "we learn to expect, especially in the longer and more purely intellectual poems, certain violations of the established rules of rhyme and rhythm," and Walter Lewin issued the order that Emerson was not to be damned because his "rhyme halts. Rules of prosody are not final." [41] Like Milton's fallen angels, two other critics suggested hopefully that if one made the best of a bad condition and simply put up with it, he would grow used to the crudities and embrace what he once had despised. As for the inelegant structure, Courtney wrote gingerly, "Emerson's poetry will be interpreted differently according to the estimation held of the value of form in poetical composition." Another said, "So rich and varied are the thoughts" that we are often able "to forget, or at least forgive, the medium through which they are expressed." [42]

The perceptive critics refused to accept such easy answers to the problems raised by Emerson's prosody and structure: they attempted to find out why he wrote as he did. Tyrer maintained that

[40] *EcRev*, n.s. III (Nov. 1862), 401; *Sp*, Feb. 2, 1884, p. 155; Tyrer, *ManQ*, III, 128.
[41] *ModR*, IV (Oct. 1883), 856; Lewin, *Ac*, Aug. 16, 1884, p. 101.
[42] Courtney, *FR*, n.s. XXXVIII, 329; Forster, *Ac*, Dec. 11, 1897, p. 533. *QR*, CLXIII, 377, agreed with Courtney.

the reason for the "roughness and wide deviation [of these poems] from the poetical standards of the day" was that Emerson was "akin to the bards, the primitive singers with whom song was a thing of nature rather than of art." "His place is rather with Taliesin and Ossian than with Tennyson and Swinburne. Nature with him, as with the bards, gives many a magical touch to his strains." Tyrer's main concern in Emerson's verse, however, was with the lack of structure in the longer poems. Such pieces as "May Day," "The Adirondacks," and "Wood Notes" were "rarely satisfactory": they lacked "that sustained power of treatment, that coordination of material, necessary to produce the unity of effect which characterizes a great work of art." In his search for the reason behind Emerson's deficiencies in poetical architectonics—a favorite term with the critics—Tyrer turned in several directions. From "such Christian mystics as Behmen and Swedenborg" Emerson "doubtless learned his abundant use of image and metaphor, his abruptness and inconsecutiveness." Another explanation lay, according to Tyrer, in the new discipline, psychology. "The grounds" for his inconsecutiveness, he wrote, "we may find probably in the constitution of Emerson's mind, which was ever catching, like the facets of a diamond, some ray of truth or beauty . . . but had difficulty in elaborating its thoughts and intuitions into connected wholes." [43]

A better place to discover Emerson's strategy would have been in his comments on poetry, and Tyrer did try to apply the "doctrine of Beauty," which he had found in *Nature* and "The Poet," to the "Ode to Beauty," "Wood Notes," and "Each and All." He seemed, however, to have little faith in Emerson's attempts to explain his poetry. "Like the other articles of his philosophical creed," the doctrine of Beauty "wants, perhaps, a clear and consistent definition." [44] If Tyrer is correct, it was not because Emerson did not try to make his theories clear: throughout his life he attempted in essays and poems devoted to the subject as well as in numerous isolated comments to explain why he wrote poetry as he did. This exposition gave critics a sounder basis for the understanding of Emerson's poetry than did their knowledge of themes and influences.

---

[43] *ManQ*, III, 110, 107, 108, 119, 109.   [44] *ManQ*, III, 114, 115, 112, 116, 114.

V

Three years before *Poems* appeared Emerson had explained in "The Poet" his theory of poetry. Early critics commented on the piece, but none was able to comprehend the organic method at which Emerson hinted in the essay or to understand the purpose of a poem, which he stated clearly. The *Biblical Review,* for instance, declared that Emerson's definition of the poet as "the sayer, the namer, and [the one who] represents beauty" meant that "the poet is by his own right the potentate of the universe, seeing that he is beauty, and that beauty, not God, made that universe. Either here is the most unpardonable impiety, or the most senseless rhapsody." To the *Dublin Review* "The Poet" was "a good specimen of the author's vagarious and illogical manner, and his perverse tendency to idle and irrelevant dreaming." [45] In this germinal essay Emerson had stated clearly that poetry is "a metre-making argument." [46] He as well as his reviewers treated poetry as a heuristic medium through which the poet set forth various moral, social, philosophical, and religious dicta. It is, therefore, ironical to find the *Critic* explaining in 1847 that Emerson failed in many of his poems because of his aims: "A poet has no right so to tax his reader's brain. A poem is not a problem ... in mathematics. ... The business of a poet is not to *prove,* but to *preach.*" Another early critic who did not do his homework reviewed *Poems* for the *Christian Remembrancer.* A poem, he implied, must mean something and not merely *be.* "We do not acknowledge a man to be worthy of the title [of poet] who only puts into indistinct dreamy words our indistinct dreamy ideas; but we hail him as a teacher" who "gives form to the vapours ... of our minds." Emerson, declared this writer emphatically, did not give form to that vapour. [47]

John Ruskin also failed to consider Emerson's critical theories. He blandly asserted that "on matters of art" Emerson's mind was "a total blank," an opinion shared in part by Henry James; and the *Athe-*

[45] *BibRev,* I (Feb. 1846) , 150; *DubR,* XXVI, 168.

[46] *The Complete Works of Ralph Waldo Emerson,* ed. Edward Waldo Emerson (Boston, 1903–4) , III, 9—hereafter cited as *Works.*

[47] *Critic,* Jan. 2, 1847, pp. 9–10; *ChR,* XV (April 1848) , 347, 348.

naeum, in its review of *Letters and Social Aims,* blindly maintained that the first essay, "Poetry and Imagination," "is but remotely connected" with poetry. The *National Reformer* declared that the essay was "peculiarly happy, both in thought and in diction," and dismissed the matter. In the Preface to *Parnassus,* Emerson had contended, as the *Westminster Review* duly noted, that "there is a poetry for bards proper, as well as a poetry for the world of readers," and that "the poet must not only converse with pure thought, but he must demonstrate it almost to the senses. His words must be pictures." The reviewer made no attempt to connect Emerson's poetry with these bards and pictures.[48]

Ignoring Emerson's poetical theories altogether, a few critics turned to other bases for judging his poetry. Earle maintained that a poet needed a definite creed to support a solid superstructure of verse, and that Emerson did not have such a creed. A handful of reviewers accepted Carlyle's dictum that "a man's sincerity and depth of vision" make him a poet. Carlyle himself wrote to Emerson the poet, according to R. A. Armstrong, editor of the *Modern Review,* "You do not fall on me like radiant summer rainbows, like floods of sunlight, but with thin piercing radiances which affect me like the light of the *stars"*—to which the critic added, "At the same time, the summer rainbows and sunshine are not altogether wanting." Judged by Carlyle's precepts, wrote *Macmillan's,* "Emerson assuredly deserves to be included among the poets," and using the same measure, Egan Mew wrote that "the author of 'Wood-notes' and 'Threnody' must by right receive that title." The *Spectator* declared that "When he succeeds, as he does occasionally, it is by virtue of an extreme sincerity and simplicity which condone all metrical imperfections." [49]

---

[48] *Ac,* June 12, 1897, p. 613; James, *MM,* LVII (Dec. 1887) , 97; *Ath,* Jan. 15, 1876, p. 81; *NatRef,* March 17, 1878, p. 1099; *WR,* CVII (Jan. 1877) , 292. In the same issue *WR,* p. 297, also carried a paragraph review of *Letters and Social Aims,* remarking only that the volume "promises to be more popular than any of his former works." For other comment on the Emerson-Ruskin relationship, see Douglas Story, *NCRev,* IV (Sept. 1898) , 196; *T. P.'s,* April 3, 1903, p. 653; *Blackwood's,* CXIII (May 1873) , 542; *NatRef,* March 9, 1861, p. 8; Foote, *Freethinker,* June 7, 1903, p. 353; *Bookman,* II (April 1892) , 15.

[49] *DubR,* n.s. XXIII (July 1874) , 75; *MM,* LXXXVIII (May 1903) , 44; *ModR,* IV (April 1883) , 327 (this article was signed, "The Editor," who was Armstrong) ; *MM,*

Some of the most interesting comments were made by students of the so-called Spasmodic School, which arose during the fifties. Members of this school dreamed of writing "a Victorian epic ample enough to embrace the manifold aspiration of the nineteenth century." [50] Unfortunately, their efforts were almost totally lacking in architectonics. An anonymous critic on the *Saturday Review* doubtless had this school in mind when, in a review of a miniature edition of *Poems,* he spoke of the volume as "the earliest and not by any means the most incomprehensible production of that mystic, harsh, condensed school of poetry which has become so prominent within the last quarter of a century." [51] Gilfillan also noted the mysticism as well as the incomprehensibility of Emerson's poetry, but as "the patron saint of Spasmodic genius," he found these aspects of the work greatly appealing.[52] Commenting on *Poems* in 1848, Gilfillan wrote that the verses "mean absolutely nothing" except to "those who have learned their cypher," and he eagerly admitted that he had not learned it. To understand what a poet was saying would have been sacrilege: to Gilfillan and the Spasmodics, the poet was "a divinely inspired creature" and his works beyond analysis.[53] "What Mr. Emerson's [poetic] creed is, we honestly say we do not know—that all we can confidently assert concerning it is, that you cannot gather it like apples into baskets, . . . nor even collect it like sunlight into a focus, and analyse it into prismatic points. . . . Beauty pitches her tents around its borders, and Wonder looks up toward it with rapt eye. . . . It is such a creed as a man might form and subscribe in a dream, and when he awoke receive a gentle shrift from wise and gentle confessors." Out of this creed came Emerson's "little volume of poems. They are not wholes, but extracts, from the volume of his mind." They are "as beautiful, changeful, capricious, and unfathomable often, as the song of the birds." [54]

Gilfillan's chief disciple in the crusade of the Spasmodics was Robert Buchanan, who dedicated his first book to his master. Rather

---

LXXXVIII (May 1903) , 44; Mew, *Lit,* Sept. 21, 1901, p. 270; *Sp,* Feb. 10, 1906, p. 220. See Buckley, pp. 37–38, for more on Carlyle's critical theories.

[50] Buckley, p. 43.   [51] Dec. 30, 1876, p. 827.

[52] Buckley, pp. 43, 50, 41–66 *passim.*

[53] Gilfillan, *Tait's,* n.s. XV, 17; Buckley, p. 42.

[54] Gilfillan, *Tait's,* n.s. XV, 18, 17.

than supplementing Gilfillan, however, Buchanan serves as a nice antidote. The American's poetry was "not great nor influential . . . , but poetry where clear vision produces just enough emotion to necessitate musical expression. There is no abandonment of personality, no dramatic force nor lyrical fervour, but there is a meditative tenderness which softens the intellectual note into tones closely resembling lyrical sweetness." Three years after writing on Emerson, Buchanan made the notorious attack on Rossetti and the Pre-Raphaelites, and in 1898 Douglas Story declared the members of that school to be Emerson's "earliest disciples." "Like them, he had gone back from the 'temper of imitation, prosaic acceptance, pseudo-classicism . . .' to the 'temper of wonder, reverence, and awe.' " [55]

Arnold protested the critical methods of his contemporaries: something was obviously wrong when head-on critical crashes like those of Buchanan and Story were common. A recent critic of Emerson, wrote Arnold attempting to stabilize the situation, praised the American because "fifty or sixty passages" from his poems have "already entered into English speech as matter of familiar . . . quotation." This kind of criticism was deplorable; rather than use it, Arnold relied on Milton's definition that poetry is "simple, sensuous, impassioned," thereby eliminating Emerson from the ranks of the poets. Almost immediately critics called that measuring rod "arbitrary" and "an absurdity." A "strict application" of the test, wrote Tyrer sensibly, "would be fatal to nearly all poetry of the reflective order, including Mr. Arnold's own"; and in a forceful rebuttal in which he refuted Arnold's whole judgment of Emerson, C. A. Ward commented astutely that the test would "make a clean sweep" not only of Emerson's poems but "of nearly all the poets in Chalmers and Anderson's collection of English poets." [56]

Like Lionel Trilling's remarks on Robert Frost, Arnold's on Emerson started a small critical war. Although the *Westminster* wrote that the article attested Arnold's "possession of the critical

---

[55] Buckley, p. 60; Robert Buchanan, *Bwy,* n.s. II (May 1869) , 226; Story, *NCRev,* IV, 196.

[56] Arnold, *MM,* L, 3; Tyrer, *ManQ,* III, 128; *Ac,* July 18, 1885, p. 35; Tyrer, *ManQ,* III, 128; C. A. Ward, *TBar,* LXXII (Oct. 1884) , 238. Ward's opinion would have pleased Emerson, who wrote that those "voluminous octavos" had "too much mass and too little genius" (*Parnassus,* ed. Ralph Waldo Emerson [Boston, 1875], p. iii) .

faculty," Lewin maintained that the classicist's judgment of Emerson as poet was "hard," and in several other articles Lewin minimized Arnoldian strictures against Emerson and emphasized the praise. The *Saturday Review* spoke sarcastically of the "serene confidence" which Arnold had shown in denying Emerson the name of poet or philosopher or writer, and Moncure D. Conway labeled the lecture as "unfortunate" and a "vague tribute." [57] Few Victorians, writes J. H. Buckley, understood Arnold's "sharper cultural insights. But from the first years of Victoria's reign his desire for an increased objectivity had been shared by more sanguine artists emerging to produce a new literature—a literature concerned not with the classic generalities Arnold commended, but seeking its universals always in the particular, through an unromantic 'realism.' " [58]

Several critics indicated that Emerson was one of these artists. At one point in his "fragmentary criticism," wrote Edith Simcox of "Poetry and Imagination," Emerson was "almost in contact with the most prosaic school of modern realists, who believe that they have only to cultivate a sufficient height and heat of enthusiasm in themselves to hoist their own prosaic surroundings into true poetic grandeur and importance." This talented feminist did not make clear where Emerson had shown such enthusiasm, but some of the other critics did: it was in "The Humble Bee." Although Underwood called "The Problem" "the high water mark" of poetry in the century, and Courtney maintained that it stood "head and shoulders above the usual stature of Emerson's muse," [59] and still others lauded (as we have seen) poems like "Concord Hymn," "Threnody," and "The Rhodora," "The Humble Bee" was praised as widely and as warmly as any of Emerson's poems. Courtney, it is true, did not like

[57] *WR*, CXLV (May 1896), 586; Lewin, *Ac*, Aug. 16, 1884, p. 101; *Ac*, July 12, 1890, p. 26; *Bookman*, XXIV (June 1903), 89; *SatR*, April 18, 1885, p. 512; Conway, *OC*, V (March 1885), 140. For other comment, pro and con, on Arnold's piece and on the Emerson-Arnold relationship, see Lewin, *Bookman*, XXIV (Sept. 1903), 215; Courtney, *FR*, n.s. XXXVIII, 330; Stephen, *NatRev*, XXXVI, 883; Story, *NCRev*, IV, 196; Foote, *Freethinker*, June 7, 1903, p. 354; *Freethinker*, May 3, 1903, p. 338; Frederick Rockell, *UM*, XI (April 1899), 183; *Blackwood's*, CLXXIII (May 1903), 716; *TLS*, May 29, 1903, p. 165. For more on Arnold and Emerson, see Chapter VI.

[58] P. 27.

[59] Edith Simcox, *Ac*, Jan. 22, 1876, p. 67; Underwood, *Good Words*, XXVIII, 814; Courtney, *FR*, n.s. XXXVIII, 330.

the piece, and a critic in 1847 could not consent to calling a bee "Yellow-breeched philosopher!" Another wrote that the "modest lines" "provoked some sharp ridicule," but as early as 1844 one reviewer compared it favorably with "L'Allegro." And others during the century singled it out as "note-worthy," "an idyl," "a sylvan idyll, full of the joyousness of June sunshine." [60] It was one of the best unified of Emerson's poems, they said. It brought "at once before the reader not only the 'burly, dozing bee,' but a witching savour of long ago." "Hearken again," urged Gallagher, "how beautifully he speaks of the humble bee!" "Its position in literature to-day," said *Belford's,* "is undeniable." [61]

This high praise for such modest lines seems extravagant until one discovers Prothero applauding Emerson for his "extraordinarily ac-curate" observation of Nature: "he has studied her with minutest care." This close, realistic observation led an anonymous critic to write, "We do not understand how any one can read these poems ["Una," "The Rhodora," "The Humble Bee," "The Romany Girl"], all marked by the true Emersonian touch, and still maintain that . . . his style is essentially obscure." Juliet Pollock made the same point when she said in praise of "The Humble Bee," "There is much described with that accuracy which gives a faithful image." Another critic praised the poem because Emerson "has descended from his stilts, and condescends to utter the impulses of the natural man." [62]

Unhappily, these comments on Emerson's realism contributed no more to the understanding of Emerson's poetry than had those by Arnold and the other critics. It was not until the mid-eighties that critics on the periodicals began freely to apply Emerson's theory of poetry to his poems, and of these only Kernahan performed the task with much distinction. Kernahan confessed "that Emerson's poetry may not be placed among the poetry of the first rank; it may not as much as be classed with poetry of the second; judged by the sternest

[60] Courtney, *FR,* n.s. XXXVIII, 330; *Ex,* May 8, 1847, p. 292; Stewart, *Belford's,* I, 224; *FQR,* XXXII (Jan. 1844) , 311; Tyrer, *ManQ,* III, 124; Stewart, *Belford's,* I, 225; *LQR,* LXXIII, 31; *NatRev,* XXXVI, 531.

[61] *DubR,* n.s. XXIII, 75; *CMM,* XVI (July 1882) , 33; Gallagher, *GT,* 4th ser. VIII, 180; Stewart, *Belford's,* I, 225.

[62] *QR,* CLXIII, 378; *ModR,* IV (Oct. 1883) , 856; Juliet Pollock, *ContR,* XXII (Aug. 1873) , 356; *Critic,* Jan. 2, 1847, p. 10.

standards, there is a great deal of it which may not claim to be called poetry at all." In fact, Emerson in his "less happy moments" "comes perilously near being the writer of the veriest doggerel ever penned by a man of genius." The reason for these lapses, continued the critic, is discernible in his imperfect poetical theories. Emerson "was not indifferent to music" in poetry, as "is clear from a fine sentence in his address at Concord." The explanation for his prosodic lapses is to be found in "his theory that 'it is not metre, but a metre-making argument that makes a poem,' [a theory which] betrayed him into a carelessness in respect to style and into an impatience of artistic detail." [63]

Three other late Victorians also recognized this important aspect of Emerson's poetic theory. Prothero wrote that Emerson "valued the thought more highly than the form, and believed that art, if over-studied, became not an aid but a chain. . . . This excess in one direction, and deficiency in the other, partly explains his enigmas, his defiance of grammatical and metrical laws, his want of constructive power." The *Primitive Methodist Quarterly* cogently observed that he does not "polish his gems." "Rather than destroy the 'argument,' he dispensed with the 'music.' " The *Saturday Review* gave the kernel of this opinion: "He philosophized like a poet, and wrote poetry like a philosopher; wherefore specialists in both kinds are disappointed with him. Yet for this very reason his work has a higher strain and a subtler charm than faultless verse or rigorous dialectic often attains." [64]

Another reason for his rough meter was, according to Kernahan, the organic theory of making poetry to which Emerson adhered. "He held that if the inward thought with which the poet's brain is pregnant be a thought of pure and perfect poetry, equally pure and perfect will be the outward form in which it bodies itself forth." Thus "not a few of his crudities . . . are in part the result of a certain wilfulness—a somewhat exaggerated dislike to the tricks of the ordinary verse-manufacturer and a contempt for everything like

---

[63] *LQR,* LXXIII, 26, 27, 28; *NatRev,* XXXVI, 524.

[64] *QR,* CLXIII (Oct. 1886), 378; Foster, *PMQR,* n.s. XXI, 295; *SatR,* May 6, 1882, p. 554. For caustic remarks on Emerson's grammar, see Stephen, *NatRev,* XXXVI, 896; Arnold, *MM,* L, 4; *NBrR,* XLVII, 329.

poetic millinery or artificial rhyme-making." The blame for the high intellectual content of Emerson's verse could also be laid to his organic theory.[65] Critics, both early and late, had censured Emerson for the excessive intellectuality of his poetry. They said that it was "cold and intellectual, destined never to reach the deeper affections of Humanity"; it was "bloodless, intellectual, not emotional." In his poems, "there seems to us very little indeed of genuine poetic passion." [66]

None of the other Victorian critics had thought to ask himself why Emerson's poems were so lacking in passion; Kernahan did ask and found a good reason. "To write true poetry," he maintained, "we must not go to work as we would in building a house, selecting and rejecting, piecing and matching." "On the contrary, Emerson believes that the poem already is—that it exists pure and simple in the mind of God." The poet "is less the author of his poem than the means ... whereby the Great Poet ... manifests Himself." Thus, "Emerson comes before us as the singer of thought rather than of passion, of the ethical rather than of the senuous." "The serene joy and starlike elevation which he finds in the contemplation of what is lovely are the joy and pleasure of the intellect." Even so, continued Kernahan, "Emerson's poems are full of genuine word-painting and sound-picturing; and equally rich is his command of beautiful symbols. . . . To him the whole Cosmos is one grand poem." Kernahan related Emerson's use of the symbol not to the meaning of the world but to the meaning in language. "In nothing is the touch of the Master Craftsman more manifest than in what I may call economy of effort. The richer a writer's command of language, the more likely is it that, when he wishes to produce a great result, his words will be simple and few. The symbol of his thought may be humble or homely—and Emerson ... could put homely objects to high imaginative use—but the words once spoken shall seem true for all time." [67]

Beautiful symbols. Symbol of his thought. Words true for all time. In these phrases lies the key to an understanding of Emerson's

[65] *LQR,* LXXIII, 28, 29.

[66] *People's,* Nov. 28 (?), 1847, p. 307; *QR,* CLXIII, 378; *Sp,* Feb. 2, 1884, p. 155.

[67] *LQR,* LXXIII, 30, 31, 33; Kernahan, *NatRev,* XXXVI, 529.

poetry, as Professor Hopkins has written [68] and as Emerson himself often tried to show. As early as 1836 he was saying that matter yields symbols of the poet's "heroic passion," and in "The Poet" he explained how symbols fit into his theory of poetry. "Nature is a symbol, in the whole, and in every part," and nature as symbol demands use of all words—mean, base, low, obscene, rude, as well as those used in "polite conversation." Most men use symbols merely for economic purposes and fail to recognize them as thoughts. Not so the poet: he is the true-namer. Although he knows that words have a function as signs and knows their function on this level, as do ordinary men, he, unlike other men, also recognizes that words convey thought and that the thought is multiform: it is conveyed by "fluent symbol." These symbols are the original language in which every word is "a brilliant picture." Symbolic language seeks to show unity in variety, to reveal concretely the essence of existence. To Emerson, as Newton Arvin points out, symbol had much the same meaning as it was later to have for Ernst Cassirer. Both philosophers held that "symbolic forms are not imitations [as are signs], but *organs* of reality." [69] Unfortunately, Emerson's attempts to explain the organic nature of symbol were lost on his critics: to them, symbol was synonymous with the vague, the abstract, the mystical.

In 1883 a reviewer made a perfect statement of the general discontent with the symbolical nature of Emerson's poetry when he wrote, "The natural fact is not enough for him; he must draw back consciously and of purpose into a *vague* region of symbol." Arnold also deplored this tendency in Emerson. "He is not plain and concrete enough. . . . And a failure of this kind goes through almost all his verse, keeps him amid symbolism and allusion and the fringes of things." Agreeing, Courtney maintained that "in its symbolic and

---

[68] Vivian C. Hopkins, *Spires of Form* (Cambridge, Mass., 1951), pp. 121–35, esp. 122, 129, 130, 133.

[69] *Works*, I, 52; III, 13, 17, 20, 26, 21; XII, 300; III, 22; Arvin, in *Major Writers of America,* ed. Perry Miller (New York, 1962), I, 482. For an expansion of this concept, see Leslie Fieldson, *Symbolism in American Literature* (Chicago, 1959), pp. 75–135, esp. 75, 120, 130–35. For other comments on Emerson's use of symbolism, see Emerson Grant Sutcliffe, "Emerson's Theories of Literary Expressions," *University of Illinois Studies in Language and Literature* (Urbana, Ill., 1923), VI, 14, 129–31; G. W. Allen, *American Prosody* (New York, 1935), pp. 93–95 *passim;* Frederic Ives Carpenter, *Emerson Handbook* (New York, 1953), pp. 96, 97.

abstract tendency, . . . the poetry of Emerson lays itself open to criticism." In somewhat the same manner, both the pragmatist Leslie Stephen and the aesthete Vernon Lee equated Emersonian symbolism with mysticism. "He tends to find a symbol in everything," wrote Vernon Lee, "a mysterious 'Open, sesame!'; he cannot be satisfied with a thing meaning only its poor self, serving its obvious purpose. . . . He has, to the highest degree, the symbolic superstition." Richard Holt Hutton, editor of the rationalist *Spectator,* found "a cant of scientific symbolism" in the language of Emerson and his followers which "makes it at once obscure and affected." An anonymous critic on this journal wrote that Emerson's chief fault "is that he makes it a sort of religion . . . to *force* a symbolic meaning in natural facts where he has not been able truly to discover one." [70]

Except for Kernahan, only a few other critics praised Emerson's use of symbol. One of these reviewed *Poems.* What concerned this early critic more than anything else was the lack of structure in the poems—they were "effusions" rather than "compositions"—and although he did not like such poetry, he made a successful effort to understand why Emerson wrote it. The poet, he commented shrewdly, was not attempting to *compose* a poem; in fact, he "ignored—perhaps despised" those "scientific harmonies which are among the mysteries of the poetic craft." Emerson "would have us recommence singing with those unaided impulses in which song began." These impulses, the critic hinted, were revealed in "many a fine image" and in "scattered symbols of deep significance." Such an effort was welcome.[71] Some forty years later Tyrer repeated this welcome when he wrote that to Emerson's "view of the symbolical meaning of nature, in its whole and in its parts, he has given a fine if somewhat enigmatical expression" in "Two Rivers." And in 1901 Gallagher commented approvingly: "He it is who verily gives . . . the thing which, panorama-like, opens up to you the talking woods; . . . shows you what a symbol is." [72]

[70] *BQR,* LXXVIII (July 1883) , 220; Arnold, *MM,* L, 4; Courtney, *FR,* n.s. XXXVIII, 330; Stephen, *NatRev,* XXXVI, 887; Vernon Lee [Violet Paget], *ContR,* LXVII (March 1895) , 346, 355; *Sp,* Feb. 2, 1884, p. 156; *Sp,* March 12, 1870, p. 326.

[71] *Ath,* Feb. 6, 1847, pp. 146, 145.

[72] Tyrer, *ManQ,* III, 117; Gallagher, *GT,* 4th ser. VIII, 179. P. C. Ward, *TheosS,* VI (1893–94) , 6, 7, appreciated Emerson's use of the symbol but did not connect it with his poetry.

VI

With so many British critics missing the essence of Emerson's cipher and so few attempting to learn it, his poetry was not widely read. This neglect is regrettable, for if Emerson had wished popularity at all, he would have wished it as a poet. Leslie Stephen quoted Emerson as saying, "I am, in all my theory, ethics, and politics, a poet." And Courtney wrote that Emerson proclaimed, "I am not a great poet, but whatever is of me is a poet." [73] Kernahan reported that "the fact that his noblest thought should so often come to him as a song . . . caused him no wonder. On the contrary, it seemed to Emerson as inevitable that the man of intellect and imagination should turn poet, and find in poetry the fittest form of expression." Poetry "is, as he says, 'the only verity.' "

Several critics believed that Emerson had found that verity. Saintsbury wrote that in his remarkable *Poems* "his real literary power perhaps best appears." "It is from his poetry," wrote another, "that we get the most pleasing impression of the writer . . .; he has no 'call' to draw obvious morals. . . . He writes to please himself." Professor C. B. Upton declared that "the works of Emerson, and especially his poems, have been for thirty years among the books which he has most read and most loved." [74]

Yet in spite of these tributes, Emerson's place as poet was not a high one in England. Certainly Benton would have been more effective in raising it if he had, as one critic said, desisted from comparing Emerson favorably with Shakespeare and Milton and "set up a more responsible claim, and to establish it by cool and judicial examination of the special qualities of the poetry." [75] Neither did Emerson's biographers add to his stature as a poet. Stewart justly complained that in *A Memoir of Ralph Waldo Emerson,* James E.

[73] Stephen, *NatRev,* XXXVI, 884; Courtney, *FR,* n.s. XXXVIII, 330.

[74] Kernahan, *NatRev,* XXXVI, 525; Saintsbury, *Ac,* May 6, 1882, p. 320; *Sp,* Feb. 10, 1906, p. 220; U[pton], *ModR,* III (April 1882) , 427. See the *ModR,* III (1882) , viii, for identification of the writer.

[75] *ModR,* IV (Oct. 1883) , 856. For other reviews of Benton's book see *Sp,* Feb. 2, 1884, p. 155; *SatR,* April 28, 1883, p. 545.

Cabot "gives us too little of the poet," [76] and Conway, who commented intelligently in *Emerson at Home and Abroad* on the organic method of making poetry, admitted resignedly in a periodical that it had long been the fashion in England to decry or ignore Emerson's verse.[77] In *Ralph Waldo Emerson: His Life, Writings, and Philosophy,* George W. Cooke devoted to Emerson's poetry a chapter which Professor Upton thought "very attractive," but the book received so few notices as to render Cooke's effort negligible.[78] In *Ralph Waldo Emerson,* which did receive respectable attention, Oliver Wendell Holmes examined the poems but in an altogether pedestrian, unimaginative manner: his main concern was to show that Emerson's verse restated the religious and philosophical doctrines of his essays. A number of British critics judged Holmes's sympathetic chapter on Emerson's poetry to be the best in the book, and several echoed the comments found in the chapter,[79] but even so, this effort as well as that of Benton and the others failed to convince the British that Emerson was much of a poet.[80]

"Except in those cases where his mind is red-hot he does not move easily in the fetters of rhyme," observed *Great Thoughts.* "His inspiration as a poet is in the highest degree fitful and fragmentary." Although Stewart expressed "great admiration for Emerson as a poet," he thought that it was "in the capacity of an essayist that his fame" would rest. Still another critic wrote that Emerson's poetry raises the question as to "whether it be a desirable thing for wise men who are not born poets to embody their thoughts in verse." One indignant reviewer asserted, "Of Emerson as a poet we do not intend to speak. . . . In taking to poetry he as much mistook the bent of his genius as George Eliot did" when she tried to write poems.

---

[76] *ScR,* XI (April 1888), 307. See Cabot, I, 45; II, 404, 480, 489, 638, 720.

[77] *Emerson at Home and Abroad* (Boston, 1882), pp. 110, 160, 221–24; *OC,* V (March 1885), 138. In his book Conway included only a few scattered comments on Emerson's poems—pp. 133, 141, 146, 148, 334, 362; he obviously was not impressed with them.

[78] *ModR,* III, 429.

[79] *Ralph Waldo Emerson* (Boston, 1890), pp. 73–74, 77, 94, 113, 170, 178, 221, 243, 246, 310–43; Lewin, *Ac,* Feb. 28, 1885, p. 143; *BQR,* LXXXI (April 1885), 440; *Sp,* April 18, 1885, p. 513.

[80] Richard Garnett mentioned Emerson's poetry only sparingly: *Life of Ralph Waldo Emerson* (London, 1888), pp. 99, 127, 130, 133, 174–78.

The only time Emerson "deliberately strove after verse for which he had little gift," said the *Spectator,* was when "he wanted not to be challenged." Courtney wrote of the American: "Nor is he a poet, though he has many poetic traits; for as a rule, though he can feel, he cannot sing; he possesses imagination, but lacks the sacred fire." Perhaps the unkindest cut came from Morley, who said that "Emerson's poems 'are the outcome of a discontent with prose, not of that high-strung sensibility which compels the true poet into verse.' " [81]

This outcome was disastrous, the critics thought. The editor of *Library,* J. Y. W. MacAlister, declared that Emerson wrote much that was "noble in the form of verse, but never wrote a line of poetry in his life," while the *Athenaeum* maintained that he "trifles with his great powers when he continues these experiments in verse." *Public Opinion* observed that although Emerson was "without question" "a poet, we think he succeeds best in prose," and after writing that Emerson's "poetical insight and rich suggestiveness are patent and undeniable," Prothero declared that he remains "rather poetical than a poet. As he philosophized like a poet, so he wrote verse like a philosopher." [82] Other critics advised him to give up versifying entirely.[83] They did not rank him very high, even among the poets of his own country.

Throughout the nineteenth century English periodicals carried bad notices on American poetry. To the early journals, it was "little better than a far-off echo of the fatherland." *Blackwood's* ascribed the scarcity of American poets to "the energetic and ceaseless industry of the people," and the *Foreign Quarterly* doubted that poetry could be written in a country where "Catholics, Unitarians, Calvinists, and Infidels, were indiscriminately mixed up," where "population was augmented" by "the needy and dissolute . . . , the criminal." The *Christian Remembrancer* argued that since America

[81] *GT,* 5th ser. III (June 1903) , 122; Stewart, *Belford's,* I, 226; *Ath,* March 8, 1884, p. 307; T. Slater, *Month,* LIII (March 1885) , 379, 380; *Sp,* Aug. 16, 1884, p. 1071; Courtney, *FR,* n.s. XXXVIII, 319; *Sp,* Feb. 2, 1884, p. 155.

[82] MacAlister, *Lit,* Sept. 29, 1900, p. 242; *Ath,* May 2, 1868, p. 626; *PubO,* June 22, 1867, p. 682; [R. E. Prothero], *QR,* CLXVI (Jan. 1888) , 152, 153.

[83] *Ath,* May 2, 1868, p. 626; [William Henry Smith], *Blackwood's* LXIX (May 1851) , 513; *Press,* April 7, 1866, p. 330.

enjoyed no language, church, history, or heroes, it needed no poets. After noting condescendingly that some American poets might not be so vulgar and worthless as many critics judged, the *Biblical Review* quickly added that it had no time to discuss further such ephemeral fare "as the poetry of a new-born country." [84] Later journals were almost as adamant as the earlier in denying poetry to Americans, "a people of low ideals." There is "infinitely little" in American poetry "that is at once thoroughly American and of permanent merit," said the *London Quarterly Review* in 1878, and in summarizing the history of American literature, Prothero in 1886 wrote rather leniently that "within certain limitations American poetry has a flavour of its own; it is racy of the soil; it remains an offspring of England, but it differs in features from its parent." American poets "do not invest still life with the inappropriate charm of English literary association, but observe for themselves." [85]

The poet most likely to observe for himself was Whitman. Earlier, both American [86] and British critics had censured Emerson, sometimes bitterly, for encouraging such "rowdy" "raving monomaniacs" as well as for echoing them.[87] But by the end of the century, the Good Gray Poet and Poe were considered America's best poets; they were exceeded in popularity only by Longfellow, "the unofficial Laureate of Victorian England." Lowell, Holmes, Whittier, and Bryant followed in that order. Although Emerson received more attention in British periodicals than any other American writer,

---

[84] *FQR*, XXXII (Jan. 1844), 291; *Blackwood's*, LXII (Dec. 1847), 643; *FQR*, XXXII (Jan. 1844), 292, 293; *ChR*, XV (April 1848), 301, 302; *BibRev*, I (April 1846), 323.

[85] Tyrer, *ManQ*, III, 105; *LQR*, L (July 1878), 493; *QR*, CLXXIX (Oct. 1886), 370, 371, 373. Agreeing with *QR*, the *Ath*, Feb. 6, 1847, p. 146, wrote that Emerson's poems were "specimens of American poetry . . . not indebted to imitation."

[86] See Rusk, *Life*, p. 373.

[87] *SatR*, Oct. 4, 1856, p. 509; *EcRev*, 8th ser. III (Nov. 1862), 394; *WR*, LXXV (April 1861), 589; *SatR*, Dec. 15, 1860, p. 762. For a somewhat different opinion of Whitman, see Harold Blodgett, *Walt Whitman in England* (Ithaca, N.Y., 1934), pp. 216–22 *passim*. On the relative merits of Emerson and other American poets, see *PubO*, June 22, 1867, p. 682; Saintsbury, *Ac*, May 6, 1882, p. 320; Gilfillan, *Tait's*, n.s. XV 20; *ChR*, XV (April 1848), 300–352 *passim*; Walter Jerrold, *TBar*, CXXVIII (Oct. 1903), 430, 436; *Truth*, Oct. 5, 1882, p. 496; *Ath*, March 8, 1884, p. 306; Story, *NCRev*, IV, 192; Joseph M. Wheeler, *Freethinker*, May 7, 1882, p. 146.

most of it was directed to his essays. As a poet and mainly because of his prosody, considered eccentric by the critics, he would perhaps have followed Bryant at the bottom of the list.[88]

Emerson was not "in any sense," contended the *Museum,* "the best" American poet. Even the critics who championed him as a great American poet did so only hesitantly. The American, Buchanan wrote, "is to be credited with most of the little actual poetry that America has produced." He was, wrote another, "the truest" of American poets, while a third observed that "Emerson in thought, if not always in expression, is the greatest of American poets." None of these poets, maintained the *Fortnightly,* "except Emerson, and perhaps Edgar Allan Poe and Whitman, is a man of such mental calibre as renders his poetry subjectively important or interesting to a large class of readers." [89] A few of the American's lyrical poems, said Tyrer, "can only be matched by some of Poe's shorter and more perfect lyrics . . . , and possibly by a very few of Whittier's more impassioned pieces." If his poetry "has not the stateliness of Bryant, the captivating music of Edgar Poe, the scholarly grace of Longfellow, or the plaintive sweetness of Whittier, it seems, more than the verse of any of these poets, a spontaneous growth of the American soil . . . , and in its buoyancy and hopeful tone reflects in a manner the boundless possibilities of the great Republic." Even Tyrer had to admit, however, that this tone was not enough to make Emerson a popular poet in England. His poetry, implied the critic, held an "attraction" only for the "thoughtful and sensitive." [90]

As early as 1847 a reviewer declared that *Poems* "is not a work that will become popular," and Earle and Stewart said that Emerson was not a "popular" poet, that his "poetry has never been sure of a wide circle of readers." [91] The public "found him an indifferent poet," asserted Underwood, who stated in words much like Tyrer's that both his prose and his poetry "can be appreciated only by those who

---

[88] Gohdes, *Amer. Lit.,* pp. 126, 134–40 *passim.*

[89] *Museum,* II (Oct. 1862) , 275; Buchanan, *Bwy,* n.s. II, 226; Gilfillan, *Tait's,* n.s. XV, 20; *SatR,* March 6, 1886, p. 342; J. Knight, *FR,* n.s. I (March 1867) , 382.

[90] *ManQ,* III, 122, 127, 128.

[91] *Critic,* Jan. 2, 1847, p. 9; *DubR,* n.s. XXIII, 74; Stewart, *ScR,* XI, 307.

share his sensibility." The *Saturday Review* wrote that *May-Day* "displays all those peculiarities which make the author's poems so attractive to his disciples, and so unreadable to the outer world." Another and more judicious critic, novelist and editor Edmund Yates, maintained that Emerson's poems were criticized by many but "cherished among the more refined scholars of our time." One of these scholar-disciples was John Tyndall, who avowed that he frequently quoted Emerson "because in him we have a poet, and a profoundly religious man. . . . In his case Poetry, with the joy of a bacchanal, takes her graver brother Science by the hand, and cheers him with immortal laughter." [92]

"Emersonidae" had existed from the time of Emerson's first literary introduction to England, and one of the early disciples described the poetry in delirious tones: "Those verse-poems which he gave us were drops of sun-rain in the Spring . . . golden almost as Tennyson's Grapes of Song; but purer, more equal, more inward, and spiritually farthrilling than they." "While we can read them, and pass into a new world of soul, we shall not need to betake ourselves to Mesmerism." Later, the littérateur William E. A. Axon declared that "there is a fine haunting ring about many of his verses, and the quality is so high that every fragment is worth preserving." It was Tyrer who perhaps best summed up this loving comment when he quietly remarked that Emerson's poems will "endure." The reason was stated very well by two critics, one of whom in comparing George Eliot and Emerson spoke better than he knew: Eliot's "Choir Invisible" "will probably live as long as anything written in our times. . . . Those solemn lines are the concentrated expression of a mood through which the mind of our century is passing, between courage and despair. But Emerson's 'Sphinx' or 'Problem' or 'World-Soul' seems to us . . . to be a mere vagueness—the kind of words to which a boy is prompted who feels for the first time thrilling through him a sense of the mystery and unity of things." Kernahan stated more clearly why a minority of critics in nineteenth-century periodicals, without quite knowing the reason,

[92] Underwood, *Good Words*, XXVIII, 808, 809; *SatR*, Aug. 24, 1867, p. 268; Edmund Yates, *Century*, May 31, 1879, p. 114 (reprinted from the *World*) .

granted Emerson the name of poet: poetry "sat with him, walked with him, worked with him. It was only when he sought to transfer her living image to canvas that she eluded him and was gone. Yet, even as she fled, she not seldom mocked him by touching brush and easel with sacred fire." [93]

[93] Gohdes, *Periodicals*, p. 240; *Jerrold'sS*, VII, 330; Axon, *Notes*, Nov. 26, 1904, p. 423; Tyrer, *ManQ*, III, 107; *Ath*, March 8, 1884, p. 307; Kernahan, *NatRev*, XXXVI, 536.

❦ IV ❧

Emerson's Rationalist Champions

MERSON'S last important work was *May-Day and Other Pieces,* and about the time of its publication in 1867 his reputation as reflected by British periodicals during his lifetime reached its apex. From then until his death British interest in Emerson was in sharp decline. *Society and Solitude* (1870) and *Letters and Social Aims* (1876) as well as the lesser works published in this period were obviously not important, and periodical literature, ever interested in current rather than past performance, had little reason to give him much space. Neither of Emerson's late collections was accorded more than a half dozen reviews.

The faithful Conway maintained that *Society and Solitude* was "warm and human, sparkling with wit and wisdom," and another reviewer said that it "ought to be read for its wisdom and gentle eloquence," [1] but nearly all the other critics found the book a repetition of the American's basic ideas. It was a "pleasant" work presenting little that was original or new.[2] *Letters and Social Aims,* noted the critics, was better. Although the *Westminster* observed deprecatingly that both books "represent the man of practical experience reviewing with complacency the work of his youth," Edith Simcox commented that the book did not show "any sense of failing power,"

[1] M. D. Conway, *Fraser's,* n.s. II (July 1870), 3; *PubO,* May 7, 1870, p. 584.

[2] *Ex,* March 26, 1870, p. 199; *BritC,* Sept. (?) 1870, p. 240. For more comment on the book, see *Sp,* March 12, 1870, p. 326; George Stewart, Jr., *Belford's,* I (Jan. 1877), 231.

and the *Athenaeum* amusingly remarked that in the book "Mr. Emerson is as crabbed, as entertaining, and as 'cock-sure' as when he first startled the Phi-Beta-Kappa Society."[3] Maybe so. But critics of the seventies did not react to Emerson's later works as violently as the earlier critics had,[4] nor did they pay marked attention to Emerson's other productions of the period. The *Saturday Review* yawned politely over Emerson's introduction to *Plutarch's Morals* (1871) (it "may probably obtain for the work a larger circulation and more general attention than its intrinsic interest would command"), and the *Westminster Review* casually remarked that the introduction was "an interesting and characteristic piece of writing." The Preface to *Parnassus* (1877), Emerson's anthology of poetry, was to one critic "most interesting," and the book itself would acquaint readers with American poetry.[5]

During these fallow years as well as those periods of Emerson's greatest popularity, a small number of Victorians never lost interest in the American, no matter how thin his production. They were the Secularists, to whom the decade of the seventies was a golden age. At this time the impact of the *Origin of Species* was just being fully felt, and when in 1871 *The Descent of Man* was published, orthodox religious doctrines began rapidly to tumble.[6] Because of cheap print and a slight relaxation in censorship, Secular writers began for the first time to reach a considerable audience. In 1873, when Emerson was becoming the forgotten man in British periodicals, the *National Reformer* ran a three-part article on him in which the Secularist Charles Cattell had great praise for "this remarkable man,"[7] and in

[3] *WR*, CLXIII (Jan. 1905), 112; Simcox, *Ac*, Jan. 22, 1876, p. 67; *Ath*, Jan. 15, 1876, p. 81.

[4] *DubR*, n.s. XXVII (July 1876), 254; *WR*, n.s. LI (Jan. 1877), 297.

[5] *SatR*, Jan. 28, 1871, p. 125; *WR*, n.s. XXXIX (April 1871), 545; *WR*, n.s. LI (Jan. 1877), 292.

[6] Noel Annan, "The Strands of Unbelief," in *Ideas and Beliefs of the Victorians*, foreword by Harman Grisewood (London, 1949), p. 150; Jerome Hamilton Buckley, *The Victorian Temper* (Cambridge, Mass., 1951), p. 208.

[7] Charles C. Cattell, *NatRef* (Part I, Nov. 23, 1873, pp. 322–23; Part II, Dec. 14, 1873, pp. 370–71; Part III, Dec. 28, 1873, pp. 410–11), Part II, Dec. 14, 1873, p. 371. Several years later Cattell, impressed by Emerson's chapter "Books" in *Letters and Social Aims*, published a short article in *NatRef*, Dec. 12, 1875, pp. 378–79. On March 17, 1878, p. 1099, *NatRef* ran a short, favorable review of *Aims*, and on Dec. 28, 1873, p. 411, it published a review of *Society and Solitude* by Cattell.

1878, when his reputation in England was at its lowest ebb, Walter Lewin vehemently denied in the *Liberal* that Emerson was "useless" and "stupid," as "the commercial British Philistines" would maintain, but a great and "universal teacher." Several years later the same kind of protest was made by Theosophists, who said that Emerson was "a most profound philosopher," "a great and a good man." [8] Other than a few Unitarians and a scattering of independent critics usually of a rational persuasion, the Secularists and the Theosophists were the only Victorians who consistently rated Emerson so highly: their interest centered in his religious and philosophical views.

While orthodox critics fulminated against the "horrid profanity" of Emerson's religious heresy and sneered at his "philosophical ignorance," these two small, iconoclastic, and highly dedicated groups showed a deep appreciation of the unorthodox aspects of the American's thought. Their devotion is understandable. Like all expounders of revolutionary doctrines, Secularists and Theosophists needed the endorsement of a widely known public figure of proven ability and integrity: Emerson was almost made to order for their need. First, he himself was a man of causes, preaching that to be great was to be noncomformist. Second, much of his genius lay in approaching nearly all questions in terms of extremes. There is almost no intermediate in Emerson: with superb legerdemain he hands the reader two ends of a stick that has no middle. Third, Emerson gave the nonconforming Secularists and Theosophists a good grip on that stick. In 1843, for example, he recorded in his journal, "We come down with free thinking into the dear institutions, and at once make carnage amongst them," [9] and ten years later he wrote to Conway, "I cannot feel interested in Christianity; it seems deplorable that there should be a tendency to creeds that would take men back to the chimpanzee." [10] He was a member of the Free Religious Association,

[8] Lewin, *Liberal*, Jan. 1879, pp. 29, 30; William T. James, *Theosophical Review*, XXII (May 1898) , 141.

[9] Clarence Gohdes, *The Periodicals of American Transcendentalism* (Durham, N.C., 1931) , p. 254. Two early church journals protested this carnage: *Macphail's* (XV [Feb. 1848], 39) deplored the "free-thinking which pervades the pages of Emerson and Carlyle," and the irascible McCarthy (*DubR*, XXVI [March 1849], 154) could "only smile when the servile 'free-thinkers' of ... [Emerson's] own country hail him as a second and a greater Moses."

[10] J. M. Robertson, *A History of Freethought in the Nineteenth Century* (London,

which promoted the scientific study of religion, and several times spoke at its meetings.[11] At one of these he declared that "we are all believers in natural religion; we all agree that the health and integrity of man is self-respect, self-subsistency, a regard to natural conscience." [12]

Yet Emerson found it difficult to resist the unnatural, often weird, and sometimes fascinating beliefs of the occultists, and although he gave short shrift to such occult sciences as mesmerism, alchemy, and astrology, he did deliver a lecture on demonology which, he said, "covers dreams, omens, coincidences, luck, sortilege, magic and other experiences which shun rather than court inquiry." Such a study, he maintained, is "no aid on the superior problems why we live," but it does open "our curiosity [to] how we live." Thus, he concluded, "far be from me the impatience which cannot brook the supernatural, the vast; far be from me the lust of explaining away all which appeals to the imagination, and the great presentiments which haunt us." "I too say, Hail! to the unknown awful powers which transcend the ken of the understanding." [13]

In order to present coherently what uses the Secularists and the Theosophists made of this kind of largesse, how the two dissimilar groups held certain doctrines in common, and, above all, how they revealed a deep respect for Emerson and his ideas, I shall begin with the Secularists, several of whom Emerson knew personally, and follow with the Theosophists, who had begun to make themselves heard just about the time of his death.

1929) , I, 107. Conway had earlier made the same kind of statement: "We were having heated debates in theology at the Divinity College....'I am not much interested in such discussions,' he said; 'it does seem deplorable that there should be a tendency in some people to creeds which would take man back to the chimpanzee.'" "Emerson spoke to me about our studies in Divinity College. I enumerated them, and he said, 'I cannot feel interested in Christianity'" (Conway, *Emerson at Home and Abroad* [Boston, 1882], pp. 356, 371) . Page 129 of this book is a list of antireligious quotations from Emerson.

[11] Sidney Warren, *American Freethought, 1860–1914* (New York, 1943) , pp. 98, 99.

[12] *The Complete Works of Ralph Waldo Emerson,* ed. Edward Waldo Emerson (Boston, 1903–4) , XI, 487—hereafter cited as *Works.*

[13] *Works,* III, 235; X, 12, 25, 3, 24, 27. For an interesting account of this subject by a moderately rational journal, see "Emerson on Dreams and Bogies," *SatR,* Jan. 26, 1884, pp. 118–19.

II

Secularism, like rationalism, may be defined as "the destructive application of reason to religious belief"; [14] the two concepts differ only in their methods of effecting the destruction. Rationalists like Bentham, Mill, Comte, Spencer, and Darwin set forth their views in tomes that seldom appealed to the general public and almost never reached the lower classes. They were content to furnish the dialectic upon which nineteenth-century rationalism rested and to leave indoctrination to others.[15] Occasionally articles of a rationalist bent appeared in the great reviews like the *Westminster* and the *Fortnightly* has well as in such magazines as *Fraser's, Cornhill,* and the *Nineteenth Century,* but these publications, like the five-foot shelves of philosophical rationalists, seldom reached the masses.[16] The chief weaknesses of the propagandists spreading rationalism among the upper and middle classes were lack of organization and, what is perhaps worse, lack of zeal. Not so with those who proclaimed the good word among the lower orders: they were zealous and they were organized.

Convinced that the destruction of Christianity could be effected only through concerted effort, George Jacob Holyoake "in 1852 convened at Manchester a Conference which led to the establishment of various Secularist groups." [17] Ten years later the *Westminster Review* wrote that "Secularism is the religion, or the no-religion, of a large minority of thinking artisans," [18] and in 1866 Holyoake's original groups expanded into the National Secular Society. Members of the society lectured against Christianity during the week, preached against it on Sunday, and published anti-Christianity pamphlets, but these activities were not so effective as the Secularist journals. Such periodicals had appeared in England as early as the 1820's, but after a year or two of publication had

---

[14] Alfred W. Benn, *The History of English Rationalism in the Nineteenth Century* (London, 1906) , II, 421.
[15] *Ibid.,* II, 418.   [16] *Ibid.,* II, 353, 354, 355; Robertson, I, 305.
[17] Robertson, I, 295.   [18] *WR,* n.s. XXI (Jan. 1862) , 67.

invariably failed.[19] The first really successful one was the *Reasoner.* Begun in 1846 by Holyoake, it was brought out (except for a brief period) under various titles for some forty years. Like all infidel papers, this one attracted no advertising, the main source of revenue for popular publications, and had to rely almost wholly on sales, which for ten or twelve years hovered around the respectable figure of 3,500.[20] The thin, bantam-sized weekly was no thing of beauty. It was poorly printed on substandard paper, little attention was paid to make-up, and publication dates and volume numbers were sometimes missing. Yet its contents were of a fairly high literary level: Holyoake seems to have recognized good writing when he saw it. This ability was important, for much of the journal was the result of an expert's use of scissors and paste. In giving an account of Emerson's English lectures, for instance, Holyoake merely clipped from his favorite newspapers: he once brassily complained of misplacing the *Daily News,* which he liked because of its brevity, and being forced to use the verbose *Manchester Examiner.*[21]

Despite its catchpenny appearance and dependence on other sources, the *Reasoner* spoke out loudly and boldly, and during nearly all of the years of Holyoake's editorship (1846–61) its voice was no small one in nineteenth-century man's struggle against revealed religion. Flying from the mast, the pennant read, "A Weekly Journal, Utilitarian, Republican, & Communist," but the feisty little paper also welcomed socialists, phrenologists, crusaders for women's rights, Malthusians, atheists, pantheists—liberals and radicals of all kinds.[22] Emerson also opposed "fossil conservatism," [23] and in his religious, political, and philosophical views the *Reasoner* found much comfort. When the American began to lecture in 1847, the journal diligently announced the time and place of the lectures, fretted over their high prices, and extolled the heretical ideas expressed in them. The lecture on Montaigne, observed the *Reasoner,* "probably" was "the most interesting ever, till then, delivered within the walls of the Athenaeum." [24] During the time that the

---

[19] Robertson, I, 298, 299, 73–75, 304–5; Benn, II, 418.
[20] *WR,* n.s. XXI (Jan. 1862), 86.   [21] *Reas,* Nov. 24, 1847, p. 640.
[22] *Ibid.,* Dec. 30, 1847, title page of bound volume.   [23] *Works,* VII, 95.
[24] *Reas,* Dec. 1, 1847, pp. 8–11; Dec. 7, 1847, pp. 17–19; Dec. 15, 1847, pp. 38–40; Dec.

Swedenborgians and the Church of England were preaching against Emerson and the newspapers were denouncing him as "a wolf [let] into the English fold," Holyoake was declaring in the *Reasoner* that he "is one of the few men to whom those who appreciate his utterances award the reverence living usually reserved for the dead." [25]

Throughout the century, Secularists pinned many similar bouquets on him: "an original genius," "the American Sage," "America's greatest voice to the world," "a great American," "the celebrated American author," "her greatest writer in prose," "the greatest of American philosophers," "high priest of the spiritual," a man of "noble, simple nature," "great without an effort." In short, Emerson was "the most comprehensive genius who has yet mirrored for us the spiritual problem of the nineteenth century." [26] While explaining this genius, Secularists usually maintained a stony silence to all that was mystical in Emerson and loudly applauded his intellect, pantheism, anti-Christian utterances, and courage: "his real and essential religion," they cried out, "was the religion of humanity." [27]

Secularists accepted no authority but that of reason, denying everything emotional and subjective. Emerson was, they claimed, of like mind. Holyoake puffed him as "the most 'distinct man' of thought this age has" and ran an excerpt from Gilfillan's *A Gallery of Literary Portraits* which praised him for taking as "his province, intellec-

---

22, 1847, pp. 45–48; Dec. 29, 1847, pp. 63–66; Jan. 5, 1847 (8), pp. 80–82; Jan. 12, 1847 (8), pp. 85–89; Jan. 26, 1847 (8), pp. 117–20; Feb. 2, 1847 (8), pp. 138–40; June 7, 1848, p. 31; June 21, 1848, p. 63; July 5, 1848, p. 95; Dec. 15, 1847, p. 38. Cattell, *NatRef*, Dec. 28, 1873, p. 410, declared that "one often regrets the clergy and other ministers of the Gospel do not devote one hour...to the reading of this one chapter ["Montaigne"] of Emerson." "Emerson shows that the sceptic is not a fool; he is the considerer, the man who weighs evidence." The *Reas*, Jan. 12, 1847 (8), p. 85, carried a flattering description of Emerson the lecturer which it had taken from the *Preston Chronicle*. The *Chronicle*, in turn, had clipped it from the *Gateshead Observer*. J. C[harlton], *Reas*, April 10, 1859, p. 117, gave still another description of Emerson on the platform.

[25] *The Letters of Ralph Waldo Emerson*, ed. Ralph L. Rusk (New York, 1939), III, 444—hereafter cited as *Letters*; *Reas*, Nov. 24, 1847, p. 639.

[26] J. M. Wheeler, *Progress*, I (Feb. 1883), 117; G. W. Foote, *Freethinker*, May 31, 1903, p. 338; *Freethinker*, May 24, 1903, p. 321; *NatRef*, March 17, 1878, p. 1099; *Leader*, June 28, 1856, p. 605; Joseph M. Wheeler, *Freethinker*, May 7, 1882, p. 146; *OC*, V (March 1885), 138; Foote, *Freethinker*, May 24, 1903, p. 321; *Leader*, Sept. 13, 1856, p. 880; *Reas*, April 10, 1859, p. 117; Collet, *Reas*, Dec. 25, 1850, p. 229.

[27] G. W. Foote, *Freethinker*, June 7, 1903, p. 353.

tuality." [28] Another writer on the *Reasoner,* Sophia D. Collet, was almost as extravagant as Holyoake in her praise of Emerson, the man of intellect. According to Conway, Miss Collet was the most scholarly writer on the journal, and her articles in it were largely responsible for the American's influence among English freethinkers. Several of these pieces can be positively identified as hers. One was a short but much quoted report on Emerson's last lecture in England; another was longer. In it Miss Collet found one of Emerson's most valuable assets to be his contempt for "spasmodic emotions." The main difference between Carlyle and Emerson, she implied, was that the latter could think more clearly. Nearly all of the heroes in his *Representative Men* were intelligent, she wrote; "We have neither God, prophet, nor priest"—only "kings of thought." [29] Of these kings, the author himself wore the brightest crown.

At the turn of the century G. W. Foote, who at the time was perhaps the most prominent Secularist in England, declared that "Emerson's real speciality was the devotion of his fine intellect to the service of the loftiest ethics." Secularists were, of course, completely smitten with Emerson's rational comment on miracles, and Foote did not miss the opportunity of quoting him and another favorite of Secularism, Thomas Paine. Paine had said, wrote Foote, "that miracles were absurdities, that it was impossible to prove them. . . . This is an admirable criticism. But it is carried a stage farther by Emerson. He invokes the moral law. 'To aim to convert a man by miracles,' he exclaims, 'is a profanation of the soul.' " Foote also argued that Emerson's censuring of historical Christianity was above reproach and highly intellectual. The American "accepted Jesus as one of the world's teachers—*only* one. . . . To claim him [Emerson] as a

---

[28] *Reas,* Dec. 1, 1847, p. 8. Holyoake showed fine impartiality in selecting his unwilling contributors. In this piece he quoted liberally from the Scottish minister, and in an article published in *Reas,* Nov. 24, 1847, pp. 639–40, he quoted even more liberally from Carlyle's Preface to the *First Series,* all the while muttering that he had not chosen Goodwyn Barmby's "admirable paper" instead of the Preface because Carlyle was "less accessible to readers in general."

[29] Conway, *Emerson at Home and Abroad,* p. 340; Collet, *Reas,* July 5, 1848, p. 95; Collet, *Reas,* Dec. 25, 1850, pp. 229, 230. Miss Collet also paid tribute to "Montaigne," p. 230, as did other Secularists. Conway, in *Emerson at Home and Abroad,* identifies "Panthea" as Miss Collet and reprints her article (pp. 324–25).

Christian is larcenous. . . . Whatever deity he believed in—and it was a shadowy one—he refused to let any person stand between him and God. He would have told Jesus to get out of the way. The only revelation he admitted was personal and rational." Foote gloried in Emerson's concept of nature, quoting from him: Nature " 'is no saint. . . . She comes eating and drinking and sinning. Her darlings, the great, the strong, the beautiful are not children of our law, do not come out of the Sunday School. . . .' The only thing that nature honors in the long run is strength," proclaimed Foote, sounding like both Emerson and Nietzsche, whose philosophy was then coming into fashion in England. "All the beauty and virtue not founded on that is hectic and unwholesome, and rapidly on its way to the cemetery." At the same time that Foote was praising Emerson's pantheism, he was careful to point out that the American never let his pantheism "overwhelm" his intellect.[30]

Emerson's concept of nature elicited some first-rate invective from British critics. Churchmen were especially abusive, as we have seen and as the Secularist J. M. Wheeler observed: "When Emerson delivered his celebrated address to the Divinity College . . . , he broke for ever not only with the churches and their creeds but with all historical Christianity." "Even the Unitarians called him Infidel and Pantheist." Wheeler, Miss Collet, and many other Secularists agreed with Foote and disagreed completely with the churchmen. These adherents of Secularism were generally rank materialists, finding manifestations of higher laws only in physical nature. Therefore Wheeler could proclaim that in Emerson's works "the student will find not only an utter absence of all distinctively Christian teaching, but a breadth of thought that leaves all its dogmas far behind." Thirty years earlier Miss Collet had voiced the same sentiments. "Those who yearn for the pure white light of religion, and who cannot be satisfied with seeing it only through the coloured windows of the Christian Church . . . find in Emerson a teacher worthy of their desire. His writings, moreover, take higher rank than the semi-polemical ones of Strauss, Parker, Newman." These instructors, declared the outspoken freethinker, had helped to emancipate England

[30] Foote, *Freethinker*, May 24, 1903, p. 321; May 31, 1903, pp. 338, 339; May 24, 1903, p. 322; June 7, 1903, p. 353.

from religious sentiment, but Emerson, assuming freedom from such sentiment, focused upon the eternal and universal: the "beauty unutterable which fills all nature." [31]

This view was shared by Holyoake, Miss Collet's editor and a more forceful writer than she. At about the time that *Essays, First Series,* appeared in 1842 Holyoake, charged with blasphemy, was languishing in jail. He was a fervent socialist, as were many rationalists, and he mildly criticized Emerson for his lack of social awareness. Holyoake was, unhappily, even more critical of this imperfection in God. "The reigning deity, considered as manager of human affairs," he remarked sarcastically, "was indicated as fitly to be placed 'on half pay.'" [32] Holyoake's first comments on Emerson were not so witty; neither was he jailed for them, as he had been for his gloss on the Deity. After judiciously scissoring from Carlyle's Preface to the *First Essays,* the Secularist expressed in strong terms the notion Miss Collet had phrased rather vaguely: "Not all the pulpits of Old and New England have thrown so much new life into reflective and progressive society as he. Weary, stale, flat, and unprofitable are Bible texts by the side of 'Wood Notes.' The Priest of Nature is far more eloquent and far more sought after than the Priests of God." [33] In 1873 Holyoake's friend Charles Cattell echoed: "Compared with the chatter of the theologians, consisting of chaff and dried chips, Emerson is as sweet and refreshing as a summer's breeze." "Compared with Emerson, the doctrines, texts, ceremonies, the parson, the beadle, and even the Church itself, sink into insignificance; . . . he has seen nature, and he interprets what he has seen; everything appears living, and full of purpose." [34]

Although the comments by Holyoake and Miss Collet do not recommend Christianity, they were not nearly so rabid as those of the Far Left of Secularism. In fact, the two were perhaps closer to agnosticism than to atheism. Holyoake had, for instance, declared

[31] Wheeler, *Freethinker,* Feb. 4, 1883, p. 34 (Wheeler had presented the same ideas a year earlier in *Freethinker,* May 7, 1882, pp. 146–47) ; Collet, *Reas,* Dec. 25, 1850, p. 229.
[32] Robertson, I, 73 *n.*   [33] *Reas,* Nov. 24, 1847, p. 639.
[34] Cattell, *NatRef,* Dec. 14, 1873, p. 370. Wheeler, *Freethinker,* May 7, 1882, p. 146, turned a similar phrase: "There are doubtless many to whom the bread of life offered in churches has become mere sawdust, who can find strength and sustenance in Emerson."

imprudently, "I am not an unbeliever, if that implies the rejection of Christian truth—since all I reject is Christian error." [35] Such heresy might have been tolerated by the early Secularists but not by the militant atheists who dominated the movement from the fateful year of 1859. Holyoake continued to assert himself after the advent of Darwin, but he was no longer a great voice in Secular affairs. His office was usurped by the leading Secularist of the Victorian era, Charles Bradlaugh. In 1858 the unregenerate atheist succeeded Holyoake as president of the London Secular Society and in 1861 graciously allowed his friend to merge the then feeble *Reasoner* (now called the *Counsellor*) with his young and vigorous *National Reformer*.[36] The hard-nosed *Reformer*, wrote one of its first editors, Joseph Barker, supported "the masses" rather than the "aristocracy," challenged "orthodox clergy" in general, and spoke out "on all subjects with great freedom." [37] Unfortunately Barker, like Holyoake, was not belligerent enough, and he was quickly shoved aside by his partner Bradlaugh. Under Bradlaugh, whose editorship covered all except four or five years of its existence (1860–93), the *Reformer* became the noisiest and most influential rationalist journal of the time.[38] It devoted many columns to Emerson, especially to reviews of his books.

If one is to believe the Secularists, the finest passages Emerson wrote are to be found in "Worship," the sixth essay in *The Conduct of Life,* a book which the *Reasoner* declared "will never be out of season." In *Conduct* Emerson had explained that the church of the future would abjure myth. Based on moral science, it would appeal to the intellect. Its function would be to serve man.[39] The *Reformer* carried a two-part review of the work, which it praised highly, and quoted with enthusiasm the famous religion-as-moral-science passage:

The religion which is to guide and fulfil the present and coming age, ... must be intellectual. . . . There will be a new Church founded on moral

35 *WR*, n.s. XXI (Jan. 1862) , 75.
36 Robertson, I, 297; *WR,* n.s. XXI (Jan. 1862) , 75.
37 "The Editorship," *NatRef*, April 14, 1860, p. 4.
38 *NatRef,* July 13, 1861, p. 4; Robertson, I, 298–301.
39 *Reas,* Jan. 13, 1861, p. 19; *Works,* VI, 199–243, esp. 203–4, 207–8, 210, 219–20, 241.

science, at first cold and naked, a babe in a manger again, the algebra and mathematics of ethical law, the Church of men to come, without shawms, or psaltery, or sackbut; but it will have heaven and earth for its beams and rafters; science for symbol and illustration; it will fast enough gather beauty, music, picture, poetry. . . . It shall send man home to his central solitude; shame these social, supplicating manners, and make him know that much of the time he must have himself to his friend. He shall expect no co-operation, he shall walk with no companion. . . . Honour and fortune exist to him who always recognises the neighbourhood of the great, always feels himself in the presence of high causes.

This "the true philosophy," commented the reviewer, was "so new yet so old, youthful as the morning of the world; beside whose august antiquity and lofty plainness . . . Christianity seems *parvenu* and effeminate." [40] In 1863–64 Cattell published, under a pseudonym, a series of articles in the *Reformer* entitled "A Secularist's Principles; or, Which Is the True Religion?" and leaned heavily on "Worship" for the religion.[41] Ten years later, in his long piece on Emerson, Cattell again quoted at length from "Worship." [42]

Still another important organ of rationalist propaganda that milked *Conduct* dry of its antireligious passages was the *Freethinker*. Upon the demise of the *National Reformer* in 1893, the *Freethinker*, which was begun in 1881, became and remains the most important Secular journal in England. G. W. Foote, its founder and editor for many years, was even further to the Left than Bradlaugh, whom he succeeded as president of the National Secular Society. An irreverent radical who "regarded himself as the last remaining bulwark of atheistic Fundamentalism," he was too blasphemous even for the Secularists. They demurred at his series of " 'Comic Bible Sketches,' " such as 'Samson and the Foxes,' depicting a repulsive Semite in striped bathing trunks, dipping the foxes' tails in a bucket labeled 'Petroleum.' " [43] Foote mellowed somewhat as he grew older and in a review of the Centenary Edition wrote the most perceptive article to

[40] *NatRef*, March 9, 1861, p. 8; March 16, 1861, p. 8.

[41] Christopher Charles [Cattell], *NatRef*, Dec. 12, 1863, p. 1.

[42] *NatRef*, Dec. 28, 1873, p. 411.

[43] Arthur H. Nethercot, *The First Five Lives of Annie Besant* (Chicago, 1960), pp. 351, 318, 313, 188.

appear on Emerson in Secular journals. In his essay review he contended that the American "pointed a ruthless finger" at the deification of Christ. "There was no authority to which he would bow." In partial support for his claims, Foote turned to the passage from "Worship," which had appeared for the first time in rationalist journals some forty years earlier.[44]

Secularists also sifted other works by Emerson, as well as works about him, for antireligious passages. A review of *English Traits* was carried by the *Leader,* a Secular journal edited by George Henry Lewes. In it an anonymous critic observed that the only chapter of *English Traits* "which can be called satirical" is that dealing with religion, and no wonder, since "it is difficult indeed to speak of religion in England without ridicule or indignation." To illustrate this ridicule the writer quoted several paragraphs in which Emerson is at his anticlerical best.[45] Although the *National Reformer* ran a paragraph on *Society and Solitude* and *Letters and Social Aims,* it did not linger, for the essays contained no unfavorable comments on religion.[46]

In 1883, however, a work did appear which rationalists could employ in their effort to spread infidelity: Conway's *Emerson at Home and Abroad.* The *Reformer* published two reviews of the monograph, the first of which was rather perfunctory. The second touched upon evolution, the most destructive blow ever delivered against Christianity. Secularists were, of course, wildly excited over the antireligious implications of this doctrine, and they were determined to bring Emerson's name into the fray. In *At Home and Abroad* Conway pleased a critic on the *Reformer* by writing, "While Auguste Comte and Mill ignored Evolution, and Carlyle reviled it, Emerson was building upon it as upon a rock." [47] Conway's main objective, though, was to see that Emerson and not Charles Darwin was credited with the discovery of evolution. "The idea of evolution, first published by Erasmus Darwin in 1794," he

[44] *Freethinker,* May 31, 1903, pp. 338, 339; June 7, 1903, p. 353.
[45] *Leader,* Sept. 13, 1856, pp. 881, 882.
[46] Cattell, *NatRef,* Dec. 12, 1875, pp. 378–79; *NatRef,* March 17, 1878, p. 1099.
[47] Dec. 3, 1882, pp. 394–95; Jan. 14, 1883, p. 22.

wrote in the *Fortnightly*, "awakened devout emotions" in Emerson. "His speculation found its first interpreter in the American scholar." Reviewing Holmes's *The Life of Emerson* in *Our Corner*, a short-lived journal of rationalism and socialism founded by a friend, Mrs. Annie Besant, Conway argued at some length that as early as 1833 Emerson had established in a lecture, "Relation of Man to the Globe," "a theory of evolution similar to that" which he set forth in his "second essay on 'Nature' " "eleven years later." Both these works, he implied, appeared much earlier than *Origin of Species*.[48] Foote and his assistant editor Joseph M. Wheeler were also convinced, as Wheeler showed in *Progress* and as they both showed in the *Freethinker*, that Emerson had understood the principles of evolution long before Darwin published them. Foote, in his long and excellent essay, was not so much concerned, however, with proving Emerson an evolutionist as in praising him as a man of great courage.[49]

This tribute was paid to Emerson fairly often by his British critics. Several of the soured church publications as well as a number of liberal and general periodicals noted the virtue,[50] but of all the journals those of the freethinking persuasion dwelt most lovingly on Emerson's courage. Foote wrote that "Emerson always insisted on the supreme value of courage. . . . Never strike sail to a fear; always do the thing you are afraid to do. . . . Emerson did not simply teach courage; he practiced it." "From first to last he displayed a steady courage, which it is not an exaggeration to call heroic." Emerson's "splendid declaration[s]" had given Cattell "courage when I wanted it," and the *Leader* praised Emerson for his "essential veracity," as did the *Liberal*. Wheeler, whose anti-Christian bias was as strong as Foote's, asserted that Emerson in all of his works had said, "Truth," "Courage," and "Love," while an anonymous critic in the *National Reformer* spoke of him as a "gentle but fearless Abolition-

---

[48] *FR*, n.s. XXXI (June 1882), 754; *OC*, V (March 1885), 140. For other comments by Conway on Emerson and evolution, see *Emerson at Home and Abroad*, pp. 148, 158.

[49] Wheeler, *Progress*, p. 118; Wheeler, *Freethinker*, May 7, 1882, p. 146; Foote, *Freethinker*, May 24, 1903, p. 322.

[50] [McCarthy], *DubR*, XXVI, 175; *Macphail's*, XV (Feb. 1847), 36; [John Nichol], *NBrR*, XLVII (Dec. 1867), 357; *Ath*, Feb. 6, 1847, p. 144; *TLS*, Aug. 28, 1903, p. 249.

ist." Miss Collet went to the heart of the Secularists' admiration of Emerson when she wrote that he spoke "words of wisdom in tones of courage." [51]

Secularists themselves were not lacking in this virtue. Defying the world which whipped them with its displeasure, these nonconformists bravely withstood verbal onslaughts, economic pressures, and social ostracism. For years they could not run for public office, make a sworn statement, or even recover stolen property. Later in the century and mainly through the efforts of Bradlaugh, Foote, and Mrs. Besant, Secularists were granted many of the privileges accorded the orthodox.[52] What J. M. Robertson, an editor of the *National Reformer* and the best historian of the Secular movement, has said of Bradlaugh can be said of a large number of the Secularists: "His courage drew the men who valued courage." [53] Emerson understood and liked such men. He had read "with much interest" the *Philosophy of Necessity*, by the eminent Secularist Charles Bray, wrote Conway, and while in England in 1847 visited the Brays. To Mrs. Bray he was "the great spirit" who "was so easy and pleasant that I wondered where all my awe had gone to." On this visit Emerson met George Eliot, with whom he was much impressed. "That young lady has a calm serious soul," he told Bray, and when Emerson departed the household, he pressed Bray "to go and see him in America." [54]

Ten years after his tour of England, in a series of interviews reported in the *Reasoner*, Emerson spoke admiringly of freethinkers like Joseph Barker, whom he called the man with "a kind of sledge hammer of his own," and Holyoake, a "brave" man. "Mr. E. talked about Holyoake's 'Self-help,' and seemed to be much interested in its theme. He said Holyoake had won a position, and was kindly

[51] Foote, *Freethinker*, May 31, 1903, p. 338; Cattell, *NatRef*, Nov. 23, 1873, p. 323; *Leader*, Sept. 13, 1856, p. 880; Lewin, *Liberal*, Jan. 1879, p. 29; Wheeler, *Freethinker*, May 7, 1882, p. 147; *NatRef*, Jan. 14, 1883, p. 22; Collet, *Reas*, May 28, 1854, p. 363. While not so radical as the journals of the Secularists, the people's organs also praised Emerson's courage: [George Cupples], *Jerrold'sS*, VII (April 1848), 323; Goodwyn Barmby, *Howitt's*, Nov. 13, 1847, p. 316; *People's*, April 21 (?), 1848, p. 210. See also Emerson's literary executor [James E. Cabot], *WR*, LXIII (April 1883), 459.

[52] *WR*, XXI (Jan. 1862), 86; Robertson, I, 304; Nethercot, pp. 190–92.

[53] I, 302.   [54] *Emerson at Home and Abroad*, pp. 337, 338, 339.

spoken of by all people." On a visit to Concord in Emerson's old age, Holyoake found his friend "still erect" with "the bright eye and calm grace of manner we knew when he was in England long years ago. . . . More than any other writer Emerson gives me the impression of one who sees facts alive." In a comparison of Carlyle and Emerson, Holyoake favored the American because of his "greater braveness of thought and clearness of sympathy." Emerson remembered Holyoake's friend Miss Collet for her close attention to his lectures and said that the rationalist George Searle Phillips had sent him "some brilliantly written things." [55] Several years earlier Phillips had declared that "from personal knowledge of Emerson, I can say that I never met with a fairer or a more beautiful soul." Phillips' biography of Emerson was brought out in 1856 by the George Holyoake Publishing Company; a review of it in the *Reasoner* read in part: "By far the fullest account (from personal observation and by quotation from his works) of R. W. Emerson, will be found in . . . [this] pamphlet. . . . What we mean is, that the publication contains the fullest material (in an accessible form) of judging the Great American." [56]

Perhaps the Secularist Emerson knew best was Charles Bradlaugh, an important figure not only in England but also in the United States. Except for the notorious Robert G. Ingersoll and a few much lesser lights such as D. M. Bennet, Benjamin F. Underwood, and Horace Seaver, America in the later 1800's depended upon England to furnish her with militant freethinkers. There were several reasons for her apathy. Rationalism flourished in highly industrialized, urbanized, and relatively homogeneous countries such as that evolving in nineteenth-century England, rather than in countries predominantly agricultural, rural, and strife-torn, as was the America of the same period. [57] America had no official church at which to take dead aim. Furthermore, the country was so large that, given the communications of the time, no effective national organization was possible. The only one that made much headway was the Free Religious Association, which was organized in 1867 by O. B. Frothingham and

[55] C[harlton], *Reas*, April 10, 1859, p. 117; *Reas*, May 13, 1860, p. 156.

[56] Phillips, *Reas*, Aug. 6, 1851, p. 174; *Reas*, Sept. 28, 1856, p. 98.

[57] Robertson, II, 445; Warren, pp. 28–34 *passim*.

a few other disgruntled Unitarians.[58] Bradlaugh came to America several times to lecture before such groups and wrote a series of letters to the *National Reformer* describing his experiences. His itinerary took him all over the East—to New York, New Haven, Boston, and other cities. Wendell Phillips "presided for me [at the Boston meeting]," wrote Bradlaugh, ". . . and William Lloyd Garrison sat by me, and repeatedly cheered me as I spoke." At another time, Emerson had been prevented by a rainstorm from attending a meeting of the Boston Radical Club, which was held at the home of the freethinking John T. Sargent and to which Bradlaugh had been invited. Later the two were brought together at the Sargents'. On this occasion, wrote Bradlaugh, Emerson "selected us to read his poem ['Boston'] on the centenary of that tea-spoiling in Boston Bay." [59]

Like several other rationalists including John Sterling and Conway,[60] Bradlaugh in his youth had been much influenced by Emerson's thought. In reviewing Conway's *At Home and Abroad* he wrote that thirty years earlier he had read "Self-Reliance," and since that time it had lost none of its "vividness." In fact, Joseph M. Wheeler wrote, Bradlaugh ascribed to the essay "my first step in the career I have adopted. . . . When too poor to buy a book, I copied parts of that famous lecture." [61] Cattell was also early drawn into the Emerson orbit. An erstwhile church school teacher, he had pointed out to "the chapel people" a few discrepancies in the Bible and had been asked to resign. Shortly afterward he "saw in a second-hand bookshop, 'Essays by R. W. Emerson.' On the front page, the book being open, I read these remarkable words 'I am owner of the sphere. . . .' I read Emerson night and day, and never since have I thought my persecutors and slanderers and enemies anything but as little children speaking." Cattell's fondest wish was that if he ever visited America he could see "Emerson and the Falls of Niagara," a

---

[58] Warren, pp. 98–106 *passim*.

[59] *NatRef,* Oct. 19, 1873, p. 242; *NatRef,* Nov. 16, 1873, pp. 305, 306; *NatRef,* Dec. 3, 1882, p. 394.

[60] Townsend Scudder, *The Lonely Wayfaring Man* (London, 1936), pp. 61–64; Rusk, *Life,* pp. 257, 373.

[61] *NatRef,* Dec. 3, 1882, p. 394; Wheeler, *Freethinker,* May 7, 1882, p. 146. Bradlaugh again notes his debt to "Self-Reliance" in the *NatRef,* May 7, 1882, p. 362.

desire expressed some thirty years earlier by the Unitarian minister Charles Wicksteed.[62]

When Emerson died, rationalists felt that they had lost not just a guide and a teacher but a friend. Bradlaugh expressed this sense of personal loss in a short, rather moving obituary in which he wrote, "To me, a stranger [in Boston], Ralph Waldo Emerson was very kindly, and his countenance made others kindly too." Years later Foote paid like tribute in his review of the Centenary Edition: Emerson "was the best beloved of American writers. . . . There is a perennial fascination in his gracious personality. He is the sweetest memory of his land and century." In a long article analyzing Emerson's works, Wheeler also paid his respects to the "loveable writer," whose death had brought him "a sense of personal bereavement." [63]

Two years before Emerson's death an article on him had appeared in the *Liberal,* a short-lived (1879–87) and fairly mild rationalist journal edited by Foote. In it Lewin treated with affection the "old man of seventy-five . . . [who] lives in Concord, Massachusetts, in his quiet contented way, much reverenced by his fellow-countrymen and very much misunderstood." He was one of "God's true prophet[s]." [64] From the beginning the Leftist element of the nineteenth-century freethinkers found that keeping God out of rationalism was no easy task. At the same time that Bradlaugh, Foote, Wheeler, and other complete atheists were denying Him a place in the universe, Holyoake, Miss Collet, Barker, and others were sneaking Him in through nature. Still others like Lewin held beliefs akin to eighteenth-century Deism, while about the fringes of the whole movement hung the more liberal Unitarians. Here Emerson himself doubtless belonged, and the reasons that his religious doctrines were never popular also account for the unpopularity of Secularism. Both Emerson and the Secularists posed for their people the dilemma of either accepting a divinity stripped of myth or refusing divinity altogether. This choice offered difficulty not only to prospective Secularists but to the converted.[65] Once delivered from the chains of

---

[62] *NatRef,* Nov. 23, 1873, p. 323; *NatRef,* Dec. 28, 1873, p. 411. See p. 12.

[63] *NatRef,* May 7, 1882, p. 362; Foote, *Freethinker,* June 7, 1903, p. 354; Wheeler, *Freethinker,* May 7, 1882, p. 146.

[64] Jan. 1879, pp. 30, 34.   [65] Nethercot, pp. 194, 197–98, 314.

Christianity, they often fell captive to the superstitions of cultists like the Swedenborgians, the Spiritualists, and the Theosophists. The most prominent of the backsliders was Mrs. Annie Besant.

Under the influence of Bradlaugh, Mrs. Besant had become in the seventies a free-thought lecturer, and from 1881 to 1887 she served as coeditor of the *National Reformer*. Later she had her own rationalist journal, *Our Corner* (1883–89), which eventually was to become a mouthpiece for the Fabians. In the early nineties longings for immortality led her away from the distressed Bradlaugh to the Theosophists. By 1895 this formidable woman was absolute head of the inner organization of the Theosophical Society and was lecturing on the subject all over the world. Her travels brought her several times to the United States, where she found her warmest welcome in that veritable Beulah of the cultists—the West Coast. She also found time to write many books on Theosophy in addition to serving as an editor of *Lucifer,* the first official English journal of the sect.[66] This periodical as well as others published by the Theosophists carried articles on Emerson.

III

As set forth in the *Theosophical Review* (a later name for *Lucifer*), Theosophy encouraged the universal brotherhood of man, "without distinction of race, creed, sex, caste or colour"; promoted "the study of comparative religion, philosophy and science"; and investigated "unexplained laws of nature and the powers latent in man."[67] In short, Theosophists were the New Mediaevalists: they attempted to solve the Cartesian dichotomy by bringing once more into balance man, nature, science, and God. They wished to heal at the religious level what T. S. Eliot has tried to heal at the aesthetic: the dissociation of sensibility. They wished to prove that man could find and abide by a reasonable faith. For the more spiritual, they provided the mysticism of Meister Eckhart and Jakob Boehme,

---

[66] Robertson, I, 305; Nethercot, pp. 67, 321, 197–98, 285, 283–399 *passim*, esp. 316, 355, 356, 378, 379, 386, 393.
[67] XXII (May 1898), back of cover.

" 'the theosophist' *par excellence";* for the more secular, the philosophy of Schelling and the New Science of Darwin.[68] For the myth that would embody both the spiritual and the rational (Madame H. P. Blavatsky wrote Bradlaugh that his becoming a Theosophist would not entail giving up "one iota of his Secularistic ideas" [69]) they turned to the religions of the Far East. Emerson himself had, at one time or another, looked in that direction as well as toward Boehme, Schelling, and Darwin.[70] The alert Theosophists were quick to seize upon this fact. In three strong articles they contended that the concepts of Emerson—then at the height of his posthumous fame in England—had anticipated those of Theosophy, that he had found Christianity as unsatisfactory as had Theosophists, and, most importantly, that he and the Theosophists had drunk from the same stream, the Sacred Ganges.

"Theosophy and Emerson," wrote P. C. Ward in *Theosophical Siftings,* are "fundamentally" in agreement, and both Ward and his colleagues remarked many parallels between the American's thought and that of Theosophy. According to this teaching, he observed, "man's consciousness manifests" itself on "seven planes," an idea "conveyed by Emerson when he says, 'Man imprisoned, man crystallized, man vegetative, speaks to man impersonated.' " And: "The distinction drawn in Theosophy between the higher self and the lower self in man . . . has a mystical parallel in Emerson." The higher self, said Ward, Emerson called Osman. The parallels are also evident in two more examples, which can at will be multiplied: "In the light of Theosophy the man of obedience is he whose personality is obedient to the dictates of the higher self. . . . Emerson tells us: 'The man of obedience is the man of power, the guide.' " Emerson held that "out of evil comes good," and Madame Blavatsky wrote: "Good and evil . . . are twins." [71]

These journals never tire of quoting Madame Blavatsky, who, with Col. Henry S. Olcott, founded in 1875 the first Theosophical Society in New York. Later she and Olcott established lodges in

---

[68] A. S. P.-P., "Theosophy," *Encyclopaedia Britannica* (Chicago, 1960) , XXII, 69, 70.

[69] Nethercot, p. 298.

[70] *Works,* IV, 49; VIII, 214; IX, 195, 292; II, 282; III, 34, 187; IV, 143; I, 162; V, 241–42; VI, 13; I, xxvi–xxxi.

[71] P. C. Ward, *TheosS,* VI (1893–94) , 3, 10, 14, 11.

India, and by 1891, the year of Madame's death, Theosophists were some 100,000 strong. Mrs. Besant, Madame Blavatsky's successor as head of the Theosophical Society, was to write that "no man in becoming a Theosophist need cease to be a Christian, a Buddhist, a Hindu," [72] but of all religions Christianity was held in the lowest esteem, as an excerpt or two from Theosophical journals will show. In *Theosophical Siftings,* Ward joyfully drew upon Edward Waldo Emerson: the church in the 1830's "seemed to his father to be the tomb of religion; he left it to come out into the living day." Emerson had shown excellent foresight, declared this Theosophist, when in 1844 he had "noted the vast changes that were to take place in this latter part of the 19th century, in regard to religious conceptions, and the havoc that science was making with the old orthodox ideas." Earlier in the article Ward had used excerpts from the religion-as-moral-science passage so often quoted by the rationalists.[73] Theosophists, however, did not press Emerson's anticlericalism with anything like the vigor of the rationalists. In their role as spoilers the rationalists could, without much further thought, seize the club of science and begin laying to: they did not have to replace the broken idols. To Theosophists the matter was not so simple. They had to acknowledge fealty to science and at the same time pay homage to supernatural power, the *sine qua non* of all successful religions.

They solved the problem in several ways. In *Lucifer,* Charles Johnston, who had helped in Ireland to prepare William Butler Yeats for Theosophy, maintained that "within the world of the physical scientist lies an ethereal, spiritual universe, with its own powers, its own prophets." Emerson, said Johnston, was "chosen by Destiny" to be one of these prophets. P. C. Ward asserted that the spirit of science was more important than the letter and then looked to Emerson for corroboration. Declared Ward: Emerson "considered that true science was to use objects 'according to the life, and not according to the form.' " [74] Still another solution was the flat declaration that spiritual phenomena could be proved scientifically.

---

[72] "Helena Petrovna Blavatsky," *Encyclopaedia Britannica,* III, 710; Annie Besant, *The Ancient Wisdom* (Adyar, Madras, India, 1954), p. 5.

[73] *TheosS,* VI, 4, 15.

[74] Nethercot, p. 301; Charles Johnston, *Lucifer,* I (Dec. 1887), 252, 253; Ward, *TheosS,* VI, 5.

James quoted Emerson: "The heart which abandons itself to the Supreme Mind finds itself related to all its works, and will travel a royal road to particular knowledges and powers," to which he added, in brackets, "[Here let me remark parenthetically that this is a fact, susceptible of experimental demonstration.]" [75]

Both Emerson and Theosophists affirmed that those able to experience complete abandonment were the Great Souls. According to Ward, Emerson referred to these souls as "rare pilgrims whereof only one or two wander in Nature at once, and before whom the vulgar show as spectres and shadows." The least in the hierarchy of Great Souls, Ward continued, were the Adepts, to whom Emerson "would seem" to refer when he wrote: "But I cannot recite . . . laws of the intellect, without remembering that lofty and sequestered class . . . the Trismegisti." The greatest of the Great Souls were the "High Initiates, the Buddhas or Christs" who, said Ward, were "alluded to by Emerson as 'a class of men, individuals of which appear at long intervals.' " [76]

Another term for the High Initiate is Mahatma, as Johnston suggested. " 'More and more the surges of everlasting nature enter into me,' " Johnston quoted Emerson as exulting, " 'and I become public and human in my regards and actions. So I come to live in thoughts, and act with energies, which are immortal.' The last words of this sentence," Johnston continued, "lead us to the occult idea of *Mahatmahood,* which conceives a perfected soul as 'living in thoughts, and acting with energies which are immortal.' The *Mahatma* is a soul of higher rank in the realms of life, conceived to drink in the wealth of spiritual power closer to the fountain-head." Looking into the Vedanta, William T. James described the Mahatma as a "fervent mystic, prophesying half-insane under the infinitude of his thought," and then by implication placed Emerson among the Mahatmas. They exhorted man, wrote James, "to find thy Self and explore thy Being, and all is thine; it can belong to none else, for thou art That, which is All. This being so," James declared reverently, "we can readily understand and believe what our mystical philosopher has here [in "The Over-Soul"] set down: 'O, believe,

---

[75] *TheosR*, XXII, 137.   [76] *TheosS*, VI, 14.

as thou livest, that every sound that is spoken over the round world, which thou oughtest to hear, will vibrate on thine ear." "And this because the heart in thee is the heart of all; . . . one blood rolls uninterruptedly in an endless circulation through all men, as the water of the globe is all one sea.' " [77]

Theosophists were as diligent as the Secularists in pointing up Emerson's pantheism, but they were even more diligent in giving it an Eastern coloration. And again they turned to the doctrine of Mahat. "The pantheistic idea of all Nature being Divine manifestation is the keystone of Emerson's philosophy," wrote Ward. "His form of belief was Pantheism; the Pantheism of Theosophy, aspectable Nature being the manifestation of consciousness." "Nature, Emerson finds to be plastic, fluid, a transparent law; the law is governed by and emanates from an Universal Mind: in Theosophy, Mahat." [78] Using "Sanscrit nomenclature," James drew many parallels between Mahat, this force which manifests itself in physical nature, and Emerson's Over-Soul. "That Emerson, in common with many of the ancients, was a Pantheist of the highest order" is self-evident. "He also held to the doctrine of Anima Mundi under a modern appellation coined by himself. . . . In his essay of the Over-Soul [he reaffirms, said James] what has already been postulated in the Vedânta of the relation of man to Mahat, the Mind of nature and the Soul of the world. 'Man is a stream whose source is hidden.' " [79]

Ward and James also carefully tied Emerson in with other Theosophical and Hindu notions. In fact, they and their brethren were inclined to make of Emerson's major concepts merely anglicized versions of the religious writings of the East, chiefly of the Indian Scriptures, "the 'Vedas,' the 'Bhagavat Gita,' and the 'Vishnu Purana.' " Complementing Mahat (Over-Soul) is Mâyâ (Illusion). In discussing this aspect of Emerson's philosophy, Ward first pointed out that since Emerson was an idealist, "he reckoned the world an appearance," and then showed in many parallels that Hindu, Theosophist, and Emersonian concepts of Illusion are the same. I shall quote only one of many examples: "The Sanskrit term 'Mâyâ,' with which Theosophical students will be familiar, is defined by H. P.

[77] Johnston, *Lucifer*, I, 256, 257; James, *TheosR*, XXII, 138, 140.
[78] *TheosS*, VI, 6.   [79] *TheosR*, XXII, 136, 134.

Blavatsky as—'Illusion; the cosmic power which renders phenomenal existence and the perceptions thereof possible. . . .' That Emerson held much the same doctrine, there is ample evidence. . . . 'The world of the senses,' he tells us, 'is a world of shows.' " [80]

Ward also showed Emerson's indebtedness to the law of Karma. This law, said the Theosophist, is "the law of cause and effect"; Emerson spoke of it under various names—"the law of compensation," "the law of balance," and "the law of action and re-action." Commenting on this same debt, Johnston wrote that "the great trilogy of friends at the beginning of this century, who rose like three mountain peaks above their contemporaries, Goethe, Carlyle, and Emerson, were chosen by Destiny as prophets. . . . The new world they have explored, is the land of hope of the future, for which we must leave the impoverished soil of theology. . . . What these three masters taught, Occultism teaches; and we propose to show them as great natural masters of knowledge." Because of space limitations, Johnston dealt only with Emerson who, as the following passages showed, was familiar with the law of Karma: "Every secret is told, every crime is punished, every virtue is rewarded." "You cannot do wrong without suffering wrong." *"What a man sows, he reaps."* [81]

Two other matters—evolution and reincarnation—reveal clearly the use to which Theosophists put Emerson. Both he and Theosophists, suggested Ward, believed in evolution on the philosophical as well as on the natural level: "The Monad is the Eternal, unchangeable reality, Atma Buddhi. . . . This subject of the evolution of the Monad is one that Emerson deals with very frequently, and his ideas upon the subject seem to be much in keeping with the doctrine expounded in Theosophical writings. He speaks of the passages of 'the Monad through all his masks as he performs the metempsychosis of Nature.' " Just as Madame Blavatsky had written, continued Ward, that "evolution is an eternal cycle of becoming," so Emerson believed that all the facts "of the animal economy, sex, nutriment, gestation, birth, growth, are symbols of the passage of the world into the soul of man, to suffer there a change, and re-appear a new and higher fact."

[80] *TheosS*, VI, 5, 7. For similar comment, see Johnston, *Lucifer*, I, 257.
[81] Ward, *TheosS*, VI, 12; Johnston, *Lucifer*, I, 252, 253, 255.

This last statement hints at reincarnation, but Ward hesitated before linking Emerson to the theory. There is "no direct evidence in Emerson," Ward wrote, "to show that he accepted this doctrine as an established fact," but Emerson did consider it "a plausible possibility," as the following quotation indicates: " 'It is the secret of the world,' he tells us, 'that all things subsist and do not die, but only retire a little from sight, and afterwards return again.' " Johnston quoted the same passage and declared emphatically that in it "we have an accurate exposition of the occult doctrine of Reincarnation." [82]

In their citations of Emerson, Ward and Johnston point up the error of many other Theosophists who quoted him: they stick to the letter but violate the spirit. The beliefs of Emerson and the Theosophists touched at a number of points, as we have seen, but Emerson would have been as wary of Theosophy as the final answer as he was of other occult sciences like spiritism, animal magnetism, or mesmerism. [83] He would have been especially repelled by reincarnation, "the most characteristic feature of ... modern 'theosophical' teaching." [84] Emerson "was assured," as Foote wrote, "that there could be no destruction of substance and force, but he had no certitude that the activities which made up his personality would be reassembled in a similar personality." [85] To him, such an assemblage would have meant still further evidence of unreality—the NOT ME. Emerson, unlike Theosophists, showed little concern either for the past or for the future: he was almost wholly a man of the present. "Life only avails," he claimed, "not the having lived." [86] A second reason for weakness in the Theosophists' treatment of Emerson lies in the

[82] Ward, *TheosS*, VI, 8, 9, 13; Johnston, *Lucifer*, I, 254. Several other journals of the occult mentioned Emerson during this period. The *Lotus Journal*, 1903–12, defined Emerson's individualism: " 'Self-Reliance,' he [Emerson] writes, 'is the attribute of the Supreme Cause, and it constitutes its measure of good by the degree into which it enters into all lower forms" (Elizabeth Severs, "The Virtue of Self-Reliance," *Lotus*, III [June 1905], 73) . "For this Emerson Centenary," wrote a critic in *Light* (Aug. 15, 1903, p. 386) , "we know of nothing better to print than his personal 'Ten Commandments,' written as 'Sealed Orders,' in 1832." These commandments *Light* duly reprinted. *Light* also published a short article, "Emerson on Materialism and Idealism," in which excerpts were used to contrast the two philosophies (January 16, 1892, p. 33) .

[83] *Works*, X, 13, 24–25.   [84] A. S. P.-P., *Encyclopaedia Britannica*, p. 70.
[85] *Freethinker*, June 7, 1903, p. 353.   [86] *Works*, II, 69.

nature of his philosophy: it was as abstruse and as unpopular as that which it was being used to explain. Although Emerson was a literary figure widely known in England in the latter half of the Victorian period and one respected as a man, his Transcendentalism was not well received. To the upper-middle class, which Theosophy was mainly interested in reaching, it was as forbidding as Hinduism.

Neither were the Secularists able to manipulate Emerson to great advantage. Unlike those pile drivers, Emerson was, as Holmes observed with some truth, "an iconoclast without a hammer, who took down our idols from their pedestals so tenderly that it seemed like an act of worship." [87] He was a philosopher who never turned dissenter; Secularists were dissenters who never became philosophers. Secondly, the lower and lower-middle classes welcomed ammunition with which to destroy the despised authority of the church, but they were sorry indeed that Emerson could replace it with nothing better than self-reliance. Rationalists like Holyoake and Miss Collet understood all too well the human being's desire to escape from freedom and had tried to substitute the security of socialism for the assurances of religion. Secularism would doubtless have fared better in Holyoake's hands than in Bradlaugh's; yet in the rashness of men like Bradlaugh, Foote, and Holyoake at his radical best, one finds something healthy and refreshing. Although Secularism failed to shake the foundations of revealed religion, it was carried on by courageous men who set liberty above self. Their influence was, like Emerson's, "eminently liberative" and "progressive." [88] Above all, both Theosophist and Secularist helped to vindicate man's right to nonconformity in matters of religion: the Theosophist upheld his belief in the occult, the bizarre, while the Secularist persisted in holding no religious belief at all. They believed in intellectual as well as spiritual freedom, and in expressing their belief they made the century more tolerant, as we shall see in the comments of late Victorians on Emerson's religious doctrines.

[87] *Ibid.*, XI, 640.
[88] Robertson, I, 106, 80; Allan Nevins, introd., in Warren, pp. 7, 9; Warren, p. 231; Janet E. Courtney, *Freethinkers of the Nineteenth Century* (London, 1920), pp. 97, 101.

❦ V ❦

In the Groves
of Academe

ROM the time of his death in 1882 until the appearance of
the Centenary Edition in 1903, Emerson received more
notices in periodicals than during any other twenty years.
Much of this attention was devoted to memoirs, biographies,
and letters that poured forth after his death. The most important of
these works were written by eminent nineteenth-century academics or by men close to the academic world: Professors Charles E.
Norton, Oliver Wendell Holmes, Richard Garnett, George Edward
Woodberry, and A. Bronson Alcott as well as the scholarly law
graduate and architect James E. Cabot contributed their share, great
and small, to an understanding of Emerson, and their contributions
were, in turn, often reviewed, or even more often utilized, by other
professors in their estimates of Emerson. Professors Matthew Arnold,
Friedrich Max Müller, Edward Dowden, W. L. Courtney, George
Saintsbury, and Leslie Stephen contributed important articles on
Emerson to British periodicals. They were joined by such excellent
Victorian critics as Richard Holt Hutton, Vernon Lee, and others
who were university trained or closely affiliated with the universities.
Around this nucleus of scholar-critics floated such independent con-
stellations as Henry James and Walter Lewin, whom Clarence
Gohdes calls "one of the ablest reviewers of American books in
England," [1] while the outer reaches consisted of a multitude of lesser

[1] *American Literature in Nineteenth-Century England* (New York, 1944), p. 134 *n.*

stars who sometimes threw a brighter light on the transcendentalist than their more illustrious colleagues. "Quite a literature has grown up on the subject of . . . [Emerson's] life and of his teaching in the course of the last half-dozen years," wrote the *Westminster* in 1887, "and one after another of his loving and admiring disciples have vied with each other in their efforts to do honour in his memory." [2] In spite of the excellent reputation of some of the disciples, much of this effort as well as that which appeared after 1887 received poor notices.

Sensing a quick profit, the newspaper editor Alexander Ireland published the first of these works shortly after his friend Emerson's death. Critics wrote that *In Memoriam* was "sketchy and scrappy," a "very pleasant volume of scraps," but that it gave an interesting glimpse of and "very pleasant peeps" into the philosopher. A year later the industrious Ireland brought out an augmented edition of the work, which was welcomed as "substantially a new book," "a rare prize." [3] Illustrating perfectly what Arnold condemned as the "provincial spirit" ("its admiration weeps hysterical tears") Moncure D. Conway threw together what surely must be one of the most embarrassing chapters in English literature, used it as the introduction to *Emerson at Home and Abroad,* most of which had appeared in English journals, and hurriedly brought out the whole disorderly production. Padded with chapters on Hawthorne and Thoreau, the book was an "ever reverent," "charming" monograph that was "a little hastily put together." Two critics compared it with Ireland's *Memoirs.* The authors, one suggested, often crossed paths in their monographs, with the Englishman's being "far superior . . . in unity and effectiveness." The second reviewer disliked both books. With these works appeared *The Emerson Birthday Book;* in it Emerson "has been dished up in scraps." [4]

For the next twenty years monographs—some anemic, many idola-

[2] CXXVIII (Nov. 1887) , 985.

[3] Mark Wyndham, *Truth,* Oct. 5, 1882, p. 496; *BQR,* LXXVI (July 1882) , 190; *LitW,* June 23, 1882, p. 389. For like comment, see *WR,* CXX (July 1883) , 266.

[4] Hugh Walker, *The Literature of the Victorian Era* (Cambridge, Eng., 1921), p. 971; *NatRef,* Dec. 3, 1882, p. 395; George Stewart, *ScR,* XI (April 1888) , 289; *Ath,* Feb. 3, 1883, p. 147; *BQR,* LXXVII (Jan. 1883) , 190; R. C. Browne, *Ac,* Aug. 4, 1883, pp. 71–72; *Truth,* Oct. 6, 1881, p. 462.

trous, and all the result of as well as a contribution to the Emerson revival—followed at fairly regular intervals. One of Emerson's chief disciples, A. Bronson Alcott, had presented to his friend as a birthday gift the small volume, *Ralph Waldo Emerson: An Estimate of His Character and Genius, in Prose and Verse,* and in 1882, some ten years later, the work was hastily reissued. One reviewer said that the book was too impersonal, another that "it is one of the best appreciative criticisms of Emerson's genius and personal life." [5] Alert publishers of the Round Table Series brought out an essay on Emerson that attempted "to give temperate and reasoned statements of his beliefs." [6] Shortly after Emerson's death Dr. William Hague, who had preached against Emersonianism from the First Baptist Church in Boston, found fault with his departed brother in a paper read before the New York Genealogical Society and immediately rushed into print. A reviewer found the effort so poorly done that he could not understand it, but Lewin was more successful: in the paper the minister had argued with little success that Emerson's "lifework as a whole, tested by its supreme ideal, its method and fruitage, shows" "a great waste of power." [7]

In 1889 Emerson's son brought out a memoir for the Social Circle in Concord, to which, said a reviewer, it should have been confined. The book furnished a few more "crumbs" "minute and . . . far from succulent" to current Emerson literary fare. A more generous reviewer called it "a welcome supplement" that attempted to clear up "odd notions that have been current about Emerson at different times" and gave "many interesting details of [his] . . . training and early life." [8] In 1890 appeared *Talks with Ralph Waldo Emerson,* by Charles J. Woodbury, who had been among the early Emerson cultists. The book revealed that Woodbury was "a hearty admirer" but no "blind worshipper." [9] In 1903 Emerson's friend, F. B. San-

---

[5] *ModR,* IV (July 1883) , 642; Walter Lewin, *Ac,* June 22, 1889, p. 422.

[6] *WR,* CXXII (July 1884) , 282.

[7] James E. Cabot, *A Memoir of Ralph Waldo Emerson* (Boston, 1887) , I, 169; *WR,* CXXII (July 1884) , 283; Lewin, *Ac,* Aug. 16, 1884, p. 101. For other comment, see *SatR,* May 10, 1884, p. 624.

[8] *Ath,* June 1, 1889, p. 695; *SatR,* Aug. 10, 1889, pp. 170, 171. For other comment, see Lewin, *Ac,* June 22, 1889, p. 422.

[9] Lewin, *Ac,* July 12, 1890, p. 26.

born, published *The Personality of Emerson,* a "slight" record of the "traits, incidents, and conversations which came within his own personal knowledge," and in 1904 Elisabeth Luther Cary brought out *Emerson: Poet and Thinker,* "a handsome volume written by one who ... has studied the Emersonian philosophy to good purpose." [10]

More important than these volumes which generally attempted, as did Edward Waldo Emerson, "to reveal his father's personal and inner life as 'the citizen and villager and householder, the friend and neighbor,' " [11] was George W. Cooke's *Ralph Waldo Emerson: His Life and Writings.* Published a year after Emerson died, this work gave a full and sympathetic account of Emerson's religious views. Unluckily, the book went almost unnoticed. George Stewart, an outstanding Canadian journalist, hastily wrote it off as a "charming" monograph, and a second critic said that it "will no doubt be greatly valued by many who have not had the opportunity of grasping the true relations of Mr. Emerson to the thought and feeling of our time. ... Cooke has shown considerable faculty and skill in firmly grasping the distinctive qualities of Mr. Emerson's mind and spirit." In 1888 Lewin commented that the book made Emerson real "in the way he was real to his personal friends," and on another occasion wrote that the Unitarian minister gave fine "analyses of Emerson's writings." Cooke, declared Professor C. B. Upton, had published "a genial and faithful guide and introduction to the study of Emerson's writings [rather than] a critical estimate of Emerson's true place as a thinker and writer." "The time for such an estimate has not yet arrived." [12]

Nor did it arrive with the publication of Holmes's *Emerson* in 1885. Several reviewers were impressed with the Autocrat's account of Emerson the poet,[13] but the book as a whole was not favorably received. Conway asserted that Holmes's hand "has not trembled, unless with awe, in achieving this fine relievo of Emer-

[10] *Ath,* June 18, 1903, p. 91; *Sp,* Dec. 24, 1904, p. 1059.

[11] Lewin, *Ac,* June 22, 1889, p. 422.

[12] Stewart, *ScR,* XI, 289; *LitW,* Feb. 10, 1882, pp. 85, 87; Lewin, *Ac,* Sept. 8, 1888, p. 149; Lewin, *Ac,* Feb. 28, 1885, p. 143; C. B. U[pton], *ModR,* III (April 1882), 429. For identification of Upton, see p. 209 of this issue of the magazine.

[13] See p. 95.

son," and a colleague wrote that the book would "not answer the high expectations which the names [of the author and subject] necessarily excite." It was, said another commentator, "uncritical," and Stewart dismissed it (as he had Cooke's) as a "charming" monograph. *Time* pithily noted, "The last word has [not] been said on Emerson." Comment in the *British Quarterly* was typical: "The book will stand as a careful, somewhat self-conscious, and laboured tribute to the memory of a great thinker . . . and will be accepted as a 'makeshift' till we can have the full-length portrait from the appointed hand." [14]

The hand was that of James E. Cabot, Emerson's literary executor. *A Memoir of Ralph Waldo Emerson* and Professor Norton's *The Correspondence of Thomas Carlyle and Ralph Waldo Emerson* received more notices than any other works on Emerson in English journals. They also received better notices.[15] Merrily whistling "A Wandering Minstrel," a reviewer on the ever-caustic *Saturday Review* wrote that the *Memoir* was "made of shreds and patches," but Lewin declared that "Mr. Cabot gives the facts, and also gives them their place and relation. . . . We had a correct outline before; now we have a finished and satisfying portrait." The *Spectator* asserted that the two-volume work furnished an "admirable memoir" that "will please nine-tenths" of its readers, and the *Westminster* said that the task was performed "with ability, with diligence, and with care." [16] Other critics wrote that "the reader will not willingly skip a line" of this "definitive memoir," which was "intelligently and carefully composed." [17] Reviewers sometimes compared the *Memoir* with Garnett's *Life,* which one critic called "a model of careful and conscientious book-making." The books, observed the *Church Quarterly,* were the best of Emerson's biographies, but whereas

---

[14] Moncure D. Conway, *OC,* V (March 1885) , 138; *ContR,* XLVII (March 1885) , 452; *SatR,* April 18, 1885, p. 512; Stewart, *ScR,* XI, 289; *Time,* XII (Feb. 1885) , 246; *BQR,* LXXXI (April 1885) , 440. For other comment, see Augustine Birrell, *Good Words,* XXVI (June 1885) , 359–63.

[15] Comments on the *Correspondence* appear in Chapter VI.

[16] *SatR,* Nov. 19, 1887, p. 708 (an allusion to *The Mikado* [1885]) ; Lewin, *Ac,* Oct. 22, 1887, p. 261; *Sp,* June 9, 1888, p. 793; *WR,* CXXVIII (Nov. 1887) , 985.

[17] Stewart, *ScR,* XI, 289; *AnnualR,* 1887, p. 73; Henry James, *MM,* LVII (Dec. 1887) , 86. For other comment, see *Murray's,* II (Nov. 1887) , 717.

Cabot's was a "full-length portrait," Garnett's was a "miniature." Lewin complained that Garnett followed "Cabot so closely," although he was "accurate as well as readable." [18]

These works, like the other offerings, presented "to the readers of Emerson [as the *Westminster* wrote of the *Memoir*] some further illustrations, some details of his outward and inward history, that may fill out and define more closely the image of him they already have." This definition was not enough. The *Saturday Review* complained of Cabot, "He gives abundant materials for forming, correcting, or filling up an idea of Emerson's character," but he neglects Emerson's "intellectual history." Henry James made the same complaint but more strongly: "We lay down the book with a singular impression of paleness—an impression that comes partly from the tone of the biographer, and partly from the moral complexion of his subject, but mainly from the vacancy of the page itself. That of Emerson's personal history is condensed into the single word Concord, and all the condensation in the world will not make it look rich." Irritated by the attention lavished upon Emerson after his death, the often-hostile *Athenaeum* observed in 1899 that "there is in reality nothing more to be said of Emerson's life and habits. That story is one of highminded simplicity—very high-minded, but also extremely simple." Reviewing Holmes's *Life,* Augustine Birrell, "a capable and versatile reviewer," gave the gist of this opinion. He quoted the American minister at the Court of St. James as querying, "How can we sufficiently honour the men who, in this secular, work-a-day world habitually breathe—'An ampler ether, a diviner air' than ours!" And then commented, "Testimony of this kind, conclusive as it is upon the question of Emerson's personal influence, will not always be admissible in support of his claims as an author. In the long run an author's only witnesses are his own books." [19]

In the nineteenth century these witnesses were questioned more as to the message they brought than the manner in which they brought it. Most late Victorian critics, as Basil Willey writes of John Morley, "subordinated 'literature' to 'life' "; literature was "a means to the

---

[18] *Ath,* June 23, 1888, p. 793; *CQR,* XXVII (Oct. 1888) , 51; Lewin, *Ac,* Sept. 8, 1888, p. 148.

[19] *WR,* CXXVIII (Nov. 1887) , 985; *SatR,* Nov. 19, 1887, p. 708; James, *MM,* LVII, 86; *Ath,* June 1, 1889, p. 695; Birrell, *Good Words,* XXVI, 359.

fuller enjoyment, or perhaps even more to the stoical endurance, of living." To them, "beauties of diction, form and treatment were . . . matters of secondary concern, unless they were accompanied by truth and seriousness of substance." This critical approach, says Willey, has been that of "the greater number of critics until recent times—not to mention most of the creative writers themselves, and the mass of readers at all times." Even recently, especially since World War II, literary critics have concentrated more and more on values other than the purely literary. They have become increasingly aware of the severe limitations of the New Criticism as well as appalled at the intellectual exhibitionism of many of its adherents. Contemporary critics are saying of their subjects, however indirectly, what Conway said of Emerson: "Few of his admirers probably would be satisfied to have him described as a 'man of letters.' "[20]

Certainly James would not be satisfied to describe Emerson as such. He had no style, said the incomparable James, "usually the bribe . . . on the journey to posterity; and if [he] . . . goes his way, as he clearly appears to be doing, on the strength of his message alone, the case will be rare, the exception striking and the honour great." James was not alone in his opinion. Emerson "was rather the prophet and teacher than the artist and literary man," wrote H. Sheffield Clapham. An anonymous reviewer declared that "to judge Emerson exclusively by his style . . . would be a great injustice." "We must consider what things he has actually said." C. A. Ward wrote, "There is no more need to ask what his position in literature is to be. It is that of a man of superlative faculty, of a man who has made it his business to seize ideas, and to assimilate them." Emerson, said the scholarly W. L. Courtney, was not "the cultivated *littérateur*, for though he cares for style, it is only as strictly subordinate to the sermonic qualities of his writings." Nothing "seems clearer than that he was bound to preach."[21]

In order to understand this preacher, Lewin contended that "what is . . . wanted is a well worked out critical study which shall display

[20] *More Nineteenth Century Studies* (New York, 1956), pp. 288, 296, 288 (see also Jerome Hamilton Buckley, *The Victorian Temper* [Cambridge, Mass., 1951], p. 216); Moncure D. Conway, *Emerson at Home and Abroad* (Boston, 1882), p. 112.

[21] James, *MM*, LVII, 98; Clapham, *MM*, LXXVI (July 1902), 188; *Ath*, March 8, 1884, p. 306; Ward, *TBar*, LXXII (Oct. 1884), 244; Courtney, *FR*, n.s. XXXVIII (Sept. 1885), 319–20. For similar comment, see *GT*, XXXIX (June 1903), 120.

Emerson as he was and his work in its correct relation to his forerunners and his contemporaries." [22] Like Birrell, James, and others, Lewin was correct in believing that none of the books appearing on Emerson had accomplished this task. Yet these critics failed to understand the great importance of the literary historians. Without the background furnished (to use J. W. Dodds's phraseology) by this "dismal series of 'official' *Lives,* reverent, discreet, commemorative," [23] Morley's essay, which Lewin sets apart as distinguished criticism,[24] would have been thin. So would a number of other essays, including those of James and Lewin. The biographers failed in significant ways to make Emerson clear to late Victorians, but they performed very well two important tasks: they furnished a solid body of factual information which a myriad of "higher journalists" [25] passed along to the British public, or, better still, they afforded a solid base upon which critics built excellent studies of Emerson's works.

No one can argue that these studies are as fresh and exciting as those from the hard-mouthed men of the forties or as entertaining as those of the fifties and sixties, or even as interesting as those few which appeared in the seventies: for these essays were, like the earlier, a product of their times. And the times were dull. The eighties sank into an "interlude of comparative quiescence which Professor Whitehead had called 'one of the dullest phases of thought since the time of the First Crusade,' a respite from intellection designed only to celebrate 'the triumph of the professional man.' " [26] Still, in the case of Emerson, this triumph did not come too soon: he had waited some twenty-five years for the first good critical estimate of his work and now, twenty years later, he was to be accorded a number of them. Karl Litzenberg has observed that the reception of Balzac, Zola, and Ibsen "illustrate[s] the Victorian proclivity for expressing violent first objection followed by friendly tolerance, and often by warm approval." [27] Emerson, too, suffered rebuff, and by

[22] *Ac,* Feb. 28, 1885, p. 143.

[23] "New Territories in Victorian Biography," in *The Reinterpretation of Victorian Literature,* ed. Joseph E. Baker (Princeton, N.J., 1950), p. 197.

[24] Lewin, *Ac,* Feb. 28, 1885, p. 143.

[25] Geoffrey Tillotson, *Criticism and the Nineteenth Century* (London, 1951), p. 9 *n.*

[26] Buckley, p. 208.

[27] "The Victorians and the World Abroad," in Baker, p. 192.

the end of the period he received warm approval. Better still, he was generally comprehended. That readers of periodicals came at last to understand Emerson's works was due mainly to the excellent studies brought out by professional scholars. The leavening provided by these essays raises the tone of the large body of criticism of the late period: they are less accusative, more critical, less argumentative, more judicial and comprehensive than those of the earlier time.

Abjuring "the bludgeon and blunderbuss" [28] critical methods of their predecessors and utilizing material from the biographers, late critics turned in fine studies of Emerson. "Scholarship was flourishing," as Elie Halévy writes,[29] and increasingly sophisticated critical techniques were making their appearance. There was little or no foaming "at the mouth," which Arnold deplored, and much that was gracious and urbane, which he sanctioned.[30] In addition to the attempt of Arnold and Garnett to test Emerson by classical standards, James turned to the canons of realism, Courtney and Henry Norman to the theories set forth by the realists and by Hippolyte Taine, Vernon Lee to the subjective impressionism of Walter Pater, Saintsbury to neoclassicism, and Leslie Stephen to "ethical humanism" — nearly the whole spectrum of nineteenth-century critical methods.

In the remainder of this chapter the effectiveness of these methods in treating Emerson's art as well as the manner in which they shed light upon his philosophy and religion will be discussed. Critical comments on other matters — Emerson's politics, his involvement in the antislavery movement, or his influence — will not be neglected, nor will the opinions of the run-of-the-mine critics who, as in earlier times, showed a lively interest in the American.

II

The late Victorian era was much more interested in the literary value of Emerson's works than were the earlier periods; at the same time late critics were just as adamant as the early in denying the

---

[28] Walker, p. 971.

[29] *A History of the English People in the Nineteenth Century* (London, 1951), IV, 435.

[30] Walker, p. 971, quotes from Matthew Arnold's *Literary Influence of Academies*.

American an important prerequisite of the successful man of letters, an instinct for style. Although some were not so negative in their judgments as James and Courtney, they declared that his style was "staccato," eccentric, lacking in finish. The diction was "abstruse" and "abstract." His sentences, which were "monotonously short," asserted one, resembled "the structure of worms." His prose was "sometimes quite platitudinous, often conceited and grotesque, and not seldom containing a stray morsel of gratuitous bad taste on which the teeth grate," observed the Neo-Augustinian Saintsbury.[31] J. M. Wheeler and G. W. Foote wrote that Emerson was "abrupt and angular," that "he has few sustained passages." "Minute critics" of all kinds complained that Emerson violated "grammatical rules," defied "idiomatic proprieties," revealed a "sententious obscurity." He was also "pretentious": much of what he wrote was "truism disguised as epigram, and commonplace uttered with an air of esoteric mystery." Even worse, said the Canadian novelist and biographer Jean McIlwraith, this epigrammatic style was "dangerous"; "Emerson is a most stimulating writer . . . [but] is apt sometimes to make you think that you have got hold of a real truth, only because he has put an old error into a novel and fascinating dress." Spoke the *Athenaeum* in imperious finality: Emerson "writes for the general public, and he has no right to envelope purposely his thought in phrases that are beyond their comprehension." [32]

Saintsbury, Miss McIlwraith, and the Secularists found certain aspects of his style worthy of praise. Emerson's prose, admitted the professor, was "nearly always suggestive, often admirably eloquent, not seldom marvellously acute." For "all its faults," confessed the lady, "the epigrammatic style of Emerson arrests the attention and stimulates the faculties as more exact writing never could." After

[31] *Sp,* Feb. 10, 1906, p. 220; [Nichol], *NBrR,* XLVII (Dec. 1867), 329; *PubO,* May 7, 1870, p. 584; Thomas Bradfield, *PMQR,* n.s. XVII (April 1895), 252; P. L[andreth], *Blackwood's,* CLV (April 1894), 481; Saintsbury, *Ac,* May 6, 1882, p. 321.

[32] Wheeler, *Freethinker,* May 7, 1882, p. 146; Foote, *Freethinker,* June 7, 1903, p. 354; *NBrR,* XLVII, 327; [R. E. Prothero], *QR,* CLXVI (Jan. 1888), 157; *SatR,* May 28, 1887, p. 780; [Richard Holt Hutton], *Sp,* Feb. 2, 1884, p. 156; *Ath,* March 8, 1884, p. 306; Jean McIlwraith, *Canadian Magazine,* I (Oct. 1893), 689; [Hutton], *Sp.* Feb. 2, 1884, p. 155; *Ath,* Jan. 15, 1876, p. 81. For other derogatory comments on Emerson's style, see *SatR,* Nov. 19, 1887, p. 708; *WR,* CXLV (May 1896), 586.

noting that Emerson "is rather a poetic . . . thinker," Wheeler said that "his unhesitating and audacious expressions" are "clear, sharp, and prismatic," and Foote declared that his English was "scholarly, fluent, and beautiful." [33] One of the nearly insoluble problems of the student sifting comment on Emerson's style from periodicals of the late period is determining which work or works the reviewer is commenting upon. This knowledge is important, for Emerson's later essays reveal a style somewhat different from the earlier.[34] When the *Spectator* acknowledged that even though Emerson's works were staccato, they also showed an interesting "poetic quality," the critic doubtless had in mind the books brought out in the forties and early fifties. This quality, the critic explained, "redeems a style" permeated by "the atmosphere of the platform." "A sudden touch of tenderness, a gleam of beautiful fancy," the "lecturer is forgotten, and we see only the poet. It is this which makes Emerson a stimulating writer." [35]

In other cases it is harder to judge which of Emerson's essays the reviewer had in mind in commenting on the style. The following glowing tributes were probably paid to the author of the *First* and *Second Series:* his style was "salient, poetical, and striking," "suggestive . . . , eloquent, . . . acute." It stimulates the mind more than an orthodox one would do; in his works lies a "wealth of imagery." Dowden wrote that Emerson's "short sentences scintillate and snap like sparks from an electrical conductor, and each gives a separate tingle of the nerves," while Hutton praised the "pithy metaphor [which] has a curious charm and sometimes a curious grandeur of its own." This style was, said James Nairn, "as condensed and epigrammatic as that of Bacon's essays." In a bountiful mood Coulson Kernahan wrote that "there is, perhaps, no writer excepting Shakespeare, whose every utterance is so packed and charged with wisdom." [36]

[33] Saintsbury, *Ac,* May 6, 1882, p. 321; McIlwraith, *CanM,* I, 691; Wheeler, *Freethinker,* May 7, 1882, p. 146; Foote, *Freethinker,* June 7, 1903, p. 354. Wheeler made a similar comment in *Progress,* I (Feb. 1883) , 118.

[34] *NBrR,* XLVII, 329. Also see p. 35. [35] Feb. 10, 1906, p. 220.

[36] *Guide,* XIV (April 1893) , 73; Saintsbury, *Ac,* May 6, 1882, p. 321; McIlwraith, *CanM,* I, p. 691; *MM,* LXXXVIII (May 1903) , 40; Edward Dowden, *ContR,* XXX (July 1877) , 314; *Sp,* Feb. 2, 1884, p. 156; Nairn, *TBar,* CXV (Oct. 1898) , 295; Kernahan, *GentM,* CCLIX (Nov. 1885) , 479.

Some critics seemed to believe that Emerson's works were composed after the fashion of the great nineteenth-century essayists who were not poets but the apotheosis of unity, coherence, and emphasis. The "elegance of diction" of his essays, wrote Henry Hemming, is "very pleasing," an opinion shared by Stewart. "There is in Emerson's style," observed T. Slater, "considerable force, and sometimes even eloquence, when it is not rendered unintelligible by being too transcendental." As an essayist, Emerson compared "in brilliancy" with Hazlitt.[37]

The more ingenious critics made comments that can be applied to any or all of Emerson's works. His prose was "chaste, lucid, and direct," "sharp, terse, compact"; "a singular power of sententious speech" characterized "his gnomic sayings"; in Emerson were found "a thousand charms of style." His books revealed "pages of brilliant writing"; as an essayist, he is "certainly a prince." His pieces "are models of condensation, a prize for a nineteenth century, which whirls so fast, that if any one has aught to say, . . . he must be brief." "Marked by a vivid earnestness, a succintness [*sic*] of expression, and a wealth of noble imagery . . . his marvellous prose writings have fascinated, dazzled, and instructed every real student of our times." [38]

These comments, good and bad, were interesting, but they failed to contribute much to an understanding of Emerson's style. Some of the critics who made them attempted to explain that style by noting the way Emerson composed his essays. R. E. Prothero probably gathered from Ireland, whose book (among others) he was considering, that Emerson's "method of working encouraged the broken and fragmentary form of this style. He jotted down his separate perceptions . . . in common place books," from which he drew material

---

[37] Hemming, *NDomM*, Aug. 1871, p. 67; Stewart, *Belford's*, I (Jan. 1877) , 231; Slater, *Month*, LIII (March 1885) , 378; *CQR*, XXVII (Oct. 1888) , 57.

[38] F. H. Underwood, *Good Words*, XXVIII (Dec. 1887) , 813; Kernahan, *GentM*, CCLIX, 472; *SatR*, July 12, 1890, p. 58; *Sp*, Feb. 2, 1884, p. 155; E. M., *Lit*, Sept. 8, 1900, p. 171; *QR*, CLXVI, 157; Mrs. M. A. Castle, *CMM*, XVI (July 1882) , 31; William R. Turnbull, *NMM*, CXXII (Dec. 1882) , 11. Other comments on the excellence of Emerson's style were made by Kernahan, *GentM*, CCLIX, 472; Ward, *TBar*, LXXII, 248; Stephen, *NatRev*, XXXVI (Feb. 1901) , 885.

for his essays.[39] The better reviewers used critical precepts of the time in an effort to explain the Emersonian manner. Vernon Lee chose those of Pater, whose criticism centered on "the quest for the exquisite moment."[40] "The relation I ... wish to set forth," she wrote in contempt of the Victorian "ethical aesthetic,"[41] "is that between Emerson's writings and one of their readers—myself. For the relation between writer and reader ... implies the originating of ideas and states of feeling such as did not exist in either reader or writer taken singly, the latent peculiarities of the one being vitalised and altered by the fruitful contact of the other." This contact led Vernon Lee to rhapsodize: Emerson's "exquisite moral and aesthetic sensibility is revealed in a thousand fragmentary utterances"; he was the "apostle of spontaneity." Unfortunately, she said, he was also rather obscure.[42]

From the start of his literary career in England, criticism of Emerson as a man of letters, as well as in other areas, had brought together strange bedfellows. Catholic and Protestant, fundamentalist and Swedenborgian, rationalist and Theosophist laid aside wide differences long enough to call for his extinction or to chant his praise. And now Pater's followers joined those of Taine long enough to deplore Emerson's obscurity. It is interesting to see "how certain predisposing forces found their proper issue in his person and character, and prefigured ... the form of the statue," explained Courtney. These forces, according to the philosopher-editor, were those which ineluctably molded Emerson for the ministry and thus set the pattern for all of his life, including the way he wrote. "In their effects on literary style there is much in common between the lecturing-desk and the pulpit, and whatever of unchastened expression or irritating phrase may be found in Emerson's prose may generally be traced to this source. The ... lecturer is never chary of his senten-

---

[39] *QR*, CLXVI, 157. See Alexander Ireland, *In Memoriam, Ralph Waldo Emerson: Recollections of His Visits to England in 1833, 1847–8, 1872–3, and Extracts from Unpublished Letters* (London, 1882), p. 33. Slater, *Month*, LIII, 377, also describes this method. He doubtless found the information in one of Emerson's biographies.

[40] *English Prose of the Victorian Era*, ed. Charles F. Harrold and William D. Templeman (New York, 1938), p. lxxvi.

[41] Buckley, p. 216.   [42] *ContR*, LXVII (March 1895), 345, 348, 346, 347.

ces; . . . the lecture, when printed in the form of an essay, irritates us by the slowness of its march and its want of adaptation to the rapid sweep of vision. Moreover, it is difficult for" the lecturer "to deliver his thoughts paragraphically, and the paragraph is the keystone of literary form. . . . Another effect, due to the same cause, is the jerkiness and want of cohesion between the sentences." [43]

Other pragmatists also complained of this want of cohesion. Stephen wrote, I do not "belong to the class which takes most freely the impression of the Emersonian stamp." The American, declared Stephen, cared "nothing for consistency. . . . His characteristic want of continuity made him as incapable of evolving a central idea as of expounding an argument." Birrell ceased his "literary flute-playing" long enough to observe soberly that if anyone had "to name the most non-sequacious author" who ever wrote, he could not "help nominating Emerson. . . . How carefully does a really great writer, like Dr. Newman, . . . explain to you what he is going to do and how he is going to do it!" "Emerson makes no terms with his readers —he gives them neither thread nor clue." This judgment was applauded by the Rev. Patrick Dillon, who quoted Disraeli the elder as writing, " 'No great work . . . was ever produced without a grand (that is a comprehensive) plan,' and this faculty it is whose absence in Emerson's writings Mr. Birrell characterizes as non-sequaciousness." To one critical realist, Emerson's style was just plain old-fashioned. "His old-world arts are powerless to retain men born under new conditions and nurtured in new creeds. For this growing neglect [his quaint and eccentric] style is, in part, responsible." [44]

Uniting with the impressionists and the realists against Emerson's

[43] Courtney, *FR*, n.s. XXXVIII, 320, 321. Walter Jerrold, *TBar*, CXXVIII (Oct. 1903) , 437–38, also traced Emerson's style to his lecturing. Of great interest to the early periodical critics, Emerson's platform performance was often noted by his biographers. See Cabot, I, 240; II, 457, 469, 496, 569, 570–71; Ireland, pp. 16, 22–23; Conway, pp. 54–55, 321–22; Oliver Wendell Holmes, *Ralph Waldo Emerson* (Boston, 1885) , pp. 132–33, 378 ff. In the *Bookman*, II (July 1892) , 108–9, Francis Espinasse devoted a good deal of space to Emerson's British lecture tour. Other late Victorians mentioning Emerson as lecturer are Stephen, *NatRev*, XXXVI, 896; Courtney, *FR*, n.s. XXXVIII, 321; Stewart, *Belford's*, I, 233; an anonymous critic in *MM*, LXXXVIII (May 1903) , 38; James, *MM*, LVII, 89.

[44] Stephen, *NatRev*, XXXVI, 883, 885, 896; Birrell, *Good Words*, XXVI, 361; Dillon, *Irish Monthly*, XXVIII (July 1900) , 416; *Ath*, Jan. 15, 1876, p. 81.

style were the classicists, whose leader was Arnold. Taking full, perhaps too full, advantage of the comparative method, Arnold declared, "I do not place him among the great writers, the great men of letters," like Cicero, Bacon, and Swift, writers with "a genius and instinct for style." Although "Emerson has passages of noble and pathetic eloquence," "shrewd and felicitous wit," "crisp epigram," "he is not a great writer; his style has not the requisite wholeness of good tissue." Garnett agreed. Adhering to Arnoldian precepts, this classicist wrote that "Emerson's peculiar gifts . . . disable him from the practice of literary art on any extensive scale. Art implies the subordination of parts to the total effect." Emerson's "disquisitions" "are incapable of this treatment." They are "deficient in architectonic." John Nichol, who doubtless had read and was influenced by "The Function of Criticism at the Present Time," in *Essays in Criticism*, summed up such comment: Emerson's "essays are bundles of loose ideas tacked together only by a common title." [45]

Less procrustean critics saw that Emerson's prose (like his poetry) could not be judged by ordinary standards. They knew, as Poe had pointed out years before, that every writer must be given his condition; [46] that the material under review was more important than the critical method. For a moment at least these sensitive reviewers scotched Strachey's poisonous comment that "to the Victorian critic 'literature was always an excuse for talking about something else.' " [47] Emerson's " 'unparalleled non-sequaciousness' as Mr. Birrell calls it," wrote a sharp commentator, "is irritating to many who would seek to judge him by ordinary canons of criticism; but in thus recording all his inspirations he has given us a multitude of tonic sentences that 'pulse as if from the veins of Spring.' " The American biographer Francis H. Underwood attained a near-miss as he sought to establish canons by which to judge Emerson's works. "If his

[45] Arnold, *MM*, L (May 1884) , 4, 5; Garnett, *Lit,* Sept. 21, 1901, p. 275; *NBrR,* XLVII, 326. Walker, p. 962, writes that *Essays in Criticism* came "to many young men . . . with much of the force of a revelation." For other comments on Emerson's lack of architectonics, see *QR,* CLXVI, 157; Egan Mew, *Lit,* Sept. 21, 1901, p. 270; *Blackwood's,* CLV, 484.

[46] *The Works of Edgar Allan Poe,* ed. Edmund Clarence Stedman and George Edward Woodberry (New York, 1914) , VII, 23–47 *passim,* esp. 38–39.

[47] Willey, p. 287.

sentences are not 'sequacious,' it is because his thoughts are prover-
bial in quality as well as form. . . . What he wrote had passed through
the alembic of his original and poetic mind, and was cast in a form
that no one could claim or imitate. . . . His thoughts touch but do not
blend. There is, however, a connection, though tenuous, or rather a
natural succession in those sentences." "It only requires some imagination to connect the thoughts, as in a chain of strength and
beauty." [48]

If Underwood himself had been a little more imaginative, he
might have discovered the connection between the composition of
Emerson's sentences and the theory of evolution: the organic method
in literature is, in essence, an extension of Darwinianism. J. H.
Buckley has written that "the doctrine of organic development was
so thoroughly diffused throughout nineteenth-century science and
philosophy that no serious thinker could escape its implications." [49]
These implications were social, political, and religious—not literary.
Comtists and Marxians, Secularists and Theosophists promoted
evolution; [50] so did less radical Victorians. *Great Thoughts* said that
Emerson expressed the doctrine of evolution thus: " 'Man is no
upstart in the creation. . . .' But it is not evolution without God.
God has been at work before the coming of man, and he traces the
Divine hand in 'the preparation made for man.' " William R. Turnbull declared that "The clergy even now-a-days can speak with
equanimity" of "the scientific demonstrations of Darwin," and
"Emerson, against whom the deepest anathema were vented because
it was presumed that he had struck at the foundations of our faith,
[is] . . . accepted as an Apostle of Righteousness." [51]

Although Stephen explained correctly that to Emerson evolution
"does not mean a blind struggle for existence but the regular unroll-
ing of a divine and benevolent drama," James Gooden insisted that
"Emerson in *Nature* foreshadowed the theory of Evolution, afterwards so ably demonstrated by Darwin independently," and the
Spectator observed that Emerson's epigraph to *Nature* anticipated
Darwin's book. Douglas Story declared bluntly that "in Science, he

---

[48] *MM*, LXXXVIII (May 1903) , 41; Underwood, *Good Words*, XXVIII, 813.
[49] P. 5.   [50] See pp. 113–14.
[51] *GT*, XXXIX (June 1903) , 122; Turnbull, *NMM*, CXXII, 8.

had taught the great theory of Evolution before Darwin understood it, and had a sounder grasp of its mysteries than appeared in the 'Vestiges of Creation.' " Of all these critics who sought to make Emerson an evolutionist, Conway was the most persistent. His master had "at the beginning of his career ... assumed the truth of evolution in nature." Once Emerson had "read a paper on 'Poetry,' in which he stated fully and clearly the doctrine of evolution. This was five years before the appearance of the papers of Darwin." Conway's comments, like those of Underwood, suggest exciting connections, and, even more than Underwood's, come closer to realizing them. "With this new heaven and new earth around it," Conway wrote, "... the least pardonable defalcations of our time [are] that pictorial art should imitate the mere outside of ancient works." Art should be organic, just as Emerson claimed. The "lack of order of which some critics complained in his earlier essays," wrote the sensitive Conway, was "the presence of a higher mathematics, like that of the climbing plants." [52]

Emerson had tried very hard, as has been pointed out earlier, to establish the organic principle as a theory of literature, but he was unable to explain it satisfactorily. Interestingly, his failure stemmed chiefly from a misunderstanding of his idol, Plato. Plato's fame does not stand on his philosophy, as Emerson asserted, but upon the "syllogism," on "masterpieces of ... Socratic reasoning": through these masterpieces, Socrates articulated to the Western world the laws of the mind. He showed man how to perform what Emerson declared to be "the hardest task in the world" — "to think." Stated simply, this task comprises man's ability to put a fact into perspective, a task which Emerson assigned to the scholar, "Man Thinking." Shortsighted, Emerson did not believe that a scholar could learn to think, and, what is worse, indicated that Plato had little to offer in this area. "Your propositions," said the transcendentalist to all logicians, "run out of one ear as they ran in at the other." "Each mind

[52] Stephen, *NatRev*, XXXVI, 891; Gooden, *ManQ*, IV (Oct. 1885) , 312, 313; *Sp*, Dec. 5, 1903, p. 952; Story, *NCRev*, IV (Sept. 1898) , 196; Conway, *FR*, XXXVII (June 1882) , 765 (part of this article was reprinted in *PubO*, July 8, 1882, p. 46) ; Conway, *Fraser's*, n.s. II (July 1870) , 9, 13. For other comments on Emerson and evolution, see the *SatR*, May 6, 1882, p. 553; *Graphic*, Sept. 12, 1874, p. 261; Max Müller, *Cos*, VI (May 1897) , 330.

has its own method." "We want in every man a long logic; we cannot pardon the absence of it, but it must not be spoken. Logic is the procession or proportionate unfolding of the intuition." [53]

In the unfolding of his literary theory, Emerson intuitively revealed many passages of profound assertion, but he did nothing to explain these assertions. He brilliantly set down the perspective, but he neglected what no teacher can afford to neglect: he placed no fact into that perspective. If he had been willing to think through his literary theory—apply the organic concept to specific works of literature—Prothero, Nichol, and an anonymous critic on *Blackwood's* would have had no reason to complain that he had "no well-marked critical standard," that he showed no "well-defined artistic standard," or that his critical "jargon" "is a mere negation of art." Leslie Stephen would have better understood why "to Emerson the value of a book is measured by its dynamic effect upon himself," and James might have been more sympathetic with Emerson's animadversions against Shelley, Aristophanes, Cervantes, Jane Austen, and Dickens.[54] Even those late Victorians who praised Emerson's critical ability—"his taste as a man of letters has . . . been underrated"; he revealed "a singular purity and keenness of critical insight" [55]— would have had something besides assertion upon which to base their conclusions. Above all, those critics to whom Emerson had given such exciting glimpses of the new critical world, brought to birth by the Germans and Coleridge and verified by Darwin, would have comprehended that world. Instead, they were aware of the organic principle behind Emerson's prose, just as they were aware of it in his poetry, without quite assimilating it.

"His thinking is 'rather organic than logical,' " said a reviewer,

---

[53] *The Complete Works of Ralph Waldo Emerson,* ed. Edward Waldo Emerson (Boston, 1903–4), IV, 81; II, 331; I, 84; II, 152, 330, 329—hereafter cited as *Works.*

[54] *QR,* CLXVI, 158; *NBrR,* XLVII, 356; *Blackwood's,* CLXXIII (May 1903), 718; Stephen, *NatRev,* XXXVI, 886; James, *MM,* LVII, 97. For other disparaging comment on Emerson as critic, see Birrell, *Good Words,* XXVI, 362; *CQR,* XXVII (Oct. 1888), 57.

[55] *SatR,* July 12, 1890, p. 58; *Sp,* Feb. 2, 1884, p. 155. For other laudatory comment on Emerson's critical powers, see [Richard Holt Hutton], *Sp,* May 6, 1882, p. 590; Story, *NCRev,* IV, 195; Lewin, *Ac,* July 12, 1890, p. 26; *RR,* I (Feb. 1890), 123. *Ath,* March 8, 1884, p. 306, treated Emerson as social critic, an aspect seldom mentioned by the late Victorians. See also *ScR,* II (Sept. 1883), 222–23.

and quoting Alcott, Lewin wrote "that the order observed by Emerson was 'the order of ideas, of imagination . . . , not of logical sequence,' " a thought repeated by several anonymous critics: "He is not to be cut up into paragraphs, or exhibited in specimen passages." An "artistic want of finish . . . leaves the reader keen at the end as at the beginning. It suggests, as few other contrivances might do, the wonderful complexity of present society." A reader cannot "clip scarlet passages" from Emerson's prose because matter and form are inseparable.[56]

The finest statement made on the Emersonian method in a nineteenth-century periodical and one of the best of all time came from an anonymous reviewer on the *Academy:* he had the method on his very finger tips. "One critic has . . . remarked," began this reviewer, "that Emerson's writing revolves round itself, rather than progresses. The remark was made depreciatingly: but we prefer to regard this trait in Emerson as a characteristic, rather than a limitation. This vortical movement of his understanding impresses itself strongly on one's mind after reading a succession of these essays." "Some one idea is suggested at the outset, and the rest of the essay is mainly a marvellous amplification of it. . . . The 'wheel-go-round' quality of his mind appears even in the detail of his style; as (in Swedenborg's image) each fragment of a crystal repeats the structure of the whole. . . . You have thus within the great volutions of the essay at large innumerable little revolutions,—wheels within wheels." "Each return of the idea reveals it in a deeper and fuller aspect. . . . So, from the first casting of the idea into the mind, its agitations broaden repercussively outward; repeated, but ever spreading in repetition. And thus the thought of this lofty . . . mind is cyclic, not like a wheel, but like the thought of mankind at large; where ideas are always returning on themselves, yet their round is steadily 'widened with the process of the suns.' "

It is unfortunate that this critic did not understand how well he had defined the organic principle in Emerson's prose; instead he rather unimaginatively suggested that the "wheel-go-round" effect in

---

[56] *WR,* CXXII (July 1884), 282 (the reviewer was quoting from the essay in the Round Table Series); Lewin, *Ac,* Sept. 8, 1888, p. 148; *DubR,* n.s. XXVII (July 1876), 253, 254; *SatR,* Feb. 26, 1876, p. 275.

Emerson's essays resulted from their development first as lectures.[57] It is even more unfortunate that these critics received almost no help from Emerson's biographers, who were not concerned with the man of letters. Most of the comments on Emerson's style seem to have come from a direct reading of Emerson's works, probably the Riverside Edition or Macmillan's. Willey chose Morley, who wrote the introduction for the Macmillan volumes, as the representative Victorian critic. Pointing to Morley's shortcomings, Willey wrote that "he seldom takes actual passages of . . . poetry for analysis, comparison or illustration." [58] Exactly the same observation can be made of the approach of Morley and his associates to prose: to them the matter was of greater interest and importance than the manner.

III

Of especial importance were Emerson's philosophical views, which a majority of the early critics had found either odious or the result of an eccentric personal preference, like eating pie for breakfast.[59] These doctrines had been formulated in Emerson's early essays and in the *Dial,* and they later cropped up in the *Memoirs of Margaret Fuller Ossoli.* Not until the publication of O. B. Frothingham's *Transcendentalism in New England* (1876) and the biographies, especially Cabot's *Memoir,* did the philosophy receive widespread intelligent attention in British journals. Late Victorian critics devoted more space to transcendentalism than the early and Mid-Victorian combined. Their comment was often based on the opinions of Frothingham or Cabot and was sometimes derogatory. Reviewing the Unitarian minister's work, the *Spectator* wrote that Emerson was "the accredited interpreter of the movement, though he confessed that it had its dangers, and made many people dreamy and listless, and excessively prone to shirk the ordinary duties of life." This movement, which added "only another to the many proofs of the folly of the man" who spurns God, had long ago lost its power, said the earth-bound Victorians, "quietly died away, and to-day it is

[57] *AcLit,* March 21, 1903, p. 280.   [58] Pp. 288, 295.
[59] *AYR,* Oct. 20, 1888, p. 378.

merely a memory." Transcendentalism had "had the effect of novelty," which soon wore off. In an article entitled "A Prophet of
Yesterday," an anonymous Victorian gently laid that philosophy to
rest: "The once widely welcomed essays ... did their admirable
transcendental work; they 'interested and instructed,' and passed, if
not into the limbo of philosophic ideals, at least into the grey ways of
the outmoded." "The new order changeth giving place to older
forms of wisdom, less transient than the fashionable philosophy of
the 'roaring forties.' " [60]

Even the more percipient critics, especially those following the
canons of realism and classicism, murmured against the philosophy.
In a day when "the shift of man's attention [was] away from his own
spiritual cultivation and control to his control and cultivation of
... nature," this murmuring was to be expected. Once again taking a cue from the scientifically oriented Holmes, Stephen wrote
condescendingly that "the name is alarming, but it represents a very
harmless and a very commendable phenomenon." James was almost
as condescending. After reading Cabot's *Memoir,* he came to the
conclusion that transcendentalism "was little else than a very decent
and innocent recreation—a kind of Puritan carnival." Arnold coldly
asserted that Emerson cannot be called "a great philosophical
writer," while Saintsbury wrote sarcastically of that "famous 'Boston
transcendentalism.' " Courtney commented that transcendentalism
was "only another form of the authoritative individual conscience
uninformed and uninformable, uncultured and incapable of culture, which has often so disastrously betrayed its disciples."

Reviewing *Letters and Social Aims,* the *Athenaeum* suggested that
"to the admirers of mysticism and rhapsody the new book will be
welcome. It is deficient, however, in the common sense which
... is everywhere lauded through its pages." After declaring in a
review of *Transcendentalism in New England* that "Fotheringham"
obviously did not know the meaning of transcendentalism, a critic
tried to enlighten him: the philosophy was "the weakest, most ego-
tistical, least intelligible part of the teaching of Coleridge, and the
entire body of the writings of Mr. Emerson, Margaret Fuller Ossoli,

[60] *Sp,* Aug. 19, 1876, p. 1044; *CongR,* II (March 1888) , 225; Stewart, *ScR,* XI, 290;
G. A. Simcox, *Ac,* April 9, 1870, p. 172; E. M., *Lit,* p. 171.

and their school." The *Times Literary Supplement* observed that the philosophy was too exclusive, and, scattering his shots, Wheeler wrote that Emerson's "mysticism is a stumbling-block to the matter-of-fact man, and foolishness to the Philistine." Even Conway criticized Emerson for leaving "himself open to some reproaches from those who shall be led by him to trust in the solidarity of that [Neo-Platonic] fog-bank." [61]

Emerson was not the only philosopher of the seventies and eighties whose works were leading adherents into the transcendental fog. In reaction against "the once almost undisputed influence of Mill," T. H. Green and F. H. Bradley "sought to reassert the permanency of human values on a higher plane than scientific analysis could reach." [62] That their "new idealism" reached only a small audience was of little consequence: critics did not need bulky volumes from philosophers to reveal "the condition of England." Manifestly alarmed at a nation which, under the impact of science, was surrendering its "dreams" and "ideals" and witnessing "the triumph of mediocrity, uniformity, monotony, mass-power, and mass-mentality," sensitive Victorians no longer spoke of transcendentalism as if it were shameful. They found "much that was repellent in 'the advancing tide of law and matter and the receding tide of spirit and spontaneity.'" Nichol wrote that "the mental philosophy of the West was limited [in the 1830's] to commentaries on Locke and Brown and the eclecticism of Cousin, when the republication of *Sartor Resartus,* backed by the . . . authority of Coleridge, gave life and voice to a new intellectual world." [63]

This voice was louder in America than in England, the British finally admitted. In the thirties and forties, observed Story, "when

[61] Harrold and Templeman, p. lxxiv; Stephen, *NatRev,* XXXVI, 883; James, *MM,* LVII, 96; Arnold, *MM,* L, 6; Saintsbury, *Ac,* May 6, 1882, p. 320; Courtney, *FR,* n.s. XXXVIII, 327; *Ath,* Jan. 15, 1876, p. 81; *SatR,* Aug. 26, 1876, p. 275; *TLS,* Aug. 28, 1903, p. 249; Wheeler, *Freethinker,* May 7, 1882, p. 146; Conway, *Fraser's,* n.s. II, 15. In *Emerson at Home and Abroad,* pp. 230, 255, 290, Conway continued his strictures against transcendentalism.

[62] Buckley, p. 197. See also A. J. Ayer, "Science and Philosophy," in *Ideas and Beliefs of the Victorians,* foreword by Harman Grisewood (London, 1949), p. 211.

[63] Harrold and Templeman, p. lxxvi; N. F. Mott, "Physical Science and the Beliefs of the Victorians," in *Ideas and Beliefs,* p. 219; *NBrR,* XLVII, 320.

the philosophy of the Old World was at fault, when man no longer found solace in the teachings of Locke, . . . the answer was found in . . . the philosophy of the New World. . . . The food that was found too strong for the most advanced intellects in Europe was but ordinary fare in Boston." "The Englishman's belief was still confined to the traditional limits of 'A Chapter of Genesis, and a leader in the *Times.*'" More succinctly, Walter Jerrold wrote that "although the Transcendental movement manifested itself in some measure in England, it was mainly a development of thought in New England." In 1903, the year Jerrold's article appeared, an anonymous reviewer asserted that transcendentalism "still lives as a vital force in the best American literature"; to this philosophy, said another late Victorian, who quoted W. P. Trent, could be traced "at least three-fifths of what is permanent and best in American literature." According to these critics, transcendentalism was ideally suited to a new country like America, which needed a philosophy that would reconcile "social conditions with high aspirations." "A boundless future seemed to open before the new philosophers." [64]

One of the most important of these philosophers was Sampson Reed, whose influence on Emerson has often been noted.[65] In the early eighties Alexander H. Japp discovered a copy of *Observations on the Growth of the Mind,* which Emerson had sent to an Edinburgh friend, Samuel Brown, and in which he had marked *"admirable passages."* These markings prompted Japp, "a versatile and prolific writer" as well as publisher and general literary adviser, to note many parallels between Reed's thought and Emerson's. "The leading idea of Sampson Reed's book is," explained Japp, "that all apprehension of truth is indirect, more a matter of moral activity than of intellectual subtlety, . . . that memory itself is nothing apart from emotion and imagination, that the language of truth is symbol, that all nature is in perpetual flux." In *Nature,* Japp found similar concepts. "Every natural fact is a symbol of some spiritual fact. Nature becomes a means of expression for these spiritual truths." Its laws "are moral laws when applicable to man." After pointing out likenesses between several ideas in Reed's book and some in "The Poet," Japp made a gesture which perhaps would not have occurred to critics writing forty years earlier: "No great writer can strictly be viewed alone. He is only the foremost point in a long perspective. . . . The greater he is, the more will he suggest what preceded him." As for bringing forward "the name of Sampson Reed in connection with that of Emerson, . . . our only purpose has been to illustrate how in some specific lines his way was prepared for him." [66]

The influence of Emerson, Reed, and other American transcendentalists was felt not only in America but also in England, as Dowden confessed when he wrote that "the soul in literature of our country, at least until comparatively recent years, has been of the kind which we have named, transcendental." A number of other Englishmen praised the philosophy. After quoting Emerson's comment that "generalisation is always a new influx of divinity into the mind—hence the thrill that attends," the great philologist and orientalist Max Müller proclaimed: "Thus one pregnant sentence of Emerson's shows . . . that he had seen deeper into the mysteries of nature, and of the human mind, than thousands of philosophers, call them evolutionists or nominalists." Even the stubborn Catholic *Dublin Review* wrote approvingly that Emerson "has long since held up to honour that philosophy which makes the spiritual true, and matter and the world false in comparison with the unseen." "He refutes . . . the vulgar superstition of materialists."

The *Times Literary Supplement* observed that "the philosophical tenets of the [transcendental] school were never very clearly defined; but the practical result of them was . . . to justify, in the face of the pessimists, a healthy delight in beauty by the declaration that Nature, and art also, are, with men, the expressions of the Oversoul." Garnett was wrong, insisted Lewin, "to think that *The Dial* 'has become a by-word for crazy mysticism,' " and Nichol wrote that the "transcendental mania" found in the journal, "shallow and affected

---

[66] *GentM*, CCLIII (Nov. 1882) , 619, 622, 627, 628.

as it in the main appears, was a valuable counteractive to the materialism round which it grew." A third observer delighted in Frothingham's assertion that transcendentalism "unquestionably had its good side, and produced earnestness, high aspirations, and enthusiastic energy." Prothero very neatly tied together such comments when he observed that no one reads Emerson's "books for the sake of clear, systematic, logical expositions. But thousands, who do not value his philosophy for itself, value it for the trains of thought which it awakens, the suggestions which he drew from it, the imagery with which he illustrated it, the inspiration of noble wishes and high aspirations which he made it breathe." [67]

The more able critics of Emerson's philosophy, like those of his style, attempted to explain his doctrines rather than merely to accept or reject them: they were, as Nichol commented on his own work, "more careful to represent correctly than to criticise." [68] The first step in representing the multistrand philosophy was to separate the elements in its composition. Where early critics had, in the main, taken a glance at Emerson's transcendentalism and without much thought or any critical analysis termed it mysticism or pantheism, later critics were able to separate, clearly define, and comment on the multiple strands of Emerson's philosophy. For a critical method, they turned to the Aristotelian category, always a favorite device of academics.

One of the earliest and best analyses was Nichol's. "In recoil from practical materialism and solid Scotch psychology," wrote this scholar, "men rushed at once to the outer verge of idealism, mysticism, and pantheism." To Nichol more than to any other British periodical critic goes the credit for separating the ideal from the mystical in Emerson's philosophy. This fine teacher gave a history of mysticism, describing its origin in India, explaining its effect upon the Middle

[67] Dowden, *ContR*, XXX, 299; Max Müller, *Cos*, VI, 329, 330; *DubR*, n.s. XXVII (July 1876), 254; *TLS*, Aug. 28, 1903, p. 249; Lewin, *Ac*, Sept. 8, 1888, p. 148; *NBrR*, XLVII, 322; *Sp*, Aug. 19, 1876, p. 1044; *QR*, CLXVI, 137. For others not unsympathetic toward transcendentalism, see Jerrold, *TBar*, CXXVIII, 433, 434; *SatR*, May 6, 1882, p. 554; Story, *NCRev*, IV, p. 196; *CQR*, XXVII (Oct. 1888), 51; *DubUM*, LXXXVIII (Aug. 1876), 245; Lewin, *Bookman*, XXIV (June 1903), 90; Bradfield, *PMQR*, n.s. XVII, 251.

[68] *NBrR*, XLVII, 341.

Ages, and showing how it "has been associated in turn with theism, atheism, and pantheism." At every stage "it has been distinguished from idealism proper ... by its exaltation of emotion above reasoning ... , by its withdrawal from active life, and generally by its tendency to submerge the individual in the universal, man in God. In most of these points Mr. Emerson ... claims affinity with the mystics of all ages." Yet Emerson cannot be classified as a mystic. Nearly all mystics "had, in the last analysis, a definite creed, and deferred to a recognised authority." But "Mr. Emerson has little of this spirit of submission." He also parts with them "in his strong assertion of individuality." He despised the "popular machinery of visions and spells." The basis of Emerson's philosophy was idealism, concluded Nichol.[69]

Emerson's biographers came to the same conclusion. From them — and for the first time in the century — a large number of Victorians learned that the main strand in transcendentalism was idealism, just as Emerson had maintained.[70] Although a handful animadverted against Emerson's "mystic overstrain" and referred to him as a "christian mystic" and one of the "mystics and symbolists," Stephen declared that the American stopped "on the threshold of mysticism." An anonymous critic used nearly all the space in his review of Cabot's and Garnett's books to explain Emerson's modified mysticism as well as his idealism; Norman wrote that "Emerson's mind exhibits throughout two distinct aspects, the first of them being an idealistic one" and the second mystical; and Courtney termed Emerson an "idealist philosopher" who frequently resorted to mysticism. Kernahan also praised him as "an idealist and a mystic," hastening to add that his mysticism "rarely" made him "unintelligible." In the end, this excellent critic seemed to forget Emerson's mystical tendencies altogether and to embrace him affectionately as a "New England idealist." Emerson was, observed *Blackwood's,* "an idealist," "an amateur of the Beautiful and the True." It was through his "Idealis-

[69] *Ibid.,* pp. 320, 332, 334, 336, 335.

[70] O. B. Frothingham, *Transcendentalism in New England* (New York, 1959), pp. 224, 226; George Willis Cooke, *Ralph Waldo Emerson: His Life, Writings, and Philosophy* (Boston, 1881), pp. 40, 77; Cabot, I, 226; II, 414, 416; Richard Garnett, *Life of Ralph Waldo Emerson* (London, 1888), p. 87; Holmes, pp. 98–100.

tic Philosophy," said the *Intellectual Repository*, "that the character of . . . [his] mind is best discerned," and the gentle editor and critic Hamilton Wright Mabie declared, briefly and finally, that Emerson was "the foremost idealist of the New World." [71]

One reason that late Victorian critics were able to treat Emerson's idealism and mysticism with so much sympathy was that the two concepts are not incompatible with Christianity. Relieved of the burden of reconciling the two strands in Emerson's philosophy with whatever sectarian views they might have held, critics were able carefully to explain transcendentalism rather than wholeheartedly to criticize it. Emerson's pantheism offered no such relief: during the years under study, it was the element in his philosophy that caused Victorians the most pain. "With very much of the mystical side of Emerson's teaching we thoroughly and thankfully sympathise," said Upton. Only when Emerson carries mysticism to the point of leaving Theism does the critic refuse to follow him.[72]

Except for the Secularists, Theosophists, and such, late Victorians made no attempt to defend this fascinating cloudland.[73] Emerson's so-called "pantheistic individualism," said a sympathetic critic, is his insistence that "it is not by self assertion but by faithfulness to self . . . that we shall successfully live a worthy life." Self should "be forgotten in reverent commune with the Universal Spirit. . . . It is assuredly a Christian doctrine that God's Spirit not only pervades every thing, but everything lives through Him, and in Him." Kernahan offered in Emerson's favor that "much that he has written is open to the charge of pantheism—that sublime conception to which all such proud self-reliant intellects inevitably more or less tend. But Emerson was no pantheist." He "does not lose God in Nature." Other defenders wrote that "his 'pantheism' is not belief in

---

[71] *Ath*, March 8, 1884, p. 306; Turnbull, *NMM*, CXXII, 20; Lee, *ContR*, LXVII, 346; Stephen, *NatRev*, XXXVI, 890; *CQR*, XXVII (Oct. 1888), 54–57 *passim;* Norman, *FR*, XL (Sept. 1883), 423, 424; Courtney, *FR*, n.s. XXXVIII, 326; Kernahan, *GentM*, CCLIX, 474, 479; *Blackwood's*, CLXXIII (May 1903), 715; *IRNJ*, XXII enlarged ser. (Feb. 1875), 65; Mabie, *MMR*, LVIII (July 1903), 17.

[72] Holmes, p. 410; *ModR*, III, 428. Henry Holbeach, *ContR*, XXIX (Feb. 1877), 482, expressed a similar opinion.

[73] See pp. 123–24.

a power superior to or indifferent to morality, but one to which the true, the good, and the beautiful are identical," and that "he has been called a Pantheist, but he never confounds God and the Universe, for to him God is the soul of the Universe." [74]

No such thing, shouted a cloud of witnesses. Emerson "may perhaps be most properly called a Pantheist," said the *Graphic* in disapproval, "rejecting, as he does, that idea of God which separates Him from Nature, and regarding Him as simply a living spiritual personality, 'One with the blowing clover and the falling rain.'" Courtney wrote that "nature, the individual consciousness, and the universal consciousness, or God, form a sort of Trinity in Emerson's creed." But, complained the philosopher, "sometimes the individual consciousness appears to be unduly exaggerated.... At other times nature is not always kept in the subordinate position." Churchmen classified Emerson's pantheism as merely another form of materialism. "When we pierce through the woven mists of Emerson's utterances about Deity and worship, we come to what is, in truth, little better than materialism," sorrowfully wrote a Methodist. "Idolatrous devotion to any conception of nature or Deity, however lofty and beautiful, which proceeds solely from our own consciousness, is not religion." The pious *Church Quarterly* bemoaned Emerson's views: "At one time he sinks God and Nature in Man, and becomes an Idealist; at another he loses God and Man in Nature, and becomes a Materialist," and the Catholic *Dublin Review* warned: "We cannot dispense with the religion of God." Emerson's pantheism "works forcibly on those whose tradition of divine things has not come from the Church. But it is ever deficient." Even the Unitarians murmured that "the Pantheistic element which peeps out here and there ... would now perhaps cause some Free Christian to doubt whether Emerson's mind is in hearty agreement with the essential idea and spirit of the teachings of Jesus." [75]

[74] Turnbull, *NMM*, CXXII, 14, 15; Kernahan, *GentM*, CCLIX, 477; Stephen, *NatRev*, XXXVI, 895; *MM*, LXXXVIII (May 1903), 42. For another sympathetic remark on Emerson's pantheism, see *NBrR*, XLVII, 336.

[75] *Graphic*, Sept. 12, 1874, p. 261; Courtney, *FR*, n.s. XXXVIII, 325, 326; Bradfield, *PMQR*, n.s. XVII, 255; *CQR*, XXVII (Oct. 1888), 58; *DubR*, n.s. XXVII (July 1876), 255; *ModR*, III, 426. For similar comment, see Frederick Rockell, *UM*, XI (April 1889), 186, 187.

IV

Emerson's religious views came in for much comment, even when dissociated from pantheism. These views, as Willey has said of Carlyle's, are almost impossible to understand without understanding "the whole of his thought"—a point brought into nice focus by Story when he said, "The universality of Emerson's genius prevents a definition of his religious belief." Attempting such a definition, one critic admitted reluctantly that Emerson "transmutes morality into a species of religion by the fire of his enthusiasm for personal purity," and then continued belligerently, "but he knew little of religion, if we use the word in the meaning of a deep sense of our relations to a Personal God." Even more truculent was the *Saturday Review,* which kicked against "the futility" "of the kind of extra-religious religiosity of which Emerson has been the most remarkable representative in our century and which still seems to attract so many good people. It is ... for these good people to decide whether, being cleverer than he was, they are likely to make a better business of religion without dogma and without ritual than he did; a conclusion which, if they come to it, will at least show that they possess the blessing of a 'gude conceit o' theirsels.' " [76]

This conceit seemed to be notably lacking. Emerson "was one of the rather large class of cultivated men who have thought fit during the last hundred years openly to abandon Christianity," a Catholic began. He was "a type of a class in whom we can trace the logical outcome of the principles of the Reformation." "Such men's thoughts are not as our thoughts, their virtue is not ours, their progress is often our decay, their faith our unbelief; we refuse then to accept them as our teachers; we are happy ... to rely, not on weak human reason, ... but on the teaching of God Himself, the Infallible Truth." Furiously stoking a quarrel with Emerson which had begun in the late forties, a Swedenborgian declared that the American had lost the more mature of his audience because he

[76] Willey, *Nineteenth Century Studies* (New York, 1949), p. 105; Story, *NCRev,* IV, 196; *CQR,* XXVII (Oct. 1888), 58; *SatR,* Nov. 19, 1887, p. 708.

"failed to satisfy their heart wants!" Sounding like the Evangelicals of the sixties, this churchman thundered: "That volume which begins with the command of the Eternal Father, *Let there be Light!* and which closes with the proclamation of an *Everlasting Gospel* and the revelation of an unending New Heaven and Earth, *'and there shall be no night there,'* for *'the Lamb is the Light thereof'* —that volume was to Transcendentalism a sealed book, for Emerson and his followers scorned to look to the LORD JESUS, the only breaker of those seals." [77]

Although less fervid than the Swedenborgians, other late Victorians, as had the early, disliked Emerson's cavalier treatment of revelation, personal salvation, miracles, and belief in a future state, as well as his attempt to place such figures as Confucius, Buddha, Manu, and Socrates "side by side our Lord Jesus Christ." [78] This theorist, declared Nichol, failed "to meet the very first conditions of the great problem, which is how to banish untruth and superstition, and still present religion in a definite and practical form to the mass of mankind." One critic seemed to be especially irked at Emerson's leaving the ministry. Even now, he wrote, after reading Cabot's sympathetic treatment of the incident, it made him "burst into a kind of subdued laughter to think" that Emerson really expected his congregation, "merely to please his whims," to "practically abolish the central rite of Christian worship." [79]

At this time when, as C. F. Harrold writes, "faith in anything whatsoever was overshadowed by doubt," Victorians also laughed at Emerson's optimism.[80] "Emersonians do not seek to dilate upon the

[77] Slater, *Month*, LIII, 374, 375, 386; *IRNJ*, XXII enlarged ser. (Feb. 1875), 68. For the continuation of the attack by the Swedenborgians, see R. M'c., *IRNJ*, XXII enlarged ser. (April 1875), 158–62, and, also, Clarence Hotson, "Emerson and the Doctrine of Correspondence," *New-Church Review*, XXXVI (Jan. 1929), 47–60; (April 1929), 173–87; (July 1929), 304–17; (Oct. 1929), 435–49.

[78] Bradfield, *PMQR*, n.s. XVII, 225; *CQR*, IX (Jan. 1880), 320; *NBrR*, XLVII, 348; Slater, *Month*, LIII, 379.

[79] *NBrR*, XLVII, 349; *SatR*, Nov. 19, 1887, p. 708. Church journals remained unreconciled to Emerson's religious views: for adverse comment, see the *CongR*, II (March 1888), 225–26; *CQR*, XXVII (Oct. 1888), 67; John Brown, *CongR*, I (Oct. 1887), 926; [John Charles Earle], *DubR*, n.s. XXIII (July 1874), 76.

[80] Harrold and Templeman, p. lxxiv. Halévy, IV, 436, notes that Victorians were especially doubtful of "the eighteenth-century optimism, which had believed that it was only necessary to remove 'superstition' to effect a vast improvement in human affairs."

corruptions of the world," declared Hemming impudently. "They would rather describe the transcendent beauties of cis-Atlantic forests in autumn. . . . They love the dilettantism of the drawing-room, the arcana of government and of science." "So rose-tinted a philosophy we might feel to be more suited to our requirements, probably, if man were living in the exalted repose of mere contemplation." A minor literary historian, G. A. Simcox, spoke against the American's "unreasoning optimism," while R. C. Browne observed that his popularity was due in part to the "cheerful optimism of his teaching." "He bade each man trust in himself with all his heart. Such a message can be rightly received only by those who, emancipated from the numbing spell of custom, prejudice, and routine, straightway proceed to the better land of higher obedience." [81]

And such a land was hard to find. Even Foote had a difficult time describing it. Emerson, said the Secularist, "was not insensible to the dark side of nature. . . . He only thought that the dark side of nature was passing into light. . . . There is a sense in which this is obviously true." But "Emerson's doctrine is open to grave discussion. It is beyond our province" to treat it here. It was not beyond the province of the aroused *Spectator* and *Athenaeum:* "The trouble is that much of life is in the dark or in the twilight, and the philosopher [like Emerson] who lives only 'at large leisure and noble mornings' is scarcely qualified to judge it." He "does not seem ever fairly to have faced the idea that the universe may . . . be *bad.*" And C. A. Ward chimed in, "The world is neither happy nor well managed, and to believe against experience, your own and that of history, that the right thing will be done and the right thing spoken, is to build castles in Spain and live on the mortgage." [82]

---

[81] Hemming, *NDomM,* Aug., 1871, p. 66; Simcox, *Ac,* April 9, 1870, p. 172; Browne, *Ac,* Aug. 4, 1883, p. 72. See also Stephen, *NatRev,* XXXVI, 891, who pointed out that many other critics disparaged Emerson's optimism but that he did "not altogether dislike the old-fashioned creed." *Guide,* XIV (April 1893), 73, and *SatR,* July 12, 1890, p. 58, were noncommittal, while Bradfield, *PMQR,* n.s. XVII, 256, concluded that since Emerson was no Christian, his optimism was unwarranted. In *Speaker,* June 27, 1903, p. 292, Arthur Rickett declared that "Emerson's optimism . . . was nothing more than the natural expression of a singularly happy, tranquil disposition," while Story, *NCRev,* IV, 197, commented mildly, "His only fault, if fault it be, is his unfailing optimism."

[82] Foote, *Freethinker,* June 7, 1903, p. 354; *Sp,* Feb. 10, 1906, p. 219; *Ath,* March 8, 1884, p. 307; Ward, *TBar,* LXXII, 247.

The foundations of these castles will inevitably rest, the Victorians of three generations believed, on the false assumption that evil does not exist. That the indignant howls of the earlier Victorians died away to the admonitory tcht, tcht, tcht of the academics, made the rejection no less complete. "When we seek to ascertain his views on the nature of *Sin*," wrote Upton, Emerson's utterances appear "to become eminently unsatisfactory, and no longer to harmonise with the teachings of Jesus." "Surely the sinful act of choice by which the soul . . . deliberately alienates itself from the Universal Mind is of all the acts of the soul the most momentous . . . and yet Emerson tells us that 'evil is merely privative.' " Nichol firmly stated, "We may safely assert that our author's solution" of the problem is "unsatisfactory." "To say that evil is negative is a play on words, which does nothing to explain its origin, and little to unfold its purpose." Evil "has always been a stumbling-block to systems which more or less identify man with God." Thomas Bradfield intoned that Emerson's implication that " 'whatever is, is right' has no other centre than the nebulous beauty of far-fetched expressions which refer to religious hopes and experiences." From such expressions "the light-hearted no less than the thoughtful may well turn away aghast." [83]

Neither James nor Morley turned away aghast, but they too rejected this Emerson world in which, as Edward Waldo Emerson wrote, the woods told him that "apparent evil or suffering were [*sic*] only 'good in the making.' " James commented that Emerson "has only a kind of hearsay, uninformed acquaintance" with life's disorders. "Hawthorne's vision was all for the evil and sin of the world: a side of life as to which Emerson's eyes were thickly bandaged." "He had no great sense of wrong—a strangely limited one, indeed, for a moralist—no sense of the dark, the foul, the base." According to Lewin, "Morley's chief complaint" against Emerson was his ignorance of "the darker facts of human life." He was "helpless in dealing with 'that horrid burden and impediment on the soul,

[83] *ModR*, III, 426, 427; *NBrR*, XLVII, 340; Bradfield, *PMQR*, n.s. XVII, 254. For further adverse comment on Emerson's idea of evil, see *CQR*, XXVII (Oct. 1888), 64–67; *QR*, CLXVI, 138, Lee, *ContR*, LXVII, 357; Slater, *Month*, LIII, 385. For a sympathetic account, see Lewin, *Ac*, June 22, 1889, p. 424.

which the Churches call sin,' " said Hutton, also quoting Morley. "Emerson lived in a pale, moonlit world of ideality, in which there was little that was adapted to tame the fierce passions and appease the agonising remorse of ordinary human nature." [84]

Even with its detractors, Emerson's religio-philosophical world of ideality found a much kindlier acceptance in the eighties and nineties than it had in the forties. "There is much that makes us smile today," admitted James, "in the commotion produced by his secession from the mild Unitarian pulpit." In these times, observed Upton in 1882, the Divinity School Address would awaken not odium but "admiration and sympathy" for the Unitarians, while Lewin stated that "his notions about religious observances were not anarchical. He felt bound to maintain his own integrity, but he was not blind to the value they possessed for others." Emerson's son wrote protectively that his father "had not turned his back on God and the truths of religion, only now they seemed to him so much greater and broader that it was out of man's power to pen them up in creeds or sects or ceremonies." He had "the sublimest faith in God," witnessed Kernahan. "Religion is to Emerson the bond between God and man . . . —a union direct and personal, and independent of all mediation. The universe is his temple." Turnbull believed that Emerson had "emphatically asserted the Divine Immanence and his belief in Eternity," and Mrs. M. A. Castle said, "Emerson seemed to stand just on the portal of that great, sublime structure, Redemption; how strange and sad, both for the world and himself, that he could not see in! To the law and will of God he was devoutly obedient; not after the polished-veneering style of pharisaical punctiliousness, but of a deep, inner, abiding principle." In a word, Emerson was, proclaimed Courtney, "above all things holy." [85]

That late Victorians were more sympathetic to Emerson's heretical

---

[84] E. W. Emerson, *Bookman*, XXIV (June 1903) , 95; James, *MM*, LVII, 89, 97; Lewin, *Ac*, Aug. 16, 1884, p. 101; *Sp*, Feb. 2, 1884, p. 156. For other periodicals mentioning Emerson and Morley, see *Ath*, March 8, 1884, p. 307; *GT*, XXXIX (June 1903) , 120; *TLS*, May 29, 1903, p. 166; *Bookman*, I (Oct. 1891) , 20.

[85] James, *MM*, LVII, 87; *ModR*, III, 426; Lewin, *Bookman*, XXIV (June 1903) , 90; E. W. Emerson, *Bookman*, XXIV, 95; Kernahan, *GentM*, CCLIX, 475, 476; Turnbull, *NMM*, CXXII, 16; Castle, *CMM*, XVI, 28; Courtney, *FR*, n.s. XXXVIII, 319.

doctrines than the earlier was due to the increasing toleration of all religious doctrines. Emerson himself had helped to bring about this tolerance. Using Λ. P. Stanley as authority, *Macmillan's* reported that " 'the pale Unitarianism of Boston,' which Emerson condemned, is becoming suffused with the genial atmosphere which Emerson has done so much to promote, and which is shared by the higher minds of all the Churches equally." Then, too, Emerson's heterodoxy seemed mild when placed beside the implications of Darwinianism and the precepts of the Higher Criticism.[86] Perhaps the greatest factor in the more kindly acceptance of the American's religious doctrines was the effort of his biographers. Nearly all of them strove heroically to prove that even if Emerson was not a Christian, he was a deeply religious man.[87] Wheeler praised Cooke and Conway for drawing "new attention to the religious views of the sage of Concord," and reviewing Cooke, Ireland, Cabot, and Holmes, Stewart wrote that Emerson's "new religion" "tinged and influenced the whole thought and movement of the best intellects in America." Jerrold contended that the American "stands as the chief figure in the great religious movement which characterised the intellectual development of America during the mid-part of the nineteenth century." Dean Stanley told President Eliot of Harvard while he was in America he had heard "some of our most eminent preachers, generally 'evangelical' in denominational position, but it made no difference what the man's name was, the sermon was always by Ralph Waldo Emerson." Huffing and puffing, Turnbull said that Emerson had "overcome the conservative prejudices and the theological traditions of the country," and the New York correspondent for the *Times Literary Supplement* declared that in America the clergy

[86] *MM*, XL (June 1879) , 113, 114; Harrold and Templeman, pp. lxxix, lxxvii. See also Buckley, p. 9; Walker, p. 976; Noel Annan, "The Strands of Unbelief," in *Ideas and Beliefs,* p. 151; Halévy, IV, 437, 438.

[87] Cooke, pp. 26–46, 66–76, 283–92, 363–84 *passim;* Ireland, pp. 5, 6, 98; Conway, pp. 58, 68–95 *passim,* 137, 167, 172–82 *passim;* Cabot, I, 100 ff., 214 ff., 298 ff.; Holmes, pp. 51 ff., 235, 411; Garnett, pp. 87–97 *passim;* Edward Waldo Emerson, *Emerson in Concord: A Memoir Written for the 'Social Circle' in Concord, Massachusetts* (Boston, 1889) , pp. 36 ff. Frothingham, pp. 183–218 *passim,* also preached Emersonian religion. So did John Beattie Crozier, *The Religion of the Future* (London, 1880) , pp. 105–57 *passim.*

"are among the first to do him honour, and the Churches of America join with singular unanimity in celebrating his centennial." [88]

These comments are doubtless exaggerated; yet Emerson's religious views did appeal to a large minority of both Americans and Englishmen. They were, like the Secularists, impressed with their rationalist basis. The *Review of Reviews* quoted President Eliot: "Emerson's great work was in the field of religion. . . . He taught that religion is absolutely natural, not supernatural. . . . For him all things were sacred, just as the universe was religious." "All the features of the contest over the higher criticism are foretold . . . in 'The American Scholar.' " These features, said Stewart, are "severely intellectual, yet founded on a simple faith." "Emerson does not believe in infallible dogmas, nor the iron sways of any creed. . . . He respects the old theology because of its antiquity, but he does not believe in it." "He is the apostle of a new Faith." [89]

The main element in this faith was ethics rather than religion, a matter which Emerson finally made clear in *The Conduct of Life*. Although Egan Mew deplored Emerson's acceptance "as an ethical light," Nichol wrote that the "essays on Wealth, Culture, Behaviour, Power . . . all contain admirable rules for the Conduct of life; inculcating prudence, suspicion of deceptions, address and tact in dealing with our fellows. . . . A chivalric nobility, in which beauty and goodness are blended, is at once the goal, the sanction, and the motive of his ethical system." "His belief in an absolute morality, and the rigid ethical criterion which he applies to men and things, are his connecting links with the old faith of New England. . . . While Mr. Emerson is Puritanic in the moral earnestness of his character and his criticisms, his own conception of the ultimate basis of morality is far removed from that of the Puritans." He acts in the line of Marcus Antonius in the setting forth "of those inherent virtues by which a man utters goodness as the mint utters coin." "This aspect of morality is what we have everywhere presented to us in Mr. Emerson's essays. He reveres the individual grandeur of Plu-

[88] Wheeler, *Freethinker*, Feb. 4, 1883, p. 34; Stewart, *ScR*, XI, 289; Jerrold, *TBar*, CXXVIII, 433; Everett Hale, *GT*, XXXIX (June 1903) , 135; Turnbull, *NMM*, CXXII, 24; *TLS*, May 29, 1903, p. 165.

[89] *RR*, XXVIII (July 1903) , 52; Stewart, *Belford's*, I, 228, 229.

tarch's heroes, who are 'natural powers, like light and heat.' . . . His pattern character needs no reminders of the law of duty." To Emerson vice is "a sign of bad blood." "To a properly constituted being he holds that a fairly moral life should be easy." [90]

The most thorough study of Emerson's ethics in nineteenth-century periodicals was that of Norman, whose article plainly reveals the wide influence of Taine. In this piece, Norman argued that the American preserved the best in both transcendentalism and empiricism "to form a new basis of ethics." The strength of transcendentalism, Norman explained in this excellent study, is that "when a man says 'I ought,' the question is settled for him for ever; 'thou shalt' is an imperative from which there is no escape." The strength of empiricism is that "every peculiarity of animal life . . . serves to illustrate some point or may be used to support some argument." The weakness of the transcendental ethic is that "it has no criterion for every-day life." The weakness of the empirical is that "it has no sufficient moral ideal." Thus, Norman declared, "the strength" of one system is "the weakness of the other." In Emerson, one finds the Platonic as well as the practical. "He gives us the most sweeping idealism, without losing sight of the fact that we are men and have to live as men on the earth." "This union of insight and sagacity . . . makes Emerson the representative of the apotheosis of common sense." We have in the union "the perfect philosophic edifice," "conscious Transcendentalism rooted in unconscious inherited Empiricism—this describes both Emerson and the new basis of ethics: . . . his mind exhibiting in one aspect mysticism, idealism, Platonism; in the other aspect, the realism of typical Yankee sense; the two combining to form an unfailing moral insight and an irresistible intellectual impulse." [91]

Although Prothero declared that Emerson had "no defined ethical ideas," Nichol and Norman were joined in their praise of Emerson's ethics by Wheeler, Stephen, and other late Victorians who, as Noel Annan suggests, realized "that to give up religion does not mean giving up morality. A man can be moral," these atheists and agnos-

---

[90] Egan Mew, *Lit*, Sept. 21, 1901, p. 269; *NBrR*, XLVII, 342, 343, 344, 345.
[91] *FR*, XL, 425, 426, 429, 430.

tics contended, "and yet not acknowledge Christian dogma." [92] Wheeler wrote in approval that "the Moral Sentiment was . . . [Emerson's] worship. His precepts are of a more than Stoic magnanimity," while Foote told readers to "note the supreme characteristic of the Emersonian ethics. It is personal, individual—some would say egoistic. But how sure and sound!" The agnostic Stephen argued that "nothing could be really less chargeable against Emerson than an approach to ethical insensibility." "He is not the man to retire to a palace of art or find in aesthetic indulgence an anodyne to dull his sympathies with human sorrow. . . . If Emerson's optimism leads him to dwell upon the 'good of evil,' and to see the use of 'scourges of God' and vulgar political scoundrels, it is because they are for him the instruments of an essentially moral force." Cabot wrote in the liberal *Westminster,* "There is a moral purpose in everything he has written," and J. A. Froude, Saintsbury, and Courtney concurred. "Emerson had just as firm a hold on morals as anybody," declared the biographer. "For me, as for him, the moral law of the universe is the one which remains binding." Wrote Saintsbury: "The general tendency of his teaching may be inferred" from his remark: " 'I am going to prove the sovereignty of the moral law and to slay the utility swine.' " Said the editor: "He is a firm advocate of the moral sentiment." [93]

Kernahan had even higher praise for Emerson's ethics: he never "lets intellectual grandeur overshadow moral greatness. On the contrary, he declares that a decline in morality is inevitably a decline in intellect. . . . He is essentially the prophet of intellectual and moral greatness." To various highly complimentary late Victorians, Emerson "has been and is a moral force of the first order," the "highest-reaching ethical teacher America has produced," "a thinker on moral matters who could mint his thoughts in golden phrases which should pass current with all thinking men." Although the rationalist

[92] *QR,* CLXVI, 158; Annan, "The Strands of Unbelief," in *Ideas and Beliefs,* p. 154.

[93] Wheeler, *Freethinker,* May 7, 1882, p. 147; Foote, *Freethinker,* June 7, 1903, p. 354; Stephen, *NatRev,* XXXVI, 895; *WR,* CXIX (April 1883), 492; *TLS,* May 29, 1903, p. 166; Saintsbury, *Ac,* May 6, 1882, p. 320; Courtney, *FR,* n.s. XXXVIII, 319. For other comments, generally noncommittal, on Emerson's ethical and moral doctrines, see Lee, *ContR,* LXVII, 354; *QR,* CLXVI, 133; Underwood, *Good Words,* XXVIII, 813; *Sp,* Feb. 10, 1906, p. 220.

Westminster took offense at Arnold's description of Emerson "as a sort of modern Marcus Aurelius" and, instead, insisted that "this over-rated American essayist was the slave of platitudes," and the *Primitive Methodist Quarterly Review* eloquently declared that Emerson "has left us vistas of indefinable beauty in which we may discover the splendours of a new ethical world, for the diversion of the intellect, but not for the . . . spirit," the *Church Quarterly* maintained that he was "a moralist who draws moral distinctions as subtle as those of La Bruyère." Another journal observed that the "lack of true speculative interest is the secret of his success as a moralist, for your metaphysician is no teacher, and can never present his conclusions in the form of a lesson." [94]

Or to state the matter positively: Emerson's teaching was of great practical value. "As a practical moralist," wrote Nichol, there is much to be said for Emerson: "when he condescends to detail he is eminently real." One of Emerson's countrymen declared that "most of his writing is of an eminently practical character, not difficult of comprehension by any serious reader, and calculated to inspire noble views of man's life, character, and destiny." And Turnbull said that his "influence was essentially moral and humanising, and his teaching, when fairly grasped and understood, was eminently practical." An anonymous critic expressed very well this aspect of Emerson's teaching: "As moralist, philosopher, prophet, we shall perhaps think him most noteworthy when he keeps nearest to definite and concrete things. He is at his best when he describes the plain living and high thinking which formed his own practical ideal." He himself, observed Cabot, "would have been prompt to confess that his life's work had been a failure if his teaching, however graceful, did not bear a practical lesson for daily life." [95]

---

[94] Kernahan, *GentM*, CCLIX, 474, 476; Lewin, *Ac*, Aug. 16, 1884, p. 101; *Ath*, Jan. 13, 1883, p. 53; Jerrold, *TBar*, CXXVIII, 433; *WR*, CXLV (May 1896), 586; Bradfield, *PMQR*, n.s. XVII, 256; *CQR*, XXVII (Oct. 1888), 57, 58; *Sp*, Feb. 10, 1906, p. 220.

[95] *NBrR*, XLVII, 342; Underwood, *Good Words*, XXVIII, 811; Turnbull, *NMM*, CXXII, 10; *Ath*, March 8, 1884, p. 306; *WR*, CXIX (April 1883), 492. For other compliments to Emerson as teacher, see Kernahan, *GentM*, CCLIX, 473; Lee, *ContR*, LXVII, 357; *MM*, LXXXVIII (May 1903), 37; *QR*, CLXVI, 159; *Sp*, Feb. 10, 1906, p. 220. See also pp. 198–200. In the *Journal of Education*, n.s. XXV (Oct. 1903), 669–71, Michael E. Sadler argued that the influence of Emerson's liberal educational doctrines

V

It is this practical ideal in Emerson's philosophy which the early critics had most neglected and which Emerson's biographers were most anxious to reveal to their "utilitarian" world.[96] Reviewing Holmes's *Ralph Waldo Emerson,* Lewin wrote that it was very satisfying "to find some prominence given" "to the practical side of Emerson's character," and the biographer seems to have taught another critic that Emerson "was by no means of the sort of idealists who are always running their heads against a stone wall for want of tact and knowledge of mankind." Rather, so Morley pointed out to a reviewer on the *Saturday Review,* the American "constantly teaches us . . . that idealism is nothing else than common sense transfigured and enthroned above sophistry." No one was "more sternly practical," said Kernahan. "So far from encouraging us to stand in dreamy abstraction . . . , he would have us see what we seek is lying close at hand." Emerson possessed "a shrewd, clear outlook upon practical life, all the sounder for his serene detachment from it," observed the *Academy.* If he "could soar into mystic regions," said

---

"has been penetrating and pervasive" (669). This influence was seen in the establishment of the elective system, de-emphasis of the classics, and the wide variety of course offerings. Although Sadler praised these innovations, he implied that such a system led to permissiveness and warned that it "fails us a little when we want a discipline which can be effectively imposed on those who are unwilling voluntarily to discipline themselves. It presupposes as normal a degree of individual energy and self-control which is really exceptional" (670). In a shorter comment on Emerson as educationist, President Eliot of Harvard wrote that Emerson "was a great believer in the education of men by manual labour" and that "Americans are only just beginning to carry into practice Emerson's" educational precepts of "sixty years ago" (*RR,* XXVIII [July 1903], 52). In general, British periodicals devoted very little space to the "new" pedagogy.

[96] Halvéy, IV, 437. "Practical works," observed a Victorian, "are the highest and most enduring monuments to genius. That is why Gladstone is now our Premier." "Gladstone is a poet, too; perhaps as much so as Emerson or Carlyle, who are prose poets, renouncing Pegasus that they may wrestle with present darkness" (*Freelight,* I [Dec. 1871], 151). See also H. G. Nicholas, "The New Morality," in *Ideas and Beliefs,* pp. 132–38 *passim.* Ireland, p. 28; Cooke, pp. 190, 191; Conway, pp. 123, 213–14, 225, 299; Cabot, II, 414, 458; Garnett, pp. 100, 102, 125; Holmes, pp. 156, 235, 236, 366, 396 — all insisted that Emerson was a practical man. One important dissenting voice was that of E. W. Emerson, pp. 198–200 *passim.*

Stephen, "he is equally delighted with the broad daylight, in which you can see the actual every-day play of human nature," a statement in which he was joined by Japp: Emerson's was "a truly original mind which could dip deep into Plato and the Oriental mystics, and yet maintain an independent foothold, transfiguring all that it borrowed and thus touching men to high practical issues." In the same vein, an anonymous critic declared, "A strong practical sense may keep his memory green when speculative philosophy has gone down before the gales of fashion," and Wheeler wrote that "to a lofty reverence of the ideal he unites a lowly regard for the real, and can meet the matter-of-fact man on his own ground." He was, said the reviewers, "a rational idealist," "his philosophy of life was entirely practical," he labored "to be practical, to translate his thought into the current language of the world." [97]

This world was not the world of the forties, and the significant difference lay in the change that had come over the common people, once the backbone of Emerson's audience. In 1847 when Emerson proudly wrote that *"my public"* filled Exeter Hall, he was speaking of a people used to plain living but insistent upon high thinking, a people eager, sensitive, understanding. Increasingly grounded in science, the cheap press, and Chamberlain democracy, this audience was by 1900 vulgar, hustling, triumphantly average.[98] Emerson's loss of the commonalty is easily the most disheartening fact in his professional career, even though a few late Victorians closed their eyes to what had happened and saw him once again a man of the people, just as Douglas Jerrold and William Howitt and Goodwyn Barmby had seen him. One late Victorian contended that Emerson was "almost the first of the people's philosophers. . . . He is the philosopher of that new renaissance which synchronises more or less closely with

---

[97] Lewin, *Ac*, Feb. 28, 1885, p. 143; *SatR*, April 18, 1885, p. 512; *SatR*, Jan. 26, 1884, p. 118; Kernahan, *GentM*, CCLIX, 475; *Ac*, March 21, 1903, p. 281; Stephen, *NatRev*, XXXVI, 888; Japp, *GentM*, CCLIII, p. 621; *Ath*, April 21, 1906, p. 472; Wheeler, *Freethinker,* May 7, 1882, p. 146; *Guide*, XIV (April 1893) , 73; Foote, *Freethinker,* June 7, 1903, p. 353; *Sp*, Feb. 10, 1906, p. 220. Other comments on Emerson's practicality may be found in *QR*, CLXVI, 150; Clapham, *MM*, LXXVI, 188; *NBrR*, XLVII, 322; *Sp*, Dec. 5, 1903, p. 952; I. A. Taylor, *Blackwood's*, CLXIV (Sept. 1898) , 365.

[98] Harrold and Templeman, pp. lxxv–lxxvi, lxix, lxx. See also R. H. S. Crossman, "The Testament of Change," in *Ideas and Beliefs*, pp. 423–32 *passim*.

the spread of cheap printing, the growth of the newspaper press, the increase of facilities of communication, the demand for universal education—for the spreading of culture over the whole surface instead of limiting it to one or two special places for hot-bed purposes. With this new renaissance of the nineteenth century, it is not surprising to find the people's philosopher arising in the great Western democracy where the effects of that renaissance have been perhaps in some ways most marked." Emerson was "a veritable Poor Richard in matters of the intellect." Accessible "to all sorts and conditions of men," he did not "belong to the Brahminical caste," avowed Dr. Everett Hale; "he was one of the Concord people." [99]

Emerson loafing around the Concord post office waiting for the mail and talking politics with the farmers, as Hale pictured him, was an image which several biographers attempted to build and to which they linked Emerson the democrat.[100] The Victorian age never "humbugged" itself into believing that it was democratic, and, except for the radicals, few Victorians showed much interest in this aspect of Emerson. Fired by reading the works of Cabot and others, Prothero declared, "Not only is he national and the representative of a new people, he is also democratic in his mental attitude." "He taught that man was capable of self-government. . . . He has all a democrat's jealousy of any exclusive claim to revelation, and he taught his countrymen to pay no false complaisance to reigning schools or the wisdom of antiquity. . . . His theory made him a democrat and a champion of republican institutions." As early as 1852 the *Reasoner* praised Emerson for his welcome to Kossuth, and in 1873 Charles Cattell commented approvingly that the American "does not urge that the Republic is 'better,' but that it is 'fitter,' " than any other form of government. In 1878 an anonymous radical praised Emerson as "a born republican," and in 1882 Wheeler termed him "a Republican, declaring, 'I will have never a noble—no lineage counted great.' " A quarter of a century later, Foote remarked that "Emerson believed in the fluid equality of his . . . nation. He hated castes and exclusions," and Lewin stated that "after

[99] Jerrold, *TBar*, CXXVIII, 430, 435; Hale, *GT*, XXXIX, 135.

[100] Hale, *GT*, XXXIX, 135; Cooke, pp. 190–91; Ireland, p. 96; Conway, p. 366; Holmes, pp. 86, 367.

the upheaval of the Revolution and the turmoil of the succeeding wars, it was chiefly his voice that guided [America] in the paths of peace and aroused her to a sense of the responsibilities she had assumed." [101]

His best and most direct contribution to democracy, proclaimed three critics, was the censuring of it. One hotly declared that "nowhere is the majority so despotic, nowhere does a minority pay so high a price for . . . independence" as in the United States. "Emerson from the beginning parted company with the majority, and . . . never took one single step to reunite himself with that omnipotent multitude which he distrusted." "It was the multitude which finally came over to him." He warned, said Conway, "that 'the true test of civilisation is, not the census, nor the size of cities, nor the crops—no, but the kind of man the country turns out.'" Notoriously antidemocratic, Arnold suggested that Emerson "exposed" courageously the "shortcomings" and the "meanness" of American politics, and denounced the corruptness of the American life.[102]

This denunciation reached a climax in Emerson's antislavery activities, which, according to the critics, were his greatest contribution to practical politics. Early Victorians had been almost unaware of Emerson's influence in the abolition of slavery; not until the eighties and nineties did his abolitionism receive much attention. Again the biographies were the main source of information. Ireland, Cooke, Conway, and Cabot were attempting, more or less, to show that Emerson was no recluse but a man of action, and in making their point often used, even exaggerated, his fight against slavery.[103] Reviewers of the biographies were delighted to find something new to say about Emerson. Reading the moderate Cooke, Cabot, and Holmes, periodical critics learned that "amid all the ferment of

---

[101] K. B. Smellie, "Victorian Democracy: Good Luck or Good Management," in *Ideas and Beliefs*, pp. 291, 291–97 *passim; QR*, CLXVI, 133, 145; *Reas*, Sept. 22, 1852, pp. 231–34 *passim;* Cattell, *NatRef*, Dec. 28, 1873, p. 410; *NatRef*, March 17, 1878, p. 1099; Wheeler, *Freethinker*, May 7, 1822, p. 146; Foote, *Freethinker*, May 31, 1903, p. 338; Lewin, *Bookman*, XXIV, 89.

[102] *TLS*, May 29, 1903, p. 165; Conway, *Fraser's*, n.s. II, 7; Arnold, *MM*, L, 10. Foote, *Freethinker*, May 31, 1903, p. 338, expressed a similar opinion.

[103] Cooke, pp. 132–43 *passim;* Ireland, pp. 25, 27, 88; Conway, pp. 56, 66, 164; Holmes, pp. 141, 145, 181, 191, 210, 302 ff.; Cabot, II, 421 ff., 574–613 *passim;* E. W. Emerson, pp. 75–86 *passim.*

novel schemes for the regeneration of society which characterised the state of New England thought during the decade which began about 1840, . . . Emerson is always found speaking the words of truth and soberness." He believed that reform "even in the case of slavery, should proceed by the gradual elevation of the human spirit, not by direct legislation and outward agitation." Emerson was "an inspirer of reform rather than a reformer"; "his calling was to supply impulse, not methods," of reform. Edward wrote that his father "was no fighter," reported the *Bookman,* "but when the day of need came he could be counted on to enter the lists spear in hand. In the stormy Anti-slavery times . . . , when personal danger was added to unpopularity, he held it a duty to be present and show his colours at a threatened meeting." [104]

All the world loves a gladiator, and late Victorians were no exception. Using Conway as a source, the radical *National Reformer* discovered that by 1837 Emerson was a "gentle but fearless Abolitionist," and taking a cue from Ireland, the *Westminster* contended that Emerson was "a brilliant exception" to the "learned men and scholars [who] do not do their duty in leading the agitations on the great social questions which stir the age." "The free expression of his views on slavery, on free trade, and on woman's rights, have had more to do with moulding the present generations of Americans than the actions of any other man; and the lectures on slavery . . . probably contributed to the issue of the Emancipation Proclamation." Quoting judiciously from Cabot, an anonymous critic declared that the only political movement Emerson took part in was slavery, on which he "gave forth no doubtful or uncertain sound. 'The last year,' he said in his address to the citizens of Concord on May 31, 1851, 'the last year has forced us all into politics. There is an infamy in the air.' " [105]

Emerson's antislavery activities were, according to the warlike, his finest hour. Turnbull boasted that Emerson "fearlessly opened his

---

[104] *ModR,* III, 429; Stephen, *NatRev,* XXXVI, 894; *RR,* XXVIII (July 1903), 52; *Time,* XII (Feb. 1885), 246 (using Holmes's phrase); E. W. Emerson, *Bookman,* XXIV, 95, 96.

[105] *NatRef,* Jan. 14, 1883, p. 22; *WR,* n.s. LXIV (July 1883), 266; *WR,* CXXVIII (Nov. 1887), 996, 997.

church ... for anti-slavery lectures; and so put the crown and seal on those philanthropic and educational labours for which the support and sympathy of the public had been secured." Stewart contended that "Emerson, as far back as 1837, was an Abolitionist, preaching and lecturing against slavery, though he was not so strong an apostle of the movement as Garrison." On the "burning question" of the times, wrote Wheeler, Emerson "was among the first to speak out." Probably after reading such comments as these, one critic growled that "Dr. Holmes does not make prominent enough for readers of a newer generation his part in the anti-slavery movement, which, though not conspicuous, was decided." Holmes, complained another, "leaves out much bearing on Emerson's attitude toward slavery." Reviewing Cabot's *Memoirs,* James, who missed the war, recalled seeing Emerson read the "Boston Hymn," which was tremendously effective. The Webster Fugitive Slave Speech was, James quotes Cabot as saying, "the one thing that ever moved him to heated denunciation." [106]

To Lewin and Conway more than to any other writers in British periodicals went the honor of making Emerson an abolitionist of the Whittier stripe. At times, Lewin the critic overcame Lewin the reformer, and he was judicious in his comments on Emerson's importance to the extremists. Reviewing the works of Edward Waldo Emerson, Lewin wrote that Emerson "had a strong aversion to political agitation. . . . [But] in connexion with the anti-slavery movement he thought he was called to this activity. He helped John Brown with money and sympathy for his work in Kansas, and when the war came he attended public meetings and addressed them and faced howling mobs. He held that the scholar was 'bound to stand.' " "Later, he was fully drawn into the movement." And in his comments on Cabot's volumes, Lewin admitted that Emerson "was neither a fanatic nor indifferent." He "lived in an age of new theories and experiments. Total abstinence, phrenology, communism, and innumerable other doctrines were being set forth." "But he rejected all 'isms.'. . . Even on the negro question Emerson maintained his accustomed critical attitude."

[106] Turnbull, *NMM,* CXXII, 4–5; Stewart, *ScR,* XI, 298; Wheeler, *Progress,* I, 118; *SatR,* April 18, 1885, p. 512; *BQR,* LXXXI (April 1885), 440; James, *MM,* LVII, 96.

At other times Lewin was not so judicious. "When Transcendentalism as a distinct effort had ceased, its influence remained," he commented in an article for the Emerson number of the *Bookman*. "Those who had been associated with it were among the boldest and most consistent leaders of the movement against slavery." Emerson was one. He expressed his views in *An Address ... on the Anniversary of the Emancipation of the Negro in the West Indies,* and "his unrest is shown in this passage from his Journal for 1852: 'I waked last night and bemoaned myself because I had not thrown myself into this deplorable question of slavery, which seems to want nothing so much as a few assured voices. ... I have quite other slaves to free than those negroes, to wit, imprisoned spirits, imprisoned thoughts. ...' Nevertheless already on special occasions he had been not inactive; and not long afterwards the call seemed clear, and he responded promptly." [107]

Lewin was a relative newcomer to the small legion of late Victorians who made liberal propaganda in the name of Emerson. Conway had been working at it for years. His crowning effort appeared in "The Python," Chapter 27 of *Emerson at Home and Abroad,* but he also wrote in the same vein in an article published in the *Fortnightly Review.* After quoting Emerson, Conway wrote that his art "in these utterances can best be appreciated by those who know how completely slavery had bound fast the conscience of the North with cotton cords, and that the pulpits and professions generally were occupied by casuists retained to justify compliance with the national wrong." He "was the first man of high social position in America who openly took the anti-slavery position. On May 29th, 1831, he admitted an abolitionist to lecture on the subject in his church." At the time that Garrison was regarded as a "vulgar street-preacher," "Emerson first drew the sympathy of scholars to that side." He did not throw himself into the movement but thought that "to elevate character" would quickly make the "atmosphere too pure for a slave to breathe." He recognized slavery reform "as a far more important reform than others." He and his brother Charles defended Harriet Martineau from violence in 1835, as she testifies in her autobiography. Emerson's *Address on the Anniversary of the Emancipation*

[107] *Ac,* June 22, 1889, p. 423; Oct. 22, 1887, p. 262; *Bookman,* XXIV, 91, 92.

in 1844 "was a bugle, and it filled the anti-slavery ranks with fresh courage." He was hissed for his speech against Webster, and he quieted obstreperous toughs in a Boston hall. While the war lasted, "no man did better service than Emerson with voice, pen, and means; and when it ended his counsels were of the utmost importance." [108]

VI

The sort of war which Emerson waged against slavery as well as against religious, social, and political conventions was, to Conway and a number of the young in both America and England, a holy one. In the early 1840's, asserted the expatriate, Emerson's "first works had begun a new revolution and crowded the village with new pilgrims from all parts of the country." He maintained that "when Emerson spoke to his generation men and women left all to follow him, made their exodus from the conventional world ... [;] creeds crumbled around him and churches were changed." These *émigrés* from orthodoxy were mainly from the ranks of youth. A critic or two denied Emerson's hold upon them or else suggested that it was a bad influence, but Conway wrote that during the Phi Beta Kappa Speech, "the wedding-guest was not held more fast by the glittering eye of the ancient mariner than were the Harvard youth by the new master," an opinion reiterated by the *Athenaeum.*[109] "More than sixty years ago," observed *Macmillan's* in 1903, "he taught the generation then growing up around him the value of faith and hope." John Skelton, essayist, public administrator, and champion of unpopular causes, was of this generation. "To speak hardly of that essay on Nature would be at once foolish and ungrateful. To how many of us did it not prove the first excitement to independent mental activity? Once more the unseen soul of the universe looked at

---

[108] See pp. 40–41. Conway, pp. 299–319 *passim; FR,* XXXVII, 757, 766, 767, 768, 769. For other comments, see reviews of E. W. Emerson's *Memoir* in *SatR,* Aug. 10, 1889, p. 171, and of Ireland's *In Memoriam* in *Ath,* Aug. 19, 1882, p. 237.

[109] Conway, *FR,* XXXVII, 748; Conway, *OC,* V, 140; Conway, *FR,* XXXVII, 758; *Ath,* March 8, 1884, p. 306. For other comments on Emerson's hold on the young, see *IRNJ,* XXII enlarged ser. (Feb. 1875), 63, 68; R. M'c., *IRNJ,* XXII, enlarged ser., 158.

us through the eyes, and spoke to us by the voice of the prophet."
Margaret Fuller also spoke of the "young men who had found in him
their highest inspiration," and the American correspondent for the
Times Literary Supplement testified that he had seen Emerson at
Harvard and life was never again the same. "There was a new earth
and a new heaven—perhaps a new divinity." Emerson's son wrote
most excellently of his father and youth: "His written and spoken
words reached young people, whom he loved because they were
gay and brave, in far distant regions, helped them, and often
brought them to him for counsel, and it was this: Be yourself; . . .
your best self. . . . Listen to the inward voice, and bravely obey that.
. . . Hear what the Morning says and believe that." [110]

A multitude of grateful Victorians recorded their early debt to the
American. "I am aware of his exceptional influence," said Vernon
Lee, "in maturing my thought." Emerson helped me to "clear my
. . . ideas, . . . to enter his presence in a mood worthy of making
me receive the inestimable gifts of his soul." In 1890 Froude declared that "it was Emerson, more than any other one influence, who
convinced me that inside the Church of England there was no place
for me. He broke the fetters. I owe my freedom to him." John Bur-
roughs when young "had been a devourer of Emerson's essays" and
found there "more mental stimulus than many a modern lad succeeds in extracting from a whole . . . university." Professor Tyndall
penned "in his copy of *Nature*—'purchased by inspiration,' " and
Conway quoted Tyndall as saying, "If any one can be said to have
given the impulse to my mind it is Emerson; whatever I have done
the world owes to him." Max Müller "dedicated his 'Science of
Religion' to 'Ralph Waldo Emerson, in memory of his visit to Oxford in May 1873, and in acknowledgment of constant refreshment
of head and heart derived from his writings during the last twenty-
five years.' " Young Fredrika Bremer, Hutton, and Herman Grimm
paid tribute to Emerson, but the most touching encomium was
Arnold's: "Forty years ago, when I was an undergraduate at Oxford,
voices were in the air there which haunt my memory still." They
were the voices of Newman and Carlyle. "And besides these voices,

[110] *MM*, LXXXVIII (May 1903), 37; [Skelton], *Blackwood's*, CXIII (May 1873), 542;
Nairn, *TBar*, CXV, 295; *TLS*, May 29, 1903, p. 166; Emerson, *Bookman*, XXIV, 96.

there came to us in that old Oxford time a voice also from this side of the Atlantic—a clear and pure voice, which for my ear, . . . brought a strain as new, and moving, and unforgettable, as the strain of Newman, or Carlyle, or Goethe. . . . Snatches of Emerson's strain fixed themselves in my mind . . . imperishably." [111]

Of more importance to late Victorians than Emerson's influence on his young contemporaries, which was incontestable, was his influence in the eighties and nineties. "There is scarcely another living writer about whom such diversity of opinion exists," one critic wrote in 1874, and Courtney suggested some ten years later that "curiously different estimates . . . have been held about Emerson from the glowing and somewhat indiscriminating enthusiasms of . . . Holmes and Conway . . . to the appreciative but critical estimate of . . . Morley, and the cold and ambiguous compliments of . . . Arnold." "Fine and almost imperceptible lines seem to divide him from the highest and the best. He is always highly commended, but rarely in the first class." Almost as an afterthought, Courtney added, "Perhaps we are too near Emerson" to judge him correctly. Another critic concurred: "The generations of those who walked with Emerson in his lifetime, or looked up to him as a living power, have had their say, and the time of posterity is not yet." [112]

These commentators were in the minority. Late Victorians were only too willing to have their say: "It would be interesting to discover . . . ," mused the *Academy* early in the twentieth century, "what influence Emerson has upon this generation. It is hardly . . . so great as the past." In 1887 it was said that Emerson "has dropped in public estimation since his death," and Bradfield wrote several years later that he was "little read by the present generation." In

[111] Lee, *ContR*, LXVII, 345, 346; *TLS*, May 29, 1903, pp. 165, 166; *RR*, XXXVII (Sept. 1905) , 282; Lewin, *Ac*, Feb. 28, 1885, p. 144; Conway, *FR*, XXXVII, 753; Story, *NCRev*, IV, 198; Gooden, *ManQ*, IV, 332; *Sp*, Feb. 2, 1884, p. 156; *Sp*, June 16, 1888, p. 826; Arnold, *MM*, L, 1, 2. Everyone seemed to quote Tyndall on Emerson: Story, *NCRev*, IV, 198; Lewin, *Ac*, Feb. 28, 1885, p. 144; Slater, *Month*, LIII, 386; Gooden, *ManQ*, IV, 313; *Sp*, Feb. 10, 1906, p. 220; *NatRef*, Jan. 14, 1883, p. 22; *IRNJ*, XXII enlarged ser. [Feb. 1875], 67. Many of these quotes came from the pages of the biographers: Cooke, p. 186; Conway, p. 150; Ireland, p. 36; Garnett, p. 196; Elisabeth Luther Cary, *Emerson: Poet and Thinker* [New York, 1904], p. 73; Frothingham, p. 243.

[112] *Graphic*, Sept. 12, 1874, p. 261; Courtney, *FR*, n.s. XXXVIII, 320; *SatR*, Aug. 10, 1889, p. 170.

1900 and in 1901 *Literature* noted that throughout Europe "during the last decade Emerson has lain neglected on the library shelves" and that he was "not greatly read in England to-day." As a reason for this neglect, one of the critics supported Amy Cruse's observation, "In the 'nineties it was still essential that anyone with pretensions to culture should know something about... [Emerson's] *Essays,* and many people who did not really appreciate him read him for that reason." Emerson, wrote the journalist, had joined the " 'admirable radicals' of the fifties"—"that class of writers spoken of by booksellers as producers of books 'which are not greatly read, but which people buy and give to one another.' " In short, he was a classic.

In 1906 the *Spectator* declared that "the centenary of the birth of a famous writer is a good vantage-ground from which to consider his position in the hierarchy of letters," and then compared Emerson's fame with Macaulay's. "Emerson's prestige has suffered something of the same fate as Macaulay's. Both enjoyed a surprising fame in their own generation; both in time fell into the hands of more eclectic critics, to whom an author's popularity was in itself ground for suspicion; and both were for the moment relegated to the shelves of Mechanics' Institutes, and condemned as food only for the half-educated mind." In Macaulay's case, the reaction was "short-lived," and he "burns to-day brighter than ever." "In Emerson's case the rehabilitation has been slower, partly because he gave us a philosophy of conduct, and the inclination of the world has rather drifted from such bequests; partly because the agreeable patriotism of his countrymen has led them to continue praising him, not always with intelligence and taste." [113]

Late critics set forth many other reasons as to why Emerson's reputation had declined. As early as 1867 Nichol had conjectured that "Mr. Emerson will never be very popular in England, where his defects and merits are alike generally uncongenial. He alarms our Philistinism by the aggressive independence and strong counter-currents of his thought, and repels our anti-philistinism by his vehe-

[113] *AcLit,* Jan. 24, 1903, p. 82; *SatR,* Nov. 19, 1887, p. 708; Bradfield, *PMQR,* n.s. XVII, 254; E. M., *Lit,* Sept. 8, 1900, p. 171; Mew, *Lit,* Sept. 21, 1901, p. 267; Amy Cruse, *After the Victorians* (London, 1938), p. 158; E. M., *Lit,* Sept. 8, 1900, p. 171; *Sp,* Feb. 10, 1906, p. 219.

mence of expression. Our middle classes rally against him round the pillars of their Church and State. Of the refined minority, those who hesitate at heart between the liberal creed and Ultramontane sympathies turn scornfully from his samplers of excellence to the 'Acta Sanctorum.' Our apostles of culture, intensifying his moral, repudiate his artistic blemishes." An American maintained that the reason for Emerson's unpopularity lay not so much in him as in the English. That his teachings were ineffective is not hard to understand when we consider "the various prejudices that inhere in the British Islands." A third pointed out that neither Emerson nor any other American writer was at the turn of the century widely read in England: "Many of us remember," said the *Bookman,* "how we were brought up on pirated editions of the American great writers. Longfellow, Hawthorne, Emerson, Holmes, and a multitude more were read even more widely and admiringly in England than our own English authors. Now with a very few exceptions no living author has a really great circulation in England." A fourth indicated that the sturdy Emerson was a little coarse for the Englishman of the *fin de siècle:* "His contempt for the connoisseur, the epicure . . . alienates . . . a class with which he had much in common." [114]

No, protested other Englishmen: Emerson himself was to blame for his ineffectiveness. First, he failed to develop a set of followers to help him carry on his mission. "Despite his marked individuality," wrote Stewart confusedly, Emerson "leaves few followers," and the *Saturday Review* pointed out that "he was neither the follower nor the founder of any school. He learnt from many and owed allegiance to none, and he taught without making disciples." In fact, said Lewin, "he was never anxious to gain converts to his opinions." [115] Second, his style had "never tempted the English into making a popular man of him." Third, his message was passé. As Harold points out, the trend toward a collective society was rapidly destroying the concept of self-reliance; foreign tariffs made free trade "less justifiable"; reason had all but dethroned the intuition.[116] Small

[114] *NBrR,* XLVII, 357, 358; Underwood, *Good Words,* XXVIII, 808; *Bookman,* XI (Dec. 1896) , 62; Mew, *Lit,* Sept. 21, 1901, p. 268.

[115] Stewart, *ScR,* XI, 307; *SatR,* May 6, 1882, p. 553; Lewin, *Ac,* Feb. 28, 1885, p. 144. Concurring was *T. P.'s,* May 22, 1903, p. 889.

[116] *Sp,* Sept. 3, 1898, p. 312; Harrold and Templeman, p. lxxiii.

wonder, then, that a late Victorian found Emerson's message "re-mote; conditions have altered; much of what he saw coming and deplored has established itself as part of our world; therefore his ideas, or some of them at least, have an air of desuetude." Another averred that "modern work and modern speculation scarcely reach him. . . . He begins to stand . . . among the men of today, a figure of the past, not yet remote enough to be venerable, but unserviceable for present needs." A third pronounced the benediction: "As a lay-preacher of wide sympathies and high aspirations his fame is assured, but the re-reading of his works inevitably reminds one of the flight of time." [117]

Less sympathetic journals proclaimed that the message had noth-ing of value for their time or for any time. Emerson "wants that last and most useful gift of genius, the power to keep young in soul, and to advance with the advancing years." In his teachings is found "no element of new or permanent instruction—nothing that will keep Emerson's work alive as representative." And finally, "the repeated and systematic perusal of his collected works has done his intellectual fame some harm by showing what only a few judges had seen before, how small was the range of his thought, how constantly he drew on the same very limited stock of ideas . . . , whether firsthand or second-hand." [118]

Encouraged by Emerson's biographers, a score of other periodical critics believed that his influence was permanent. One wrote that his influence in America "can scarcely be exaggerated," while Egan Mew noted that "his popularity in the United States flourishes ex-ceedingly." [119] Reviewers called him the "great American," [120] "one of the greatest of Americans," and "first amongst Americans." He was "the most American of Americans," "the most universally be-loved and honoured man in America." [121] He was honored both as a

[117] *AcLit*, Jan. 24, 1903, p. 82; *Ath*, Jan. 15, 1876, p. 81; E. M., *Lit*, Sept. 8, 1900, p. 171.
[118] *Ath*, Jan. 15, 1876, p. 81; *Ath*, March 8, 1884, p. 307; *SatR*, Nov. 19, 1887, p. 708.
[119] *CQR*, XXVII (Oct. 1888), 53; Mew, *Lit*, Sept. 21, 1901, p. 267. For a similar opinion, see *QR*, CLXVI, 143.
[120] Turnbull, *NMM*, CXXII, 14; *Blackwood's*, CLV, 480; *Truth*, Oct. 5, 1882, p. 496; *AnnualR*, 1887, p. 73.
[121] *RR*, V (Jan 1892), 47; Lewin, *Bookman*, XXIV, 89; *IRNJ*, XXII enlarged ser. (Feb. 1875), 61; Conway, *FR*, XXXVII, 770. For similar comments by the Secularists, see pp. 107–8.

man of letters and as a thinker. A great task of English literature, observed the *Athenaeum* in 1884, was the education of America, "a nation at once the most materially powerful and the most susceptible of literary influences which the modern world has seen." One of the most prominent of these educators was Emerson, "the chief of American philosophy and letters"—"an American John the Baptist, proclaiming tidings of great joy to the American Israel." [122] He "is to the whole civilised world the representative of all that is most profound and most inspiring in American literature," wrote Nairn, whose estimate received support from Prothero and others: Emerson was "on the whole, the most striking figure in the American republic of letters"; "the most noted of American authors"; "beyond all doubt, one of the most impressive figures in American literature." This adulation was approved in the *Times Literary Supplement:* "The revolution in American opinion about him ... has turned censure into homage and has, within half a century or less, placed him once for all at the head of American literature and thought." [123]

As a man with a message, Emerson was "the mouthpiece of the national mind," "the greatest thinker of his nation," "the finest and deepest thinker in America." He was "the greatest of American philosophers," "the great transcendental philosopher," "one of the most celebrated of American philosophers." He "has exercised a profound influence on American thought; ... he has done much—more perhaps than any other American writer—to ennoble his countrymen's conception of life." From the publication of *Nature* in 1836, wrote Japp, "dates the birth of an original literature of thought in America." Emerson's " 'substance, sinews, arms, strength,' " declared Conway, "... are distributed in America in innumerable moral and intellectual activities; in schools, colleges, pulpits, journals." His influence was, observed *T. P.'s Weekly,* "galvanic rather than dynamic." "Hawthorne put the case well when ... he said, 'it was impossible to dwell in his vicinity without inhaling more or less the mountain atmosphere of his lofty thought,

[122] *Ath*, March 8, 1884, p. 306; *MM*, LXXXVIII (May 1903), 38; *T. P.'s*, Jan. 6, 1905, p. 12 (this critic quoted Henry James, Sr.). For an opinion similar to *MM's*, see *Chambers's*, July 29, 1882, p. 483.

[123] Nairn, *TBar*, CXV, 290; *QR*, CLXVI, 158; *Ath*, May 6, 1882, p. 569; *CongR*, II (March 1888), 221; *TLS*, May 29, 1903, p. 165.

which, in the brains of some people, wrought a singular giddiness—new truth being as heady as new wine.' " His "rhapsodies," averred Max Müller, "did more good than any learned disquisitions or carefully arranged sermons.... Socrates or Plato, if suddenly brought to life again in America, might have spoken like Emerson, and the effect produced by Emerson was certainly like that produced by Socrates in olden times." [124]

As early as 1867 Nichol was writing that "the time has come when well-educated Englishmen of all sects ought frankly to acknowledge the high qualities of [Emerson's]...mind, on the whole the loftiest that the world of letters in New England has hitherto produced." He "has been very widely read in this country," said the author and minister, W. B. Rands, in 1877, and twenty years later, Max Müller wrote that Emerson's "influence was not confined to the American mind. I have watched it growing in England." [125]

But many Victorians would not be satisfied to confine Emerson's great influence to England and America: he was a man of his age and a man for all time, they said. "There is not a living writer in sympathy with 'the spirit of the age' who has not gained strength and illumination from him; for he more than any man represents that spirit," wrote Underwood. Prothero commented that "in the intellectual history of the 19th century, Emerson is not a man to be skipped," a thought echoed by Nichol. Speaking of the transcendental movement, the *Times Literary Supplement* suggested that "one great man [Emerson] made it, and with one great man it ended." Norman declared him to be "one of the controlling minds of our age." Kernahan maintained that "Emerson's influence upon his own generation, and upon generations to come, will be second to none," and the usually hostile *Spectator* that he held "a high place among the high thinkers of the world." All the noted writers of the period

---

[124] *CQR*, XXVII (Oct. 1888), 54; Turnbull, *NMM*, CXXII, 25; *PubO*, May 7, 1870, p. 584; Conway, *OC*, V, 138; Nairn, *TBar*, CXV, 291; *Graphic*, Sept. 12, 1874, p. 261; *SatR*, May 28, 1887, p. 780; Japp, *GentM*, CCLIII, 621; Conway, *FR*, XXXVII, 749; *T. P.'s*, May 22, 1903, p. 889; Max Müller, *Cos*, VI, 329. For other critics who recognized Emerson's greatness as an American, see Alex. Ireland, *Ath*, Jan. 13, 1883, p. 53; *Sp*, Aug. 16, 1884, p. 1071; Stephen, *NatRev*, XXXVI, 882; *AcLit*, Dec. 26, 1903, p. 718; James, *MM*, LVII, 94; *GT*, XXXIX (June 1903), 120. See also pp. 24–25.

[125] *NBrR*, XLVII, 358; Holbeach, *ContR*, XXIX, 481; Max Müller, *Cos*, VI, 329.

had expressed "indebtedness" to Emerson, whose "influence was far-reaching and profound." Ireland wrote that he "exercised on some of the most thoughtful minds of his age an influence probably not exceeded by that of any other writer of the century," a viewpoint shared by Nairn. His "position in literature . . . ," urged C. A. Ward, "is that of a man of superlative faculty, of a man who has made it his business to seize ideas, and to assimilate them." Emerson's working life "coincided . . . with the two mid-quarters of the century, on which his mind has left its impress in such a way as he himself would have chosen," wrote Walter Jerrold, who had edited a volume of Emerson's essays for the Temple Classics. And his "thought has thus become so largely assimilated by the children and grandchildren of the contemporaries whom he originally addressed, that it is difficult to realise the freshness of his work when he began." Foote maintained that Emerson was "read now by more persons than when he was living," while Wheeler predicted "that his name will remain among those the world will not willingly let die." An anonymous critic declared that "no man who looked out on life with such clear, charitable eyes can be forgotten by posterity" and Lewin that "a hundred years after the birth of Emerson, . . . his fame seems assured." [126]

To describe Emerson as a famous and influential figure was not enough for some late Victorians: they were bent on canonizing him. Throughout his career Emerson had been for some an object of worship. In 1838 Harriet Martineau had hinted at his eminence, and several critics of the fifties and sixties also spoke of it.[127] Among them was Conway, who in three long articles appearing in the sixties contributed more than any other periodical writer, English or Ameri-

[126] Underwood, *Good Words*, XXVIII, 813; *QR*, CLXVI, 137; *NBrR*, XLVII, 356; *TLS*, Aug. 28, 1903, p. 249; Norman, *FR*, XL, 422; Kernahan, *GentM*, CCLIX, 476; *Sp*, Sept. 3, 1898, p. 312; Story, *NCRev*, IV, 198; Ireland, *Ath*, Jan. 13, 1883, p. 53; Nairn, *TBar*, CXV, 295; Ward, *TBar*, LXXII, 244; Jerrold, *TBar*, CXXVIII, 430, 431; *Lit*, April 27, 1901, p. 343; Foote, *Freethinker*, May 24, 1903, p. 321; Wheeler, *Freethinker*, May 7, 1882, p. 147; *Sp*, Feb. 10, 1906, p. 220; Lewin, *Bookman*, XXIV, 89. For similar views, see *Ath*, March 8, 1884, p. 306; Turnbull, *NMM*, CXXII, 24; Lewin, *Ac*, Aug. 16, 1884, p. 102.

[127] Lucian Paul, *Critic*, Aug. 1, 1851, p. 347; *Critic*, July 15, 1853, p. 379; *LondR*, Aug. 24, 1867, p. 205; *Ath*, May 2, 1868, p. 626.

can, to Emerson hagiography. Unlike the other critics who hastily conferred upon him the title of wise man and passed on to other matters, Conway carefully set the stage and placed Emerson upon it. The first of the articles pictured the sage strolling about Concord with his disciples and discoursing on profound metaphysical and intellectual problems. He was, recorded the awestricken Virginian, "the first great man I had ever seen." With loving care Conway described Emerson's library and told of the "most notable American['s]" love for Hafiz, the Bhagavad-Gita, and Plato. In the second article Conway discussed the latest works of the wise man, who showed notable interest in contemporary reforms and had such a grasp upon religion that listening to him "would be more helpful to a young minister than a theological course in any university." The concluding article, in which Conway gave a reverent account of Emerson's incunabula and how it fitted into the master's later thought, also afforded him an opportunity to end the series on a suitably elevated plane. After thirty years Emerson had once more been invited to speak at Harvard, and he closed his address with words Conway quoted at the end of his article: "Gentleman, I draw new hope." [128]

Conway's adumbration of Emerson the Saint had left Mid-Victorians unimpressed, but it was readily filled in by the biographers of the eighties [129] and, in turn, accepted by other late Victorians. "Emerson, by his nature and disposition, came near to realising that perfection which is at once the ideal and the goal of humanity," said an overwhelmed reviewer. "We are lost in admiring wonder while viewing the aerial height to which he attained, and we search in vain for some flaw in his character." The hard-boiled *Westminster Review* wrote that "he survived to a green old age, retaining all his faculties, with the exception of his memory, to the last." "His body

[128] *Fraser's*, LXX (Aug. 1864), 245, 246, 256, 263, 259 (*SatR*, Aug. 13, 1864, pp. 205–6 ridiculed this article); *Fraser's*, LXXV (May 1867), 586, 590; *Fraser's*, LXXVIII (July 1868), 2–9 *passim*, 19.

[129] Ireland, pp. 25, 39, 42; Holmes, pp. 356, 367, 369, 418–20 *passim*; Cabot, I, 6, 337; II, 678. Conway himself continued in *Emerson at Home and Abroad*, especially in Chapter I, to add new hagiographical detail and repeat the old, a procedure which led Browne, *Ac*, Aug. 4, 1883, p. 71, to remark sarcastically that in Emerson the expatriate had portrayed "a new Messiah with all the latest American improvements."

rests in Sleepy Hollow. In his books will be found 'the precious life-blood of a master spirit, embalmed and treasured up on purpose to a life beyond life.' " Forgetting all that had gone before in criticism of Emerson's religion, Story told of "Emerson's pure life—that life that has been called 'the likest Christ's.' . . . Unhampered by poverty, and untried by wealth, he lived his eighty years without struggle—a beautiful life, the parallel of which is not found in our literature." He was "one of the purest intellects and fairest lives known to our century," declared the *Times* (a newspaper not given to sentimentality), and Rossetti called him "one of the finest souls of our time." Mrs. M. A. Castle spoke of his "pure, noble, conscientious, honest life," while C. A. Ward described "his beautiful mild face fluttering with illuminated change to every passing breath of thought." In the *Modern Review* William Henry Channing, who had helped Emerson put together the Fuller *Memoirs,* cried out, "This Man of the Future incarnate, this Golden Age revived" it was my aim "to enshrine for others' love, by proving how . . . he actually had 'annulled the adulterous divorce between Intellect and Holiness' and in his own person 'reconciled' the Poet-Seer and Mystic-Saint in living oneness with the wedding-ring of Beauty." [130]

Emerson's friends—biographers [131] and periodical critics alike—worked diligently at making a shrine of Emerson's home. Their picture was in perfect keeping with what Harrold has called "the placid surface of late-Victorian life" [132] and light years removed from the place where the hobgoblins met. Every day, to borrow from the rationalist Grant Allen, was Sunday at Concord. "From the peaceful village home . . . a man who lived in, but not of the world in which he moved . . . [,] has been borne hence," wrote Turnbull of Emerson's burial, "and now the world is busy with the story of the imperishable teachings of the life so closed." In 1898 Nairn rejoiced that "hundreds of pilgrims have made their way from distant Eng-

[130] *MM,* LXXXVIII (May 1903), 38; *WR,* CXXVIII (Nov. 1887), 997; Story, *NCRev,* IV, 196, 197; Slater, *Month,* LIII, 386 (quoting the *Times* and Rossetti but also commenting sardonically: "He seems to have been a moral man"); Castle, *CMM,* XVI, 27; Ward, *TBar,* LXXII, 243; Channing, *ModR,* III (Oct. 1882), 853.

[131] Ireland, pp. 29, 93, 95, 111; Conway, pp. 229 ff.; Holmes, p. 72; Cabot, I, chap. viii and x.

[132] Harrold and Templeman, p. lxvii.

land to that spot . . . which is now sacred for all time to those who have loved and learned from Emerson." This spot is comparable to Wordsworth's home in England. To the world, said Nairn, Emerson was "a poet and a prophet, to them of his own household he was a saint. . . . The home of such a spirit becomes a temple." Three eminent Victorians who knew Emerson personally testified to his saintliness: Max Müller spoke of him as "this wonderfully gifted man," Stephen said that he was "made of the finest clay of human nature," and James could not understand why people were shocked at Emerson's "ceasing to care for the prayer and the sermon. They might have perceived that he *was* the prayer and the sermon." [133]

[133] Allen, "Sunday at Concord," *FR*, XLIX (May 1888), 675–91; Turnbull, *NMM*, CXXII, 3; Nairn, *TBar*, CXV, 290, 295, 296; Max Müller, *Cos*, VI, 328; Stephen, *NatRev*, XXXVI, 898; James, *MM*, LVII, 88. For similar comment, see Lewin, *Ac*, June 22, 1889, p. 422; *Ath*, Feb. 3, 1883, p. 147; *AnnualR*, 1887, p. 73; *Art Journal*, n.s. XIX (Feb. 1880), 55; Rev. Stuart J. Reid, *ManQ*, I (Jan. 1882), 1–13.

◄ VI ►

Emerson and Carlyle

THE most notable literary friendship between an American and a British author in the nineteenth century was that of Emerson and Carlyle. Both writers won recognition in the forties and for the next twenty years were the leading men of letters in their respective countries. Carlyle's last major work, *Frederick the Great,* appeared in 1865, and two years later Emerson published *May-Day and Other Pieces,* his last major work. Both writers died in the early eighties, within two years of each other. During their lifetime Carlyle and Emerson revealed great respect for each other in their books, letters, and private conversations, and biographers of the two men as well as other critics have commented on the close relationship. A number of references to the friendship appeared in British periodicals. Comments begin with the first notices of Emerson and continue throughout the century. This material is especially important, for it not only sheds fresh light upon two remarkable men but also contributes an important chapter to the history of Anglo-American cultural relations.

In the introduction to *The American Writer and the European Tradition* the editors write that America "needs to perceive more clearly the source and nature of formative influences, both past and present, upon its literature." [1] Critics have pointed out that from colonial times America has tended to look to England for these sources. The metaphysical poets exerted a strong influence upon Edward Taylor, and Locke influenced such diverse figures as Jon-

[1] Margaret Denny and William H. Gilman, eds. (Minneapolis, 1950), p. v.

athan Edwards and Benjamin Franklin. So powerful were these literary and intellectual currents that by the first part of the nineteenth century Washington Irving was being referred to as the American Addison, Cooper as America's Scott, Whittier as her Burns, and Bryant as her Wordsworth. At the very time, however, that America was using England as a literary warehouse, writers like Philip Freneau, William Cullen Bryant, William E. Channing, and even Longfellow were calling for demolition of the edifice. In 1838 Emerson offered his services as a one-man wrecking crew: "Our day of dependence," he cried in the famous "Address," "our long apprenticeship to the learning of other lands, draws to a close. The millions that around us are rushing into life, cannot always be fed on the sere remains of foreign harvests." "We have listened too long to the courtly muses of Europe." [2]

Before Emerson issued this bold declaration, the British critical constabulary had looked with amused tolerance on America's efforts to cut literary and intellectual ties with the Mother Country. Emerson's address brought this attitude to an abrupt halt: Great Britain began working overtime to keep America within her literary compound. Appropriately enough, she began with Emerson. He was charged with borrowing from such English writers as Wordsworth and Toland.[3] He was accused of pilfering from the German Kant and the French Rousseau.[4] He was, above all, denounced as an imitator of Thomas Carlyle: his works were "Massachusetts Carlylery," he closely resembled the "weird Carlyle." [5]

Even as British critics charged Emerson with these sins, they found it difficult to sustain the charges: the question of America's cultural and intellectual debt to Europe in general and to England in particular is a complicated one. In order to answer it, Margaret Denny and William H. Gilman suggest, other questions must first be answered. One of these is, "Does the excellence of American writers of undisputed merit rest to an appreciable degree upon their debt to or

[2] *The Complete Works of Ralph Waldo Emerson*, ed. Edward Waldo Emerson (Boston, 1903–4) , I, 81–82, 114—hereafter cited as *Works*.

[3] R[ichard] M. M[ilnes], *LWR*, XXXIII (March 1840) , 194; *EcRev*, 4th ser. XII (Dec. 1842) , 667.

[4] *Tait's*, n.s. VIII (Oct. 1841) , 667.

[5] *LitG*, Sept. 25, 1841, p. 621; *EcRev*, 8th ser. III (Nov. 1862) , 387.

their independence of the European tradition?"[6] In dealing with Emerson, the early critics gave this query an ambiguous and interesting answer. They were thoroughly exasperated with the "Phi Beta Kappa Oration," yet they somehow felt that the author was America's first really original writer. Emerson had been greatly influenced by Continental idealism; nevertheless he was free of the storm and stress of a Goethe or the rigid system of a Hegel. He seemed to be a good deal like Carlyle; still the differences were perhaps more striking than the similarities. On only one issue were they in complete accord: it was Emerson who sought out Carlyle.

When the American visited Great Britain in 1833, he wished to meet an obscure writer whose works he had first read in English journals. He went to Craigenputtock, observed Alexander Ireland, to acknowledge "in person his indebtedness to Carlyle for the spiritual benefit he had found from some of his articles in the *Edinburgh* and *Foreign Quarterly Reviews.*" The Scotsman described the meeting in a letter to his mother: "Of course, . . . we could do no other than welcome him; the rather as he seemed to be one of the most lovable creatures in himself we had ever looked on." Emerson, too, "was enchanted with his visit," and soon afterward he laid the groundwork for the American edition of *Sartor Resartus,* for which he wrote a preface.[7] This recognition of Carlyle was to Englishmen, said a late Victorian critic, "one of the most endearing features of Emerson's character." In 1841 Carlyle returned the favor by writing an introduction for the English edition of *Essays, First Series.* His kindness probably did more harm than good. In the first place, the Preface, which was written in "a half-laughing, half-patronizing air," may have led such a critic as the one on the *Athenaeum* to treat the essays in the same manner. Secondly, some reviewers read the Preface very carefully and neglected the essays;[8] thirdly, and most importantly, a number of reviewers were tempted by the Preface to form

    [6] Denny and Gilman, p. v.

    [7] Ralph L. Rusk, *The Life of Ralph Waldo Emerson* (New York, 1949), pp. 164–65; Alexander Ireland, *Ac,* April 7, 1883, p. 231; [Richard A. Armstrong], *ModR,* IV (April 1883), 319. For another description of Emerson by Carlyle, see *LeisH,* XXXIV (April 1885), 288.

    [8] *Chambers's,* July 29, 1882, p. 483; [Charles Wicksteed], *ProsR,* I (May 1845), 256; *Ath,* Oct. 23, 1841, pp. 803–4 *passim; LWR,* XXXVI (Oct. 1841), 491–93.

exaggerated notions of Carlyle's influence on Emerson, especially on his style.

II

Victorians often disparaged the Scotsman's "peculiar or discursive" manner of expressing himself, and to find Emerson copying him was insufferable. "CARLYLE's style," wrote the *Critic* derisively, "is not his own invention, but taken from the German; EMERSON's is not his own, but borrowed partly from the German and partly from CARLYLE." [9] In reviewing the *First Essays,* the *Monthly Review* stated that Carlyle's praise in the Preface "has been considerably influenced by Emerson's mannerism of . . . diction, partaking as it does of Carlyle's own." The *Literary Gazette* agreed. "Mr. Carlyle approves of this book," it declared, "and no wonder, for it out-Carlyles Carlyle himself, exaggerates all his peculiarities and faults, and possesses very slight glimpses of his excellences. It imitates his inflations, his verbiage." "As the master, so the pupil; . . .—only that the latter is often more quaint, more stilted, and more unintelligible." As late as 1888 a critic wrote that "Carlyle influenced rather the form than the substance" of Emerson's teaching.[10] Two critics, one early and one late, found Emerson's style less affected than Carlyle's, and another said that it was more spiritual. If tried by Arnold's "extreme test, Emerson falls somewhat short," wrote C. A. Ward, and "Carlyle breaks down altogether." [11]

Arnold himself had rated Carlyle's "gift of speech . . . not so very much below 'even Shakespere himself,' " and though few critics, including Ward, would agree to such a comparison, they seemed to prefer the Scotsman's manner, bad as it was, to "the mosaic method of Emerson." Carlyle's "wind-in-the-orchard style" was at least "coherent," whereas "his followers, among whom Mr. Emerson

---

[9] *Sp,* Jan. 12, 1850, p. 42; *Critic,* Feb. 1, 1850, p. 60.

[10] *MR,* n.s. III (Oct. 1841) , 275; LitG, Sept. 25, 1841, pp. 620, 621; *CQR,* XXVII (Oct. 1888) , 56. Emerson himself was rather offended by Carlyle's style, as Leslie Stephen, *NatRev,* XXXVI (Feb. 1901) , 884, and J. C[harlton], *Reas,* April 10, 1859, p. 116, pointed out.

[11] Goodwyn Barmby, *Howitt's,* Nov. 13, 1847, p. 315; Douglas Story, *NCRev,* IV (Sept. 1898) , 197; *GT,* XXXIX (June 1903) , 122; C. A. Ward, *TBar,* LXXII (Oct. 1884) , 240.

is the most conspicuous, do not possess this coherence ... ; doing, in fact, little more than repeat themselves." Carlyle "has a style, odd as it may be; Emerson's is more a mannerism than a style.... The diction, which with Carlyle is merely a mode, ... is with Emerson a thing in itself." Carlyle was, wrote the *Biblical Review and Congregational Magazine,* "not grotesque for the sake of grotesqueness." He "forgets himself in his subject, and so his attitudes are unstudied; the other forgets his subject in himself, and so the matter of his thought is unnatural." [12]

Not all the criticism was so thorny. Both writers showed "an uncompromising aversion" to "stereotyped modes of expression," and in their prose both used techniques ordinarily reserved for poetry. Emerson and Carlyle, observed *Freelight,* "are prose poets, renouncing Pegasus that they may wrestle with present darkness." Several critics suggested that Carlyle was the better writer of prose poetry and thus the more effective. He was, said R. E. Prothero, "a great artist ... detesting abstractions." "Emerson is ... a generaliser and abstract thinker." Agreeing, *Macphail's* declared in striking imagery of its own that "Carlyle made more of young Samuel Johnson's 'old shoes,' than Emerson could of all the articles of human apparel." In a rather backhanded compliment to the Carlyle manner, C. A. Ward wrote that "his 'French Revolution' will live, not because it fathoms history like Machiavelli ... [but] because it is a portrait gallery." R. A. Armstrong praised the "vivid bits of portraiture" which Carlyle gave in *The Correspondence of Thomas Carlyle and Ralph Waldo Emerson,* and an anonymous critic commented that "what is poetic ... [Carlyle] strangely intermingles with what is didactic; his drama is philosophy, and his philosophy is a drama." Richard Holt Hutton draws the matter to a close with the observation, "Some of Carlyle's prose is as touching as any but the noblest poetry, while Emerson never reaches the same profound pathos." [13]

Nearly all the comments on the poetry in the two writers' prose

---

[12] Matthew Arnold, *MM,* L (May 1884) , 6; Ward, *TBar,* LXXII, 240; Walter Jerrold, *TBar,* CXXVIII (Oct. 1903) , 433; *Sp,* Jan. 12, 1850, p. 42; *BibRev,* I (Feb. 1846) , 149.

[13] [John Nichol], *NBrR,* XLVII (Dec. 1867) , 349; *Freelight,* I (Dec. 1871) , 151; [R. E. Prothero], *QR,* CLXVI (Jan. 1888) , 156; *Macphail's,* XV (Feb. 1848) , 35; Ward, *TBar,* LXXII, 241; *ModR,* IV, 336; *BibRev,* I (Feb. 1846) , 148; [Hutton], *Sp,* May 6, 1882, p. 590.

were made by the early critics—those of the forties who, with some justification, pointed out stylistic parallels between works like *Sartor Resartus* and the *First* and *Second Essays*. Later critics found it somewhat difficult to compare the styles of Carlyle and Emerson. Books like *English Traits, The Conduct of Life,* and *Letters and Social Aims* exhibit a more pedestrian, less allusive and poetic manner than the first essays. So different is the style of these books from that of *Sartor Resartus* or *The Life of Frederick the Great* that one finds little reward in dealing with them, as several critics inadvertently reveal. Carlyle's manner, wrote Professor Nichol, is "often fragmentary, sometimes grotesque," but it is better than Emerson's, which was "graceful and clear, but colourless." W. R. Turnbull found in Emerson's works a "positive disrelish for . . . those *outré* similes and masquerading images so freely used" by Carlyle. As if looking at *Sartor* and *Traits,* Prothero said, "Carlyle is incomplete, fragmentary, and often grotesque. Emerson is easy, graceful, and sometimes self-complacent." And, finally, the American's "language [was] less harsh, his imagery . . . more rounded, more perfect" than that of the Scotsman, commented George Stewart. "He is never . . . coarse. He never offends." [14]

Emerson in his early period looked for rather than avoided the *outré* simile; his manner often offended. The later works are fairly typical examples of an excellent and inoffensive prose style, and though these works received, in general, an increasingly respectful reception, British critics did not regard Emerson as a great stylist. Neither were they greatly impressed with Carlyle.

Victorians—especially the earlier—also deprecated Emerson's and Carlyle's philosophy and religion. Nor were they—at least the earlier —willing to say that Emerson's transcendentalism was much more original than his style.

III

"The republication of *Sartor Resartus,* backed by the elder authority of Coleridge, gave life and voice to a new intellectual world," wrote Nichol. "Coleridge and Carlyle were hailed as prophets in

[14] *NBrR*, XLVII, 350; Turnbull, *NMM*, CXXII (Dec. 1882), 10; *QR*, CLXVI, 156; George Stewart, Jr., *Belford's*, I (Jan. 1877), 222.

Boston." And Douglas Story averred that "three years before Emerson had delivered his oration to the Phi Beta Kappa Society, *Sartor Resartus* had taught the world that, not this man and that man, but all men, make up mankind." [15] The essays of *First Series* were, the early critics declared, full of such transcendent thought. In this book, wrote the *Literary Gazette* in 1841, Emerson imitates Carlyle's "metaphysics and mysticism; but wants the originality, the soul, the high and searching intellect." The *Monthly Review* wrote that Carlyle lauded the book because it was in "thought" like his own works, but the *Critic* found both writers guilty of parroting. "There can be no question," it proclaimed, "that EMERSON is an imitator of CARLYLE, but not more so than CARLYLE is himself an imitator of certain of the German philosophers." The main differences between the two imitators, wrote the *Journal of Sacred Literature,* were that Carlyle did not go so far as Emerson in "pantheistic mysticism" and that he "does not assert," as does Emerson, "that man is the highest being." Still, "his principles . . . lead to that conclusion." [16]

Several critics, notably the later Victorians, were not so sure that the philosophies of the two writers were wholly bad or that Emerson was a plagiarist. In 1884 the *National Review* wrote approvingly that Carlyle and Emerson unhesitatingly ranged themselves against the cause of materialism. Charles Johnston asserted in 1887 that "the new world they have explored, is the land of hope of the future, for which we must leave . . . the arid deserts of materialism." [17] These commentators made no distinction between the transcendentalism of Emerson and Carlyle, but other late Victorian critics did. "Emerson has been sometimes sneered as a 'Yankee pocket edition of Carlyle,' " wrote the *Graphic* in 1874, but although "he has studied deeply the works of the great Scotch philosopher, his own writings bear the most unmistakeable marks of original and independent genius." Juliet Pollock had written a year earlier that Emerson "has by such as have not read him been quoted as an imitator. This is an error. . . . Emerson, whether as a poet or as a philosopher, is essentially

[15] *NBrR,* XLVII, 320; Story, *NCRev,* IV, 195.

[16] *LitG,* Sept. 25, 1841, p. 620; *MR,* n.s. III (Oct. 1841) , 275; *Critic,* Feb. 1, 1850, p. 59; M. G. E., *JSL,* 3rd ser. VI (Jan. 1858) , 307.

[17] R. C. Seaton, *NatRev,* III (Aug. 1884) , 777; Johnston, *Lucifer,* I (Dec. 1887) , 253.

original." Stewart declared in 1877 that Emerson did not copy Carlyle: he "is an independent thinker." In 1903 *Macmillan's Magazine* observed that "it is hardly necessary at this time of day to deny the accusation once made against Emerson that he was indebted to Carlyle," and Prothero maintained in 1888 that "they should rather be contrasted than compared"—especially in their philosophies.[18]

Emerson had obviously studied the works of Carlyle in formulating his philosophical doctrines, but the conclusions of the two philosophers differed. Carlyle's transcendentalism was that of a hardheaded, pragmatic Scotsman from Auld Caledonia; Emerson's was that of a naïve, idealistic American from New England. One was the philosopher of the Old World, the other of the New. Although Emerson was, as an early journal observed, "a transcendentalist distinguished for sound common sense," he was much more "prone to soar into universals, to deal with abstractions, to suggest indefinite rather than concrete possibilities," than was Carlyle.[19] The Scotsman "remained to the end," writes David Masson, "a *Realistic Transcendentalist* or *Transcendental Realist.* . . . He was satisfied to think of the world of space and time, and of all physical and historical realities, as having substantially existed." Emerson's transcendentalism, on the other hand, was highly idealistic. "Carlyle complains gently that his friend is in danger of parting from fact and soaring into perilous altitudes," wrote Leslie Stephen. "Come back to the earth, he exclaims." [20] Disregarding this advice, the American would not be satisfied with a world of time and space: to him the earth was a symbol of the mind. The idealist's "manner of looking at things transforms every object . . . from an independent and anomalous position . . . into the consciousness," he said. The world was the NOT ME: it had no real, true existence.[21] This concept was as broad, as expansive, as inchoate as the young nation from which it took its peculiar coloration and for which it was formulated.

[18] *Graphic*, Sept. 12, 1874, p. 261; Pollock, *ContR*, XXII (Aug. 1873) , 357; Stewart, *Belford's*, I, 222; *MM*, LXXXVIII (May 1903) , 40; *QR*, CLXVI, 156, 142.

[19] *Macphail's*, XV (Feb. 1848) , 34; [R. E. Prothero], *QR*, CLXIII (Oct. 1886) , 377.

[20] Masson, *Carlyle: Personally and in His Writings; Two Edinburgh Lectures*, in *English Prose of the Victorian Era*, ed. Charles F. Harrold and William D. Templeman (New York, 1938) , p. 1559; Stephen, *NatRev*, XXXVI, 886.

[21] *Works*, I, 331.

In treating the subject of the American writer and tradition, recent critics frequently maintain that, instead of turning his back on foreign ideas, the writer restates them in his own terms.[22] Emerson's noble expansion of Carlyle's philosophy is an excellent example of such a restatement, just as critical reaction to this statement was typical of the British tendency to embrace the narrower, manageable concept—even when that concept was transcendental. Carlyle, declared Prothero, is at his best in his philosophy, Emerson at his worst. "Emerson misses his mark, because he aims too wide. Carlyle, on the other hand, strikes with tremendous force to the core of the subject." Complained the *New Quarterly Review*, "Mr. Emerson's philosop_, not only begins but ends in wonder. He conducts us through a series of cloud-scapes," whereas "Carlyle rends the mountains and breaks in pieces for our actual gaze the rocks and barriers of truth." Armstrong reported that Carlyle, in criticizing American transcendentalism, had called Emerson "a *Soliloquizer* on the eternal mountain tops only," and had written to him, "I love your *Dial*, and yet it is with a kind of shudder. You seem to me in danger of dividing yourselves from the Fact of this present Universe, . . . and soaring away after Ideas."

Perhaps Hutton best revealed British periodical opinion on Carlyle and Emerson as transcendentalists. Like Prothero and Carlyle himself, this critic also deplored Emerson's tendency to aim at the million and miss the unit. Carlyle, wrote the critic, is "much the greater of the two. Emerson never seems . . . so little secure of his ground as he is in uttering his transcendentalisms,—Carlyle never so secure." Emerson "aims too wide, and hits only the vague." Carlyle, on the other hand, "stuck to the very truth and reality of nature. He showed us how small a proportion of our life we can realise in thought; . . . how infinite the universe. . . . This was but a narrow aim, compared with that of Mr. Emerson's philosophy, but it succeeded, while Emerson's did not. The various philosophic essays in which Emerson tried to assert the absolute unity of the material and

[22] Robert E. Spiller, "Benjamin Franklin: Promoter of Useful Knowledge," in Denny and Gilman, pp. 29–44, esp. 39, 43; Stanley T. Williams, "Cosmopolitanism in American Literature before 1880," *ibid.*, pp. 45–62 *passim*, esp. 45, 49, 51, 56; Leon Howard, "Americanization of the European Heritage," *ibid.*, pp. 78–89 *passim*.

spiritual laws of the Universe, have always seemed . . . , though decidely interesting, yet unquestionable failures." [23]

IV

The essays in which Emerson expressed his religious views were also, according to British commentators, unquestionable failures. Although the radical Norman Britton approved of these doctrines as well as Carlyle's,[24] most critics disparaged them. Of the two writers, Emerson was considered the more blameworthy. Speaking of his heresies, a religious journal observed reproachfully that he was "either of a bolder spirit or has a more definite creed than Carlyle's." *Hogg's Instructor* concurred: "If Emerson never repels by misanthropic lucubrations like those of Carlyle . . . , he gives all our holiest feelings . . . at times a deadlier shock." A Canadian church journal observed that Carlyle took "a somewhat higher range in the scale of faith" than Emerson.[25] Even as the century progressed and religious controversy centered upon the Higher Criticism and Darwinianism, Carlyle and Emerson still came in for much abuse. Critics never failed to arraign these writers for their animadversions against Christianity. Carlyle once declared that it was "inconceivable . . . that any man of real intellect could be found in that camp without something of conscious insincerity," a comment with which Emerson would agree.[26] "Long ago," wrote Turnbull, "Carlyle hailed" Emerson as "the one man among the millions of the New World whose faith did not impinge on the 'withered traditional' Church yielding dry catechisms." [27]

Such a salutation could easily have led the *Congregationalist* in

[23] *QR*, CLXVI (Jan. 1888), 156; *NQR*, V (1856), 450; *ModR*, IV, 323, 324; *Sp*, May 6, 1882, p. 591.

[24] *Progress*, I (May 1883), 283–85. For an excellent early comparison of Emerson's and Carlyle's religious and philosophical views, see John Beattie Crozier, *The Religion of the Future* (London, 1880), pp. 105–57 *passim*.

[25] *Macphail's*, XV (Feb. 1848), 41; *Hogg's*, 3rd ser. IV (Feb. 1855), 91; Henry Hemming, *NDomM*, Aug. 1871, p. 68.

[26] Masson, *Carlyle*, in Harrold and Templeman, p. 1560; J. M. Robertson, *A History of Freethought in the Nineteenth Century* (New York, 1929), I, 107.

[27] *NMM*, CXXII, 12.

1883 to lament, "Here are two of the seers of the time." "They do not treat the faith of others with any particular consideration: have they anything to put in its place?" No. There is "something inexpressibly sad in the absence of those brighter hopes which cheer the Christian heart." According to R. C. Seaton in a long and excellent article on Carlyle's and Emerson's religious views, the Scotsman's "conception of the character of Christ" was "higher" than Emerson's, but, even so, he rejected Christianity: it was not in accord with "experience." Emerson rejected Christianity on even less valid grounds: he took "from the Gospels what chimes in with his *à priori* notions of what Christ said and did, in preference to what he finds there recorded. . . . While vastly superior to Carlyle in breadth, he has no consolation for the afflicted soul." [28]

One reason that Emerson brought no consolation to the afflicted was, the critics indicated, his disbelief in the power of evil. This treatment, they suggested, was too exclusive, too complacent.[29] Victorians did not accuse Carlyle of such complacency. Although he erroneously treated evil "as being rather the result of outward circumstances than of anything inherent in human nature," as Seaton observed, he did admit its presence. To this Scotsman brought up under the strict mandate of Calvin, evil was a blood-freezing reality. He "recognises the truth that underlies all the formulae about human corruption," wrote Nichol, "and acknowledging the necessity of a law of duty with definite sanctions, takes for his watchword the Christian self-sacrifice" instead of Emerson's "Pagan self-reliance." [30] But both Carlyle and Emerson, for all their picture-making ability, failed to put their beliefs in a manner that the public could grasp. Man must have something concrete upon which to base his religion: he must be able imaginatively to render his God. No successful system of worship has existed without its myth. God of mercy or God of wrath, Deity must be seen, heard, felt, and touched. Emerson and Carlyle failed to recognize this necessity. In the place of Deity, Emerson set forth vague abstractions like the "Over-Soul," "Universal Being," "Original Cause," while Carlyle spoke fuzzily of "Immensities,"

---

[28] *Cst*, XII (April 1883) , 333; Seaton, *NatRev*, III, 779, 780, 781, 776.
[29] Seaton, *NatRev*, III, 775, 776; George Gilfillan, *Tait's*, n.s. XV (Jan. 1848) , 22.
[30] Seaton, *NatRev*, III. 775; *NBrR*, XLVII, 350.

"Silences," "Infinite Unnameable." "Behind everything in Carlyle," wrote Hugh Walker, "lay an unalterable belief in the Law of the Universe, which was his Religion, and a conviction that this law was identical with Truth and Justice." "No one ever preached this doctrine more consistently." [31]

Except for a few radicals, the pragmatic Victorian remained cold to the effort of these writers to preach, as Masson said of Carlyle, "synonyms or verbal shifts by which he could hope to bring back the essential notion" of Christianity. One early critic who understandably misinterpreted their religious views declared that Carlyle "inculcates the worship of genius; Emerson denounces all adoration save that of self: Carlyle is by nature a mental slave; and Emerson the embodiment of self-glorification. The one commands us to kneel in the dust before *force* . . . ; the other forbids us to set the most glorious actions . . . above . . . our own private notions of them. Which of these creeds is more mischievous, it were difficult to say: the cant of either is disagreaable; but we should say that that of the idolworshipper was the more odious, that of the self-idolator the more absurd."

More perceptive and less abusive but still missing the mark was the *Eclectic,* which observed in 1862: Emerson "has a lively, comfortable faith." His "mood . . . is one of infinite hope, whilst Carlyle's is oftenest one of infinite sadness. One believes in eternal ideas, the other in God's facts." "Both are earnest men, and find different avenues for it. Carlyle bursts out into melting tenderness and self-sacrificing love; he would fold all men to his bosom and assuage their tears. Emerson is colder, calmer, more brilliant, knows mankind well, and will not give himself over to aught save the rapture of the future." Perhaps the most cogent comment of all came from the *Athenaeum,* which suggested in 1887 that "the true analogy between Carlyle's position and Emerson's, [is] that they each assumed the moral government of the world without appealing to any revelation." "Carlyle assumes as little as possible—only Infinities and Eternities in a general way, and a sort of final triumph of Right." "Emerson, on the other hand—shall we say with a shallower or with a

[31] *Works,* II, 265–97; I, 10, 31; Masson, *Carlyle,* in Harrold and Templeman, p. 1560; Walker, *The Literature of the Victorian Era* (Cambridge, Eng., 1921) , p. 79.

deeper insight into the eternal problems?—was ready at once to believe a great deal more than this himself, and to encourage you . . . , to believe pretty nearly whatever you had a fancy for." [32]

V

Emerson's great tolerance was even more manifest in his political than in his religious doctrines, while Carlyle was, much more than in his religious views, restrictive. In their politics the two men were complete opposites. One was a liberal democrat in the best sense of the word; the other was vehemently opposed "throughout his whole life, and especially in his later life, to the modern faith in Democracy." [33] As G. W. Foote wrote, "it was inevitable that Emerson should be a democrat, as it was inevitable that Carlyle should be an autocrat," and Nichol said of the American, "At every crisis of his country's history, he leaves his 'intellectual throne,' to say . . . the aptest and truest things, as the spokesman of a liberty at once ideal and practical. . . . He approves of free-trade, a wide suffrage, a national education, a popular literature, a mild penal code." [34] Several other critics praised Emerson on the same grounds, while shaming Carlyle. Unlike the Scotsman, declared the feminist Edith Simcox in 1876, the American "seems to feel himself increasingly *en rapport* with his countrymen." And Armstrong stated, "Emerson at Concord was in much closer contact with his people . . . than was Carlyle in London, where he was able to live in disdainful isolation from the whole world of politics and human society around him." [35]

Not only was Emerson more in tune with his own country than

[32] Masson, *Carlyle,* in Harrold and Templeman, p. 1560; *EngR,* XII (Sept. 1849) , 141; *EcRev,* 8th ser. III (Nov. 1862) , 387; *Ath,* Oct. 29, 1887, p. 561.

[33] *Works,* III, 199, 207, 213, 214, 215, 219, 210; A. I. Ladu, "Emerson: Whig or Democrat," *NEQ,* XIII (Sept. 1940) , 419–41, esp. 423; Masson, *Carlyle,* in Harrold and Templeman, p. 1562.

[34] Foote, *Freethinker,* May 31, 1903, p. 338; *NBrR,* LXVII, 351, 352. Seaton, *NatRev,* III, 787, commented that "we are rapidly arriving at the reign of *laissez-faire* which Carlyle foresaw." Seaton might have added "and deplored." See Richard Holt Hutton, "Thomas Carlyle," in Harrold and Templeman, p. 1556.

[35] Edith Simcox, *Ac,* Jan. 22, 1876, p. 67; *ModR,* IV, 323.

was Carlyle, said most of these critics, but he was more in tune with the spirit of the age. "He sympathised ardently with all the greatest practical movements of his own day, while Carlyle held contemptuously aloof," wrote Hutton. "He had a genuine desire to see all men really free, while Carlyle only felt the desire to see all men strongly governed,—which they might be without being free at all." [36] Prothero made a similar judgment and was sustained by Alexander H. Japp and J. M. Wheeler. The American "advocated human development through liberty, Carlyle under authority." "Emerson exhorts to self-reliance, Carlyle to hero worship; the one is hopeful, the other despondent, of human potentialities." Carlyle, wrote Nichol, "takes his stand as a retrograde politician, and, seeing only decay where his fellows are seeing progress, advocates a purely ideal and impractical despotism." And C. A. Ward commented, Carlyle did not seem "to be in actual contact with the great world-movements, and they came . . . as *images* of things[,] not things."

Finally, the *Illustrated London News* cogently wrote: "The sympathy of an age which cherishes Liberal principles and humane dispositions, and which trusts to find them still hallowed by a true religion, was not estranged from the gentle and placid sage of Concord, as latterly it was, in a great measure, from the rugged Chelsea preacher of a less charitable creed." This creed, said the *News*, often drove away the stanchest of Carlyle's disciples. They were "rudely checked and shaken . . . by harsh and perverse tendencies of the Master, in after years, to the arbitrary exaltation of despotic or revolutionary violence, outraging the sentiments of equity and of human brotherhood." "How much of Carlyle's sorrow and bitterness," asserted another journal, "was due to the absence of . . . [a]

---

[36] *Sp*, May 6, 1882, p. 591. One great practical movement with which Emerson and Carlyle sympathized was that of labor. "It is difficult not to see," wrote *CQR*, XXVII (Oct. 1888), 56, "in the dignity of labour so strongly enforced in *The American Scholar*, some more direct trace of Carlyle's teaching." Carlyle was much the stronger in the socialistic movement. "Mr. Carlyle, when he talks of 'Captains of Industry,' 'Organised Labour,' . . . seems to discern dimly the great Constructive Truth of the Nineteenth Century; but it is not yet a leaven of conviction in his mind." "Mr. Emerson, meantime has fled to the mountain-tops" ([Parke Godwin], *People's*, Nov. 28[?], 1847, p. 308). As for evolution. "Carlyle always rejected it." "Emerson, on the other hand, welcomed it as a valuable addition to human knowledge" (Seaton, *NatRev*, III, 777).

visible and appreciable influence on national life and institutions!" [37]

VI

Although the majority of British critics remained unconvinced of the efficacy of Emerson's and Carlyle's philosophical views and deplored their religious doctrines, they recognized that all these doctrines—bad as well as good—were the outpourings of inspired men, men who could justly be called seer and prophet. Such men often come in for great praise as teachers, just as did Emerson and Carlyle. One critic who did not appreciate them was Judge Oliver Wendell Holmes, who said that neither writer "comes up to exactly what I want. Underneath them, behind them, and before them, come the great metaphysicians and men of science, who attack more directly, acutely, logically, and profoundly, the fundamental problems of thought and nature." Emerson and Carlyle "chose a different path . . . , laying the stress on the moral and practical, the aesthetic and religious, aspects of the whole matter." A more sympathetic commentator wrote that "neither of them was fitted to build up a great system . . . , but both left an impress upon the minds of those who came under their influence which could not easily be effaced." [38]

One of these minds maintained that "it would not be easy to find two men who have exercised so wide and deep an influence on the thought of the two continents." Another, Wheeler, wrote that "the words of both, appealing as they do to both heart and brain, have come as inspiration to many to whom the bread of life offered in older revelations has become as fossilised sawdust." And a third, Ireland, declared that Emerson and Carlyle "were two of the most notable men of letters and spiritual forces of their time." Walter Jerrold wrote approvingly that each "had a message disquieting to smug self-satisfaction; each was in a sense an iconoclast." They be-

[37] *QR*, CLXVI, 156; Japp, *GentM*, CCLIII (Nov. 1882), 628; Wheeler, *Progress*, I (Feb. 1883), 119; *NBrR*, XLVII, 350; Ward, *TBar*, LXXII, 240; *Illustrated London News*, May 6, 1882, p. 438; *Ath*, March 17, 1883, p. 335.

[38] Henry G. Atkinson, *SecR*, May 19, 1883, p. 316; *CongR*, II (March 1888), 221.

lieved, so the *Spectator* stated, that they had "some of the most vital truths of the day." Nichol also believed it: "There are," he asserted, "many now of middle age to whom the first reading of Carlyle and Emerson brought the sense of a new revelation." [39]

Of the two teachers, Nichol believed the Scotsman to be the greater: "Perhaps Carlyle," he said, "has stood the test [of time] better than Emerson." Others were of the same opinion. "Carlyle was feared," commented Story, Emerson was "universally loved. Still, for practical benefit to the world at large, he has probably been the least useful." In England, wrote Stewart in 1877, "Emerson is almost as much appreciated as Carlyle and Matthew Arnold. Indeed the men of the Carlyle school of thought rank Emerson as one of themselves." Although a critic declared that neither Emerson nor Carlyle was able to "found a school of disciples," *Macphail's* said that, next to Carlyle, Emerson "possesses the power of making disciples of those who are brought into intercourse with him. Speaking with fewer airs of *prophetic* authority than Carlyle, he subdues and persuades by the softer spell of a *poetic* influence. The one uses the rod of an enchanter; the other that of a schoolmaster." [40]

Conversely, other critics indicated that, for good or bad, Emerson was the superior teacher. "Originally kindled into morbid life by Carlyle," Emerson, asserted one, "overpassed him far in extreme views, and exerted correspondingly greater influence over the young and the doubtful in mind." Another wrote that "literary sects," led by such figures as Macaulay, De Quincey, and Carlyle, "are now more numerous than the religious. . . . But the most exclusive and bigoted of superstitious disciples are those who enter the Emersonian." [41] Other critics contrasting Emerson and Carlyle as teachers were not quite so acerb, but they too awarded the prize to the American. After writing in 1884 that "as sage and teacher we have probably heard the last of Thomas Carlyle," C. A. Ward maintained that Emerson was "brimful of genius, cosmopolitan, suggestive,

[39] *Cst*, XII (April 1883), 325; Wheeler, *Progress*, I, 120; Ireland, *Ac*, April 7, 1883, p. 231; Jerrold, *TBar*, CXXVIII, 433; *Sp*, March 24, 1883, p. 387; *NBrR*, XLVII, 324.

[40] *NBrR*, XLVII, 324; Story, *NCRev*, IV, 198; Stewart, *Belford's*, I, 232; *CongR*, II (March 1888), 221; *Macphail's*, XV (Feb. 1848), 37.

[41] *ScR*, XII (Jan. 1862), 128; Atticus [William Maccall], *Critic*, Dec. 22, 1860, p. 779.

foodful." Even though Carlyle was "the greatest moral teacher of the age" to J. H. Buckley, some late Victorians thought Emerson to be even greater. One declared that "there is no thinker of our day who, for sentences that have the ring of oracles, can quite compare with Emerson." "He has the art of saying things with a tone of authority quite unknown to Carlyle, who casts his thunderbolt, but never forgets that he is casting it at some unhappy mortal whom he intends to slay." And the *Saturday Review* averred that the American was "a more deadly enemy to formulas than CARLYLE, because a profounder one. . . . CARLYLE taught men to mock at formulas, EMERSON to rise above them. CARLYLE's prophesyings . . . became at last a string of opposition formulas." "EMERSON leaves one with the hopefulness of man's estate." [42] Carlyle's opposition formulas and Emerson's hopes were illustrated, suggested British critics, in two of their books— *Heroes and Hero Worship* and *Representative Men*.

Carlyle had first presented his heroes in a series of lectures in 1841, while Emerson's appeared (also as lectures) four years later. By the end of the century British periodicals judged *Representative Men* to be Emerson's best contribution, followed closely by *English Traits* and belatedly by *The Conduct of Life*. [43] Although several of the

---

[42] Ward, *TBar*, LXXII, 241, 244; Buckley, *The Victorian Temper* (Cambridge, Mass., 1951), p. 38 (Harrold and Templeman, p. xlvi, affirm this judgment); *Sp*, May 6, 1882, pp. 591, 590; *SatR*, May 6, 1882, p. 554.

[43] Lewin said that *"The Conduct of Life* is, probably, the high-water mark of Emerson's literary achievement, and is certainly his most finished and, excepting *Representative Men,* his most systematic work." Hutton observed that *"Representative Men,* and the critical passages which abound in . . . *Conduct of Life* and *English Traits,* seem to us his best literary achievements." Commenting on *Traits,* Arnold declared that the work lacked the principal element of all good criticism—"the disinterested quality"—but a reviewer on the *Academy* said that "the English nation was never passed through so understanding and complete an analysis . . . as by this casual visitor to our shores," a judgment substantiated by *TLS.* Other critics also praised the book. *English Traits* was better than Taine's chapters on the same subject, said the *Athenaeum,* and Prothero wrote that it gave "a generous appreciation of the national character." Underwood argued that "considering its brevity," *Traits* "is perhaps the most weighty and best-considered estimate of the country in existence," and Francis Espinasse said that it was "of all Emerson's books the most interesting to English readers" (Lewin, *Ac,* Sept. 8, 1888, p. 149; [Hutton], *Sp,* Feb. 2, 1884, p. 156; Arnold, *MM,* L, 7; *AcLit,* March 21, 1903, p. 281; *TLS,* May 29, 1903, p. 166; *Ath,* March 8, 1884, p. 306; *QR,* CLXVI [Jan. 1888], 151; Francis H. Underwood, *Good Words,* XXVIII [Dec. 1887], 811; [Francis Espinasse], *Bookman,* II [July 1892], 108).

biographers gave elaborate précis of the *First* and *Second Series,* critics failed to enter them in the sweepstakes, just as they ignored *Society and Solitude* and *Letters and Social Aims.* F. H. Underwood wrote that *Representative Men* was "probably the most popular of his works," and Saintsbury contended that it was the "best known of all his books," an observation echoed by an anonymous critic on the *Literary World* and by C. A. Ward, who added that in the book Emerson "perhaps has not built up much, but he has commented much, felicitously, and sometimes profoundly." The volume was "considered to be," observed the *Graphic,* "the most vigorous and intelligible of his writings." It was, declared the *Westminster,* "an English classic," which the editor and biographer, Clement Shorter, maintained should have been included among Lord Acton's hundred best books. Jean McIlwraith devoted an essay to Emerson's choice of men. Although disagreeing on occasion with that choice, she concluded that "his original manner of treating these great men introduces them in a new light, and they gain greatly in human interest viewed through the spectacles of the New England seer." Turnbull also commented on the originality of the *Men,* but he did hear an echo: the work was "as powerfully original, as full of profound thought, as replete with ingenious metaphors and brilliant epigrams as the famous 'Lectures on Heroes.' " [44]

While other critics, especially the earlier, made a good deal more of the similarities between *Heroes* and *Men* than did Turnbull,[45] nearly all of them agreed that the works were meant to furnish models for precept and imitation. Commenting on these models, Nichol, echoed by an anonymous critic, argued that Emerson regarded his men "as inspired mouthpieces of universal or national ideas rather than as controlling forces. Their mission is not so much to regulate our action as to 'fortify our hopes.'. . . Their examples . . . are perpetual encouragements. . . . It is obvious that this view is in essential antagonism to Mr. Carlyle's. His heroes are

[44] Underwood, *Good Words,* XXVIII, 811; George Saintsbury, *Ac,* May 6, 1882, p. 320; *LitW,* May 5, 1882, p. 285; Ward, *TBar,* LXXII, 244; *Graphic,* Sept. 12, 1874, p. 261; *WR,* CLXII (Sept. 1904) , 352; Shorter, *Pall Mall Magazine,* XXXVI (July 1905) , 10; Jean McIlwraith, *CanM,* I (Oct. 1893) , 691; Turnbull, *NMM,* CXXII, 9.

[45] See pp. 32–33.

men with divine mandates, which they have . . . to impress and enforce upon their fellows." Emerson "loves an easy greatness which has its grace by nature, and 'lives in a sphere of thought which others get at with difficulty.' To force . . . he prefers beauty, rounded outline, and mental grasp." Foote pointed out that Emerson "shared Carlyle's view of the importance of great men," but whereas the Scotsman believed that the world should be governed by "heroes," "Emerson believed that the less government . . . the better. Carlyle believed in force. Emerson believed in influence." To Carlyle, a great man "was any man he chose to call so." Emerson defined a great man as one "who inhabits a higher sphere of thought, into which other men rise with labor and difficulty." The American's "view of great men was in every respect sounder than Carlyle's." In a less balanced judgment than Nichol's or Foote's, Edward Dowden declared that Emerson "loves [light] better than warmth, and [he] lacks the strong humanity of Carlyle. His heroes do not concentrate and contain the divine force, they represent qualities; therefore they do not claim our worship or obedience. . . . Or we obey and worship, but then go onward, since it is not permitted us to forfeit the indefeasible freedom of our advance." [46]

VII

These words—grace, light, freedom; warmth, force, obedience— form a contrapuntal theme that runs through periodical comment on the Emerson-Carlyle relationship, a theme brought into sharp focus when, in 1883, Professor Norton published *The Correspondence of Thomas Carlyle and Ralph Waldo Emerson.* For the first time the personalities of the two writers were placed in close juxtaposition, and it was mainly upon their personalities that the Victorian age based its final estimate of the American and Scotsman. Only a few reviewers complained that the letters failed as self-portraits of the correspondents. The volumes added little to that which "was not known before" about the writers, said one. The work "has fallen

[46] *NBrB,* XLVII, 353; Foote, *Freethinker,* May 31, 1903, pp. 237, 238; Dowden, *ContR,* XXX (July 1877), 314.

very dead to us." There is little "real answering of one mind to the other," a second grouched. Emerson and Carlyle "live in such different planes that neither really helps the other at all with the thoughts with which he is struggling. . . . This correspondence is not so much a correspondence in any true intellectual sense as a deliberate exchange of monologues." [47]

On the other hand, many critics praised the book, some effusively. The sensible G. S. Venables moderately wrote that "the correspondence on both sides is remarkable for its good taste and for its grateful courtesy," an opinion repeated by Armstrong: Carlyle and Emerson tacitly avoided questions on which they would be in essential disagreement. The volumes, said Stephen, were "charming." [48] A less moderate and more excitable commentator asserted that "with opinions wide as the poles asunder on most of the great questions that stir the hearts . . . ; separated from each other . . . by an eternal 'cliff of difference'; there nevertheless subsisted between them a deep-seated, firm, and most tender affection, which never knew 'shadow of turning.'" The book was "the record of one of the most beautiful friendships furnished by the annals of literature," wrote another excited critic. "We doubt," declared a writer for the *Congregationalist,* after reading *The Correspondence,* "whether either of the men will appear anywhere in character more attractive, or give a more correct revelation of himself, or become to us more admirable and lovable because of this more intimate knowledge of them." [49]

Certain critics seemed to be attempting to surpass all the rest in hymns of praise. "These letters," sang the poetaster Richard Herne Shepherd, form "a history of one of the most beautiful and remarkable friendships hitherto recorded in literary annals." The work, effused James E. Cabot, "is a beautiful supplement and key to the lives and writings of its authors; a book not to be skimmed, but read again and again." The *Athenaeum* lovingly affirmed, "These two volumes shed a beautiful light upon a friendship as warm as it is

---

[47] *SatR,* March 24, 1883, p. 368; *Sp,* March 24, 1883, p. 386.

[48] Venables, *FR,* XLII (Nov. 1884) , 598; *ModR,* IV, 321; Stephen, *NatRev,* XXXVI, 884.

[49] Ireland, *Ac,* April 7, 1883, p. 231; *WR,* CXXVIII (Nov. 1887) , 986; *Cst,* XII (April 1883) , 332.

singular. It is doubtful if the history of literary friendships presents any instance comparable with this 'sacred covenant'... between thinkers ... representing contrary tendencies." The *British Quarterly Review* asserted that "the work furnishes a series of notes on the writings of both men ... such as is hardly to be found in any other case, unless it be in that of Goethe and Schiller." There was no doubt at all in Ireland's mind as to which correspondence was the greater: the "unfailing sincerity" and "absence of the merely literary or philosophic tone" gave the letters "higher value than the Goethe-Schiller correspondence, with which alone they can be compared." Writing in the *Academy* a year earlier, Ireland had been even more extravagant: "For living reality and face-to-face truthful outspokenness, these letters stand quite by themselves. An extensively read friend asserts that he has met with nothing to match them in any European literature." Britton was also overcome by these letters wherein "we seem to catch the very ring of the human voice, the very sparkle and moisture of the eyes, so clear and calm in the one, so deep and mournful in the other." [50]

In an age noted for inflated prose, these comments are outstanding in their flowery exaggeration. Certainly the rather pedestrian correspondence could not have been the sole reason for them. Some of the encomium was due, no doubt, to the universal custom of speaking well of the dead. Some of it resulted from a sense of loss at the passing of one of the last of the Eminent Victorians. "By the early eighties," writes C. F. Harrold, "there had been a change in the intellectual climate; the public could no longer be held in raptures by a sermon, whether by a clergyman or by Ruskin. It no longer placed so much faith in great personalities, or in their dogmas: the doctrines of Carlyle, Newman, Arnold, and Ruskin began to lose their hold on the public mind, which now wished to be entertained or given a veneer of culture rather than to be challenged by a moral ideal." Yet when J. A. Froude insisted that one of their gods had feet of clay, they quickly protested and attempted to counterbalance the picture which he had revealed in the *Reminiscences* and *Thomas Carlyle: A History of the First Forty Years of His Life, 1795–1835*

[50] Shepherd, *GentM*, CCLIV (April 1883), 415; [Cabot], *WR*, CXIX (April 1883), 452; *Ath*, March 17, 1883, p. 335; *BQR*, LXXVII (April 1883), 481; Alexander Ireland, *Ath*, Nov. 8, 1884, p. 593; Ireland, *Ac*, April 7, 1883, p. 232; Britton, *Progress*, I, 281.

and *A History of His Life in London, 1834–1881.* Throughout Carlyle's career, critics were, like Froude, unable to treat the Scotsman coolly and dispassionately. Several characterized him as magnanimous and genial, while others saw in him a "savage souredness and raw rabid rage," his works marred by "brutalities" and "howling effeminacies." [51] Froude, according to the critics, had wrongly exaggerated the raw edge. After reading the first two volumes of *Thomas Carlyle,* Professor Norton wrote, "I have never read a book that gave me more pain, or that seemed to me more artfully malignant." "Carlyle's letters will, I hope, do something to set right public opinion concerning him, which the questionable Froude has had such success in misleading and perverting." [52]

Norton's hopes were realized, if one is to believe the reviewers. "Carlyle has been foolishly decried of late," wrote Cabot, and the letters helped prove that he was not altogether bad. The *Congregationalist* was "prepared to give a special welcome to anything that would justify us in returning to something like our old estimate of Carlyle. . . . Mr. Norton has succeeded . . . in showing that there was a different side to Carlyle from that to which prominence has been given in the 'Reminiscences.' " The letters revealed that if the Carlyle of the *Reminiscences* "was acrid and unpleasant" his early struggle "against poverty" was enough to make him so. In the biography Froude had pictured Carlyle as "a bitter cynic, whose tendency [is] to sneer even at those with whom he is on terms of friendship." But in *The Correspondence,* "we get closest to the true heart of the man, and come to understand what a fund of real tenderness and affection lies hidden under the rough exterior of the man." *Vanity Fair* shared these views, as did the *Fortnightly.*[53]

Other journals reviewed *The Correspondence* without mention-

---

[51] Harrold and Templeman, p. lxxv; Walker, pp. 33 ff.; [George Gilfillan], *Pm,* I (July 1850), 55; Robert Buchanan, *Bwy,* n.s. II (May 1869), 226.

[52] Waldo H. Dunn, *Froude & Carlyle* (London, 1930), pp. 78, 80. Norton's volumes were not the only work dealing with the Emerson-Carlyle relationship that showed Carlyle's more genial side: see Moncure D. Conway, *Emerson at Home and Abroad* (Boston, 1882), pp. 77, 79, 123, 233, 355; Alexander Ireland, *In Memoriam, Ralph Waldo Emerson* (London, 1882), pp. 7–9, 28, 69, 71, 115; James E. Cabot, *A Memoir of Ralph Waldo Emerson* (Boston, 1887), I, 193–96 *passim,* 241–43 *passim;* II, 530–31.

[53] *WR,* CXIX (April 1883), 453; *Cst,* XII (April 1883), 325, 326, 327, 329, 330; *Vanity Fair,* April 28, 1883, p. 223; Venables, *FR,* XLII, 596.

ing either *Thomas Carlyle* or the *Reminiscences,* and, except for the *Saturday Review,* had high praise for Carlyle's part in it. The *Review* sarcastically called the letters a continuation of Carlyle's "Lamentations," but a more enthusiastic critic wrote that "Carlyle's share in the correspondence . . . is characteristic of what was most humane and magnanimous in him." Another said that "Carlyle's finest moods are here represented, . . . his kindliness, . . . his steadfastness under personal trials." "Nowhere in all literature," asserted Ireland, "can one find words more tender or vivid" than in "Carlyle's expressions of affections." Here we find, continued this critic, "passages of tenderness, of pathos, of unstinted regard . . . , of grim struggles." Said still another, "Carlyle's manner and temper" are displayed "at their best." [54]

In their flattering comments, British critics gave much of the credit for the more pleasant side of Carlyle's character to Emerson. Although several early critics denied that the American was "a sort of echo of" Carlyle, they had generally assumed the Carlyle-Emerson relationship to be one-sided, that Emerson was Carlyle's "protégé." [55] To these critics, influences flowed in one direction only: from Europe to America. This view was not entirely discarded by 1900, but some late Victorians did admit in their comments on Carlyle and Emerson that an American could impress a European. During the early years, wrote Venables, whose essays on social problems were models of style and thought, the relationship had been "inspired on one side by admiring enthusiasm, and on Carlyle's part by a feeling of gratitude to the sympathetic student who had, as he thought, been the first to understand him. . . . This early devotion of the disciple to his master lapsed gracefully into a more equal relation." Cabot maintained that the "friendship was not one-sided: both were givers and both receivers." Reviewing Ireland's *In Memoriam,* a critic observed that many Victorians thought they saw in Emerson an American Carlyle, but Ireland showed "in how many respects the two were the antipodes of each other, though clearly perceiving in

---

[54] *SatR,* March 24, 1883, p. 367; *ModR,* IV, 320; *Ath,* March 17, 1883, p. 336; Ireland, *Ac,* April 7, 1883, pp. 231, 232; Venables, *FR,* XLII, 596.

[55] [William Henry Smith], *Blackwood's,* LXII (Dec. 1847), 648; *MR,* n.s. III (Oct. 1841), 275.

each other the elements of true greatness." Indeed, wrote Armstrong in 1883, Carlyle owed much of "his first assured successes, to the zeal of his devoted admirer," an opinion shared by *Leisure Hour*.[56]

One of the great factors in helping critics to realize Carlyle's debt to Emerson was *The Correspondence*. "Without reference to the letters of Carlyle it is impossible," stated Ireland, "to realize the value [Carlyle] ... set upon Emerson's friendship." The letters should have been published much sooner, said the *British Quarterly Review*. "It is surprising to see in ... [them] how the smoother, softer, more accessible and insinuating genius of Emerson tends to transform the harsher, gloomier ... nature of Carlyle." When Carlyle's letters complained "of the tiresomeness and tyranny of his hopeless, self-imposed task on the history of Frederick the Great," said Shepherd, Emerson condoled with him. In the correspondence, said Armstrong, we see Carlyle coming "out of the gloom and the shadows into the light of the cheerful day to talk with his friend." Emerson brought the dour Scotsman the "sunshine of hope and enthusiasm." Summarizing this opinion is Britton's comment that "critics have confronted Mr. Froude's volumes with those of Professor Norton, very much to the disfavor of the former, asking how it is that Mr. Froude's Carlyle is such a different man from the Carlyle of the Emerson correspondence." Carlyle answered the question, said Britton, when he wrote, "I admit that you [Emerson] were like an angel to me ... and absorbed in the beautifulest manner all thunderclouds into the depths of your immeasurable aether." [57]

Carlyle, implied the reviews, came increasingly to need this angel. He "poured out his heart" to Emerson, asserted the *Athenaeum*. The Scotsman "repeats again and again," declared Venables, "that Emerson's utterances are to him the most *human* which he has known." In his relations to Emerson he was, said Cabot, "toned into unwonted tenderness." Said Britton, he was "never so lovable as in some of ... [the] letters; probably because the invincible sweetness

---

[56] Venables, *FR*, XLII, 597, 596; Townsend Scudder, *The Lonely Wayfaring Man* (London, 1936), p. 59; *WR*, CXIX (April 1883), 457; *BQR*, LXXVII (Jan. 1883), 190; *ModR*, IV, 328; *LeisH*, XXXIV (April 1885), 288.

[57] Ireland, *Ath*, Nov. 8, 1884, p. 592; *BQR*, LXXVII (April 1883), 480; Shepherd, *GentM*, CCLIV, 425; *ModR*, IV, 320, 319; Britton, *Progress*, I, 278.

of Emerson's nature wrung from him something like a genuine, unselfish, ungrudging love." [58] Carlyle loved Emerson above all except his own kin, according to Ireland, even more than he loved Sterling. This love "was immeasurably heightened by his consciousness of Emerson's spiritual insight, his intellectual loftiness, his unconquerable independence of thought." "Carlyle was like a lover," continued this critic in singularly inappropriate imagery, "tormented by the seeming lofty indifference of the proud beauty." Emerson "could more easily have dispensed with *his* love and friendship than Carlyle could have dispensed with the affection and sympathy of Emerson." [59]

The secret of Emerson's hold over Carlyle, according to these critics, was that he "understood his friend well, his shortcomings as well as his strength," and he "learnt to separate . . . the true genius of Carlyle, and the qualities for which he had always loved and reverenced him, from the alloy of Carlylese prejudices, animosities, and wilful extravagances. . . . Carlyle might well be grateful for one who could never look at him and his work with any eyes but those of affectionate admiration." And the Scotsman was grateful: "Whatever it might be on other subjects, Carlyle's manner when he spoke of Emerson was gentle and affectionate." Attempting to reveal the affection between the two men, the *Academy* quoted an anecdote from Moncure D. Conway. Before going to America in 1880, the expatriate dropped by to see Carlyle, then "feeble and depressed" but "still alive in his heart. He whispered to Mr. Conway: 'Give my love to Emerson.'" Sometime later when Conway delivered the message, Emerson's memory "was gone; but the one name that required no suggestion was that of Carlyle . . . [and] 'his face beamed with the old intelligence.'" [60]

More knowledgeable critics than the foregoing were aware that toward the end of Emerson's and Carlyle's lives, their friendship cooled. Contrary to opinions that they will "always be thought of

---

[58] *Ath*, March 17, 1883, p. 335; Venables, *FR*, XLII, 596; *WR*, CXIX (April 1883), 455; Britton, *Progress*, I, 279.

[59] *Ac*, April 7, 1883, pp. 232, 233.

[60] *WR*, CXIX (April 1883), 455; *ModR*, IV, 332; *TLS*, May 29, 1903, p. 166; Ireland, *Ac*, April 7, 1883, p. 232.

together henceforth as inseparably united in the bonds of a true and beautiful friendship" or that the friendship "continued through life," a sharp critic noted that in Cabot's *Memoir,* one "can trace in the mind of the American philosopher the . . . process of disenchantment with Carlyle." Walter Lewin also pointed out that dissension had come between Emerson and Carlyle, and he regretted that Cabot and Norton had not been more "explicit" as to why.[61]

One reason for the break between the two writers was doubtless their divergent views on slavery, which Carlyle "was not known to disapprove." Although Britton maintained that Emerson's "sweetness of temper prevented the constraint [imposed by slavery] from ever degenerating into a coolness," the *Athenaeum* wrote that it was "a sore trial" for Emerson to read Carlyle's comments on the subject. Had the American been in England during the war, said the *Saturday Review,* "they would almost certainly have quarrelled, owing to Mr. Carlyle's decided opinion about the proper treatment of 'Sambo.' " Armstrong speculated that Carlyle's *"The Occasional Discourse on the Nigger Question,* and *The American Iliad in a Nutshell,* must have been difficult for [Emerson] . . . to forgive." At the time that "Carlyle was shrieking out an insolent lie, putting the American Iliad in a nutshell," asserted Robert Buchanan, "and instructing many little voices to echo him for echoing sake, Emerson could calmly look at the American conflict, and say—'Here, friends, we are proving ourselves great.' " [62]

According to other critics, the breach between Carlyle and Emerson went back further than the war. The second visit, suggested Venables, "produced some disillusion" between the two. Mrs. Carlyle had never held Emerson's "genius" in high esteem, Venables said, and by 1847 Carlyle was expressing a like opinion. "We had commenced talking with him here," wrote Carlyle, "but found he did not give us much to chew cud on—found in fact that he came with the rake rather than the shovel." "He is a pure, highminded man, but I think his talent is not quite so high as I had anticipated."

---

[61] *ModR,* IV, 340; *Truth,* Nov. 10, 1887, p. 780; Lewin, *Ac,* Oct. 22, 1887, p. 262. Wheeler, *Progress,* I, 119, expressed an opinion similar to Armstrong's.

[62] Venables, *FR,* XLII, 599; Britton, *Progress,* I, 281; *Ath,* March 17, 1883, p. 335; *SatR,* March 24, 1883, p. 367; *ModR,* IV, 321; Buchanan, *Bwy,* n.s. II, 226.

Another commented that when Emerson left the Carlyles' "it was soon plain that he had sore feelings from [the] ... intercourse," a view shared by Lewin. Francis Espinasse suggested a reason that the "second meeting had not been quite so satisfactory as their first one. ... To say nothing of other differences, Carlyle, still full of Cromwell, resented with needless heat Emerson's refusal to fall down and worship the Puritan hero. There was just a trace of irritation, the only one which I ever perceived in Emerson. ... 'Carlyle's heart is as large as the world, but he is growing morbid.' " [63]

Still another critic traced "the root of divergence" between Emerson and Carlyle back to the first two letters, which showed "Emerson's world ... [to be] a mad world to Carlyle." The whole correspondence, said the critic, revealed two men of completely "contrary tendencies." [64] Many other commentators pointed to these tendencies. Emerson was, they said, "a most gentle yet self-reliant and hospitable-minded man, glad to receive as quick to bestow." His was "a singularly happy, tranquil disposition." He was "patient, enduring, suave," "benignant and gentle," serene, tolerant, "cheerful and hopeful." [65] Carlyle was the antithesis: "gey ill to live with." He was "intense," "gloomy and dyspeptic," "impatient, domineering, aggressive," "arrogant and bitter," "the polemic, the sophist, the scorner." [66] One was "at bottom an aristocrat ... of refined culture," wrote the *Spectator*, the other "at bottom a sans-culotte, with a huge contempt for refined culture." One was "all ice," the other "all fire." One was "ever haunted by great and sinister images"; "the other is filled with a cheerful, reverent faith." Carlyle was, wrote Henry James, Sr., an "egregiously secular person," "a gross human reality,

---

[63] Venables, *FR*, XLII, 599; P. L[andreth], *Blackwood's*, CLV (April 1894), 485; Lewin, *Ac*, Oct. 22, 1887, p. 262; *Bookman*, II, 108.

[64] *Ath*, March 17, 1883, p. 335.

[65] *BQR*, LXXVII (Jan. 1883), 190; Arthur Rickett, *Speaker*, June 27, 1903, p. 292; *QR*, CLXVI (Jan. 1888), 156; *Sp*, May 6, 1882, p. 590; Ireland, *Ac*, April 7, 1883, p. 232. Using Ireland's *Ralph Waldo Emerson*, Japp, *GentM*, CCLIII, 628, repeats many of these thoughts.

[66] Wheeler, *Progress*, I, 119; *BQR*, LXXVII (April 1883), 481; C. E. Tyrer, *ManQ*, III (April 1884), 127; *QR*, CLXVI (Jan. 1888), 156; *Sp*, May 6, 1882, p. 590; Walter Lewin, *Ac*, June 22, 1889, p. 423. Lewin quotes A. Bronson Alcott, *Ralph Waldo Emerson: Philosopher and Seer* (London, 1889), pp. 26–27. Japp, *GentM*, CCLIII, 628, again borrowing from Ireland, sets forth much the same opinion.

suggesting . . . nothing to your devout imagination, but appealing with . . . vivacity to your sensuous wonder and love of fun." "Emerson, on the other hand," was "an eminently sacred person," "a tender, divine personality, making a most modest appeal to your senses, but brimful of significance to your imagination." Max Müller "found something in Emerson which was not to be found in Carlyle, particularly his loving heart, his tolerant spirit, his comprehensive sympathy with all that was or was meant to be good and true, even though to his own mind it was neither the one nor the other." In brief, one was a member—to use Mark Twain's celebrated phrase—of "the damned human race"; the other had risen above it.[67] It was this membership more than any other factor that moved Victorian critics to place Carlyle higher among world figures than Emerson.

In treating the style, philosophy, and religion of the American and Scotsman, most British critics had peevishly declared that both were a good deal less than perfect and reluctantly indicated their preference for Carlyle's views. Many of the same critics, on the other hand, quickly and easily recognized Emerson's political views as superior. Both men were, thought the critics, eminent teachers; yet there is throughout the period abundant evidence that Victorian critics were more interested in the men than in their message. This preoccupation with personality led critics, when they were discussing Emerson and Carlyle, almost always to devote more space to the Scotsman than to the American. Their interest is not hard to understand, especially toward the end of the period. Late Victorians had come to look upon Emerson as the Sage of Concord—calm, serene, aloof—but when they attempted to find the human being behind the Sage, he was somehow always missing. "Fed on nectar and ambrosia from the tables of the gods," Emerson makes one imagine, wrote Britton,

---

[67] *Sp*, March 24, 1883, p. 386; Seaton, *NatRev*, III, 776; Turnbull, *NMM*, CXXII, 21; *T. P.'s*, Jan. 6, 1905, p. 12; Max Müller, *Cos*, VI (May 1897), 329; Henry Nash Smith, "Mark Twain," in Miller, II, 57. W. L. Courtney, *FR*, XLIV (Sept. 1885), 323, gave a novel explanation of the reason for the difference in the American's and the Scotsman's vision of life: "Emerson, with his lecturing instincts, . . . becomes naturally optimistic, and believes in the evolution of the better. Carlyle, with his solitude, . . . is more of the pessimist." "Carlyle, if he had lectured oftener, might have lightened some of the darker elements of his creed."

"that some cool ichor must have replaced in his veins our seething human blood with its fervors and torpors." [68] Critics loved and admired the American, but he escaped them: he remained somewhere in the middle distance.

Not so Carlyle: he was always front and center. Critics could touch this highstrung, arrogant, aggressive, bitter man. And they could be touched by him, especially by his humor, a rowdy, boisterous, wry, humanizing humor that was much different from Emerson's. After the American's visit to Craigenputtock, Carlyle wrote that his friend was "full of lively anecdote, and with a streaming humour, which floated everything he looked upon." Several other critics also noted this humor. Emerson, said Lewin, inherited the "brightness of humour" from his father, and Hutton wrote that both Emerson and Carlyle "were in their way humourists." [69] But a third flatly contended that "the defect of humour in Emerson is notable." Others noted that "he is not quick in humour," that his "spirit" was "less rich in . . . humour" than Carlyle's, that "his eloquence had none of the humour which permeates and enlivens the mysticism of *Sartor Resartus.*" The *Athenaeum* suggested that in the famous conversation at Stonehenge, Carlyle "amused himself [at Emerson's expense] with his drastic humour and frolicsome make-believe." [70]

Carlyle's sense of comedy was doubtless beyond Emerson's ken. Stung by the "outbreaks of Carlyle's humour upon his lecturing tour," the American retaliated with a thrust of his own: Did not "Carlyle's originality often lie in his rhetoric, rather than in his ideas?" However annoying, such cold, detached irony was far removed from the sort of "rich humour" exhibited by the Scotsman. This humor, said Nichol, redeemed the "incompleteness" of his style, while the *British Quarterly Review* found "his humour" to be his "medium of unity." Another journal praised Carlyle's "capacity for laughter" and then quoted Margaret Fuller, who gave perhaps the best indication of the value Victorian critics set upon this capacity in their comparison of the American and Scotsman. "Carlyle is worth a

[68] *Progress*, I, 279.

[69] *LeisH*, XXXIV (April 1885) , 288; Lewin, *Ac*, Oct. 22, 1887, p. 261; *Sp*, May 6, 1882, p. 590.

[70] *BQR*, LXXVII (April 1883) , 481; Stewart, *Belford's*, I, 226; Japp, *GentM*, CCLIII, 628; Venables, *FR*, XLII, 597; *Ath*, Sept. 6, 1856, p. 1111.

thousand of you . . . ,'' she wrote Emerson; "he is not ashamed to laugh, when he is amused, but goes on in a cordial human fashion." [71]

According to the British, Carlyle shared the lot of common humanity in yet another way denied Emerson. An impoverished childhood, a difficult marriage, prolonged physical illness—all combined to make his life one of "grim struggles." [72] Emerson had not been subjected to such humanizing misery. Lewin and Edward Waldo Emerson noted the poverty of Emerson's childhood, but the Englishman admitted in a well-turned phrase that "Emerson's faith was that the drift of all things is goodward," and Ireland commented on the American's "long and serene life." A host of Victorians agreed with the editor. Armstrong observed that Emerson's life was "singularly bright, harmonious, and altogether sweet and wholesome," and C. E. Tyrer wrote that "the calamities of life hardly ruffled the clear current of his being." He "led 'a life . . . of nearly untroubled happiness,'" said Egan Mew; in his pages, Wheeler wrote felicitously, "serenity and sunshine dwell." "There is not one jarring note," maintained Story, "not one false quantity, to break the sweet harmony of his eighty years." [73] Somehow, these critics felt, Emerson was a lesser human being for this sweet harmony. Arnold believed that Emerson's "holding fast to happiness and hope" made his work "more important than Carlyle's," but Nichol wrote that "Mr. Emerson seems to have bought his experience cheaply. . . . His 'Threnody' and 'Dirge' are indications of his having passed through the 'valley of the shadow,' but he has encountered no Apollyons, and assumes

---

[71] *Blackwood's,* CLV, 485; *Ath,* March 17, 1883, p. 336; *NBrR,* XLVII, 350; *BQR,* LXXVII (April 1883), 481; *Bentley's,* XL (Oct. 1856), 540. See *Memoirs of Margaret Fuller Ossoli* (Boston, 1852), II, 185. Other critics commented indirectly on Emerson's lack of humor when they pointed to his aloof manner, his lack of "warm-blooded intensity" (*Ac,* Jan. 24, 1903, p. 83; *GT,* XXXIX [June 1903], 121; Rickett, *Speaker,* June 27, 1903, p. 292; Thomas Bradfield, *PMQR,* n.s. XVII [April 1895], 254; see Tyrer, *ManQ,* III, 105, who suggested that Emerson had "little of that humour . . . of Lowell and Holmes").

[72] *WR,* CXIX (April 1883), 455; Ireland, *Ac,* April 7, 1883, p. 232.

[73] Lewin, *Ac,* Oct. 22, 1887, p. 261; E. W. Emerson, "Ralph Waldo Emerson," *Bookman,* XXIV (June 1903), 92; Lewin, *Ac,* Aug. 16, 1884, p. 102; Ireland, *Ath,* Jan. 13, 1883, p. 53; *ModR,* IV, 334; Tyrer, *ManQ,* III, 127; Mew, *Lit,* Sept. 21, 1901, p. 272; Wheeler, *Progress,* I, 118; Story, *NCRev,* IV, 197. *AnnualR,* 1887, p. 73, also noted that Emerson's life was not easy.

himself in the Celestial City without having crossed the dark river." [74] Carlyle—"the 'sick giant' of the old world" [75]—had encountered Apollyon and had crossed the dark river.

Perhaps the most important question posed in *The American Writer and the European Tradition* is, "What . . . makes an American author peculiarly American?" [76] A corollary question might well be, Why have European critics so often denied greatness to American writers? Part of the answer to both questions lies in Nichol's comment on Emerson: the American writer has bought his experience too cheaply: he has not crossed the dark river. His land and his civilization are too young, too brash, too undeveloped; he is too gay, too ebullient, too naïve. The more cosmopolitan of nineteenth-century American writers sensed the thinness of American civilization and of the writers it was producing. Washington Irving wrote, for example, "I longed . . . to wander over the scenes of renowned achievement—to tread . . . in the footsteps of antiquity—to loiter about the ruined castle—to meditate on the falling tower—to escape, in short, from the . . . commonplace realities of the present, and lose myself among the shadowy grandeurs of the past." [77] Henry James, the most famous Anglophile of them all, said that "one might enumerate the items of high civilization, as it exists in other countries, which are absent from the texture of American life, until it should become a wonder to know what was left." [78]

James enumerated some thirty-three of these items, including "no sovereign," "no church," and "no literature," [79] but he left out the most important one: one which he himself and Carlyle possessed in great degree and one which Emerson lacked almost completely: the tragic vision, a profound sense of the evil in life. Saintsbury was reaching for the difference between the two cultures and the products of those cultures when he wrote, "Emerson may be said to have been an essentially irreligious person, just as Carlyle was an essentially religious one. A cheerful process of exploration within his own soul, and a confidence in its power of comprehending the universe,

---

[74] Arnold, *MM*, L, 11; *NBrR*, XLVII, 350.   [75] Britton, *Progress*, I, 279.

[76] Denny and Gilman, p. v.

[77] Quoted by Stanley T. Williams, "Cosmopolitanism in American Literature before 1880," in Denny and Gilman, p. 57.

[78] *Ibid.*, p. 46.   [79] *Ibid.*, p. 47.

was the note of the one; a sense of the vast and terrible unknown surrounding the *ich,* and of a presence pervading the unknown, was the note of the other." [80] Carlyle himself revealed the chasm between the two. Taking Emerson to a slum in London, he turned to him and "with deep intensity" inquired, " 'Do you believe in the devil now?' " [81] It was the vision, the presence, and the devil that weighed heavily in Carlyle's favor when Victorian critics came to make their final estimates of the man from sunny Concord and the one from the dark moors of Ecclefechan and Craigenputtock.

Four of these critics tried with varying degrees of success to put this final estimate into a nutshell. "Carlyle has the rude energy of one battling with things evil," wrote Wheeler, "Emerson the calm serenity of one who sees the soul of goodness shining through them. Emerson has more of light and less of lightning. His stream is broad, and placid; Carlyle's, foaming, rushing in narrower bounds. Carlyle had the stronger grip of real life." Turnbull judged that "probably Carlyle is the more colossal figure of the two." He is the "Jupiter," Emerson is the "Apollo." "Emerson is ever soft, gentle, impersonal, shedding abroad the freshness of perpetual youth.... Carlyle is rugged, dyspeptical, clamourous.... Carlyle may more readily carry conviction with him; but he lacks the fascination, and somewhat of the inspiration to boot, of the great New Englander." W. L. Courtney used fewer words but arrived at, perhaps, a more valid conclusion: Carlyle overflowed "with terrible beauty, ... and so he is the greater, the deeper, the more authoritative man, even though he is not the happier and the more sun-like." Reviewing the letters, the *Spectator* said much the same thing, but said it better: "Emerson's nature, on the whole, comes out of this correspondence the more disinterested, saner, and wiser, though not the stronger and grander of the two." [82] This evaluation by the *Spectator* states fairly the final estimate of the two writers in nineteenth-century periodicals and, possibly, the judgment of posterity. It will always be the judgment, other factors being equal, when, as with Emerson and Carlyle, an eminently good man is placed beside an eminently human one.

[80] *Ac,* May 6, 1882, p. 320.   [81] Quoted by Buckley, p. 37.

[82] Wheeler, *Progress,* I, 119; Turnbull, *NMM,* CXXII, 23; Courtney, *Time,* **XIV** (June 1886) , 654; *Sp,* March 24, 1883, p. 387.

⊶ VII ⊷

The Secret

IN 1861 Matthew Arnold maintained, writes Geoffrey Tillotson, "that 'the main effort [of the intellect of the Continent], for now many years, has been a *critical* effort; the endeavour, in all branches of knowledge—theology, philosophy, history, art, science—to see the object as in itself it really is.' " Arnold, Tillotson goes on, "noted the laggardliness of English writers who continued to exhibit that absolute and insular thing, a 'strong tendency . . . to bring to the consideration of their object some individual fancy.' " [1] Throughout the century Emerson had suffered from this provinciality; yet the critics are not wholly to blame. Emerson's own practical criticism was highly subjective, and he himself had declared that books were only for the scholar's idle times, not to be studied and analyzed but used as a means of inspiration. Aside from Emerson's not so shining example, however, there is another and more urgent reason why British critics were not successful in bringing Emerson under critical control: it was the object itself.

Some authors, observes Tillotson, "make one sort of demand only" and can be criticized "whole." "But the writings of many authors are various enough within themselves to outwit any single critic. There are no critics equal, singly, to giving them criticism that has a uniform authority." [2] Emerson is such an author. Henry James, Sr., called him "a man without a handle," while the New York correspondent for the *Times Literary Supplement* expressed something of this opinion in writing, "The beauty in Emerson's thought,

[1] *Criticism and the Nineteenth Century* (London, 1951), p. 92.
[2] P. 38.

like that in his life, does not lend itself readily to analysis." Herman Grimm was reaching for the same point when he quoted "with something like approval, the judgment of an America journalist that 'only Shakespeare can be named with Emerson,' " and C. A. Ward stated that "to treat Emerson as Emerson, such is the rarity of the man, . . . would be like treating America, or immensity, or eternity, or any other subject that has practically neither beginning nor end." [3]

In the eighteen forties this immensity had touched the raw nerves of a people made jittery by religious, political, and social upheaval; they were more interested in exterminating Emerson than in understanding him. Church journals were especially vehement. They fumed at Emerson's unorthodox religious views; they declared that his philosophical speculations contaminated all of life. Lay journals were also disturbed at the implications in his religious and philosophical views as well as in his politics. Many of these periodicals equated Emersonian democracy with anarchy; even liberal organs warned against it, as did the people's journals where Emerson found, at this time, his most sympathetic audience. These journals, which were often written by the young for the young, discovered in Emerson's radical vision an expression of their longing to cast off all restrictions—religious, philosophical, and social. This longing was never to bear much fruit, as the next twenty years show.

Mid-Victorian critics as well as the earlier had found difficulty not only with what Emerson said but with the way that he said it. His literary style, they asserted, was extravagant, tedious, and likely to be as opaque as the doctrines it was attempting to express. With the publication of *English Traits* and *The Conduct of Life* critics found an improvement in style, but they were more highly incensed than ever at Emerson's religious and philosophical doctrines. Only a small minority—Secularists, Theosophists, and a few other Victorians of radical persuasion—were ever to give much acclaim to these aspects of Emerson's thought. Even these radicals refused to accept Emerson as poet. Only a handful of critics found in his poetry any intimations

[3] F. W. Dupee, ed., "Henry James," *Major Writers of America,* ed. Perry Miller *et al.* (New York, 1962) , I, 139; *TLS*, May 29, 1903, p. 166; *Sp*, June 16, 1888, p. 826; Ward, *TBar,* LXXII (Oct. 1884) , 236.

of greatness, and of these, only two or three indicated that the direction of this greatness lay in symbolism.

By 1870, three years after the appearance of *May-Day and Other Pieces,* Emerson's reputation had begun to decline, and for the next ten years little was heard of him in Victorian periodicals. At his death in 1882 he once again was a subject of wide discussion, but the commentators were much more respectful than they had been earlier.

The new Emerson had been adumbrated as early as 1867, when Professor John Nichol brought out a long, scholarly article setting forth judicially, critically, and somewhat dully an estimate of the American's works. The last two decades of the nineteenth century saw a plethora of such articles. Abjuring the blunderbuss approach of earlier critics, Matthew Arnold, Henry James, Jr., W. L. Courtney, and others explained Emerson's political, religious, and philosophical doctrines rather than merely reacting to them emotionally. More often, however, late Victorian critics ignored the doctrines altogether and concentrated on the man. This treatment was eminently safe: early critics had paid homage to the earnest American, and though Mid-Victorians were apt to sneer at his ideas, they seldom questioned his lofty character and impeccable morals. Late Victorians, encouraged by a number of reverent biographies, helped to drape over Emerson the mantle of holiness visible even to this day.

Yet these critics were still not sure what lay under that mantle. Nichol had given an excellent account of Emerson's philosophy but understood only vaguely or not at all his literary style and theory of criticism. In the 1880's Arnold could not account for the romantic elements in Emerson's works, James's effort to understand Emerson's philosophy was in vain, and Vernon Lee failed to see that she was not treating an "introspective, brooding nature" [4] such as that of her mentor, Pater. In perhaps the best article on Emerson to appear in British periodicals, Leslie Stephen wrote that after a long talk with the American he had been "left with a problem unsolved." "The question remained: what was the secret of his power?" [5]

[4] Hugh Walker, *The Literature of the Victorian Era* (Cambridge, Eng., 1921), p. 1021.

[5] *NatRev,* XXXVI (Feb. 1901), 882.

For the writer who has no handle, the term *secret* is an altogether necessary one. "In general criticism," said Tillotson in 1951, " 'secret' has had a longish history, not yet ended. Carlyle and Newman used it. Arnold was fond of it. And Pater too." [6] So is Tillotson: "Arnold can [at times] be so good a critic . . . that he can make us feel that the object of the criticism is itself speaking with his words, saying, 'This is my nature: my "secret," for better or worse, is out.' " [7] Basil Willey also defends the use of such terminology, which, Tillotson admits, "strikes a modern reader as rather too coy a term." [8] "The Victorian attitude to Wordsworth," writes Willey, "was summed up once and for all by Arnold when he invented the phrase 'Wordsworth's healing power.' This may not qualify as a literary *aperçu,* but it says something both true and important about Wordsworth, and if it is not 'criticism' need we greatly care?" [9] Arnold as well as Stephen and others also tried to sum up Emerson, to put into words his nature, his secret, and in doing so, they said something that is true and important about him.

One Victorian believed in the secret of Emerson but despaired of finding it. "EMERSON leaves one with . . . the hopefulness of man's estate, combined with a modest, but not abject, resignation to the imperfection of all individual achievement. The happy composition of spiritual forces by which this is brought about is precisely the secret of EMERSON, and it is incommunicable. He would have said of himself that the only clue of it is to go about one's own business, and work altogether in one's own way." He was "a thinker the operation of whose works is more easily reflected on than described, more easily felt than reflected on." Not to be put off, bolder critics set forth a number of hypotheses: two of them found the clue to Emerson in his religion. In an article entitled "The Secret of Emerson," Richard Garnett said that he would try "tersely expressing" that secret: Emerson was "a seer without pretensions to the supernatural." The *Athenaeum* observed that the American "was not one of the original thinkers who suggest new truths, nor of the solid reasoners who prove them. Rather he was the continuator of the old tradition of faith in its widest sense; of an idealistic conception of

---

[6] Tillotson, p. 37 *n.*   [7] P. 43.   [8] P. 37 *n.*

[9] Willey, *More Nineteenth Century Studies* (New York, 1956) , p. 293.

nature; of a confidence that the meaning of the world is good." The *Spectator* turned to the American's democratic tendencies: "the keynote of Emerson's teachings" was his ability to make individuals out of the masses, while the *Times Literary Supplement,* quoting Froude, wrote that "his freedom from all desire to influence others directly was one secret of his influence on others." A Swedenborgian declared that when Emerson declared that Goethe "seemed to see through every pore of his skin, he used a remark equally applicable to himself. In this lies the chief secret of his popularity." Saintsbury believed that Emerson's power was derived mainly from two sources: "partly from the fact that, with the most egotistic of all possible creeds in literature, politics, and philosophy, he was personally not in the least an egotist; partly from the sheer literary merit of even his most unequal work." [10]

Only the most daring contended that the American's strength lay in his power of expression, one critic declaring that one secret of his "writings" was that "he addresses *you,*" but a number did find Emerson the man wonderfully effective. "Emerson's fame will probably be independent of any single contribution to the world's literature," wrote Courtney. "For his merit does not appear to consist either in his rhetoric, or his philosophy, or his poetry, but rather in the genial spirit of the man, and in the generous and wholesome influence which he diffuses around him." "It 'does one good' to read him; for he braces the sinews and sets the blood coursing more freely through the veins." Another said that "Emerson did everything gently, whether as sympathiser or moraliser. Surely never existed a . . . softer-tongued Radical than he. . . . Herein lay his great influence with other men." Walter Lewin also found that his "distinguishing quality was the largeness of his sympathy." "This breadth of sympathy explains much in his character, and must be the starting-point upon which to base a true estimate of the man and of his work in the world." Stephen allowed Emerson to "explain his own secret": " 'The true preacher,' he says, 'can be known by this, that he deals out to the people his life.'. . . His simplicity and sincerity

---

[10] *SatRev*, May 6, 1882, p. 554; Richard Garnett, *Lit*, Sept. 21, 1901, p. 274; *Ath*, Oct. 29, 1887, p. 562; *Sp*, Sept. 3, 1898, p. 313; *TLS*, May 29, 1903, p. 166; *IRNJ*, XXII enlarged ser. (Feb. 1875) , 61; George Saintsbury, *Ac*, May 6, 1882, p. 321.

moved congenial hearers to aspire to regions of thought higher than those of the counting-house . . . , and impressed upon them at least the beauty and dignity of Emerson's own character." The *Spectator* shaped to a nice point this British comment on the persuasiveness of Emerson the man: "The writings of Emerson fail to explain adequately the effect which he produced upon his contemporaries, and the secret of his influence was expressed by Harriet Martineau, in words which Mr. Cabot quotes with approval: — 'It is a man so *sui generis* that I don't wonder at his not being apprehended till he is seen.' " [11]

Arnold and James believed that Emerson's secret lay not altogether in the man nor in his message but in a combination of the two: his ability to inspire. "Yes, truly, his insight is admirable," wrote Arnold; "his truth is precious. Yet the secret of his effect is not in these; it is in his temper. It is in the hopeful, serene, beautiful temper wherewith these, in Emerson, are indissolubly joined. . . . One can scarcely overrate the importance of thus holding fast to happiness and hope. It gives to Emerson's work an invaluable virtue." Although James "laughed" at the idea of trying to find writers' secrets, he could not help joining the fascinating game long enough to speculate on Emerson's: "He did something better than anyone else: he had a particular faculty, which has not been surpassed, for speaking to the soul in a voice of direction and authority." [12] Others agreed. Vernon Lee wrote that to Emerson, "the real life is that of the soul: the life, so to speak, at head-quarters, to which all other subordinate lives do but bring their necessary tribute of well-being, of experience, of sensation, of facts." R. E. Prothero observed that "Emerson's undoubted influence in suggesting thought and inspiring noble ideals of life" is "his highest title to fame." Coulson Kernahan asserted that "perhaps the most valuable and lasting of Emerson's characteristics is his intense suggestiveness," and Henry

[11] G. W. Foote, *Freethinker*, May 24, 1903, p. 321; W. L. Courtney, *FR*, XLIV (Sept. 1885) , 331; Arthur Rickett, *Speaker*, June 27, 1903, p. 292; Lewin, *Ac*, Feb. 28, 1885, pp. 143, 144 (Lewin expressed the same view in *Ac*, Oct. 22, 1887, p. 262, as also did an anonymous critic in *Ath*, Feb. 3, 1883, p. 147) ; Stephen, *NatRev*, XXXVI, 896; *Sp*, June 9, 1888, p. 793.

[12] Matthew Arnold, *MM*, L (May 1884) , 10, 11: Tillotson, p. 37*n*; James, *MM*, LVII (Dec. 1887) , 98.

Norman believed "Emerson's great secret [to be] the secret of his stimulating power. . . . That it does so is . . . its chief merit." [13]

The chief merit of Norman, Vernon Lee, and the other critics was that they could be stimulated by the American. To lose Emerson meant, as a Victorian had commented almost half a century earlier, losing "an important, informing fact, out of the nineteenth century," but, more significantly, losing him means losing a fact in life itself. "The purpose of human life," wrote one of Emerson's admirers, the British philosopher Alfred North Whitehead, "is to grasp as much as we can out of . . . the infinity of the possibilities that confront humanity—the limitless variations of choice, the possibility of novel and untried combinations, the happy turns of experiment, the endless horizons opening out. As long as we experiment, as long as we keep this possibility of progressiveness, we and our societies are alive; when we lose them, both we and our societies are dead, no matter how externally active we and they may be, no matter how materially prosperous they and we may appear. And nothing is easier to lose than this element of novelty. It is the living principle in thought, which keeps all alive." [14] Emerson presented his times with a few variations of choice: his secret was that he helped the nineteenth century to live a little.

[13] Lee, *ContR*, LXVII (March 1895), 358; [R. E. Prothero], *QR*, CLXVI (Jan. 1888), 152; Coulson Kernahan, *GentM*, CCLIX (Nov. 1885), 476; Norman, *FR*, XL (Sept. 1883), 432. For other uses of the word secret in connection with Emerson, see Courtney, *FR*, n.s. XXXVIII, 323; M. D. Conway, *Fraser's*, LXXXII (July 1870), 11.

[14] *Ex*, June 17, 1848, p. 388; *The Dialogues of Alfred North Whitehead*, recorded by Lucien Price (New York, 1956), pp. 134, 135.

Index

[Books other than Emerson's are identified by the author's name in parentheses except when they appear as subentries under the author's name. Titles of books, articles, and periodicals are usually given in full when they form main entries. Shortened forms are used in the subentries and cross references. Journal abbreviations are listed on pages xiii and xiv.]

Castle, Mrs. M. A., see under *CMM*

Catholicism and "Divinity School Address" compared, 14

Cattell, Charles C. ("Christopher Charles"), 102, 112, 117-18; see also under *NatRef*

Censorship, 102

Century, Edmund Yates: E's poetry, 99

Cervantes Saavedra, Miguel de, 144

Chambers, Robert, *Vestiges Nat. Hist. Creation*, 143

Chambers's Edinburgh Journal: E, 35, 47, 178; *Mems of MFO,* 35, 37; E and Carlyle, 186

Channing, William Ellery, 2, 32, 185

Channing, William Henry, 37, 39, 182; see also under *ModR*

Chapman, John, 2, 12, 61

Charles, Christopher, *see* Cattell, Charles C.

Charlton, J., see under *Reas*

Chartism, 45

"Choir Invisible" (Eliot), 99

Christ, Jesus, 42, 182

Christianity: E and, 108-9; Theosophy and, 121; and idealism and mysticism, 153

Christian Observer, 29; E's style, 35; E's philosophy and religion, 35, 36, 42, 44; caricatures of E, 39; sarcastic about E, 61; pirated editions, 61

Christian Remembrancer, 8; *Poems*, 8, 70, 74, 84; E's theology, 8; E's pantheism, 17; E's influence, 26; American poetry, 96

Christian socialism, 22

Church journals: circulation, 44; E, 109, 114, 217; *see also denomination or sect*

Church of England: journals of, 8; preaching against E, 10, 107; E's character, 24; *see also* Established Church, England

Church of Scotland: journal of, 8

Church Quarterly Review: E's poetry, 81; biographies of E, 131-32; E's style, 138; E's literary criticism, 144; transcendentalism, 151; E's philosophy and religion, 153, 154, 155, 156; E and evil, 158; E's ethics, 164; E's influence, 177, 179; E and Carlyle, 187, 197

Cicero, 141

Circulating libraries, 1

Clapham, H. Sheffield, see under *MM*

Clarke, James F., 37

Clemens, Samuel L., 211

Clough, Arthur Hugh, 63, 67

Coleridge, Samuel Taylor: E's debt to, 17, 19, 32; *Ode on Dej*, 18; *Aids to Refl*, 19, 37; *Friend*, 37; influence, 37, 189; theory of literature, 144

Collet, Sophia D. ("Panthea"), 26, 108; characterized, 32, 40, 109, 110; and E, 116; see also under *Reas*

Comte, Auguste, 105

Comtists, 142

Conduct of Life, The: critical opinion of, 31, 46, 52-55, 70, 111-13, 161, 200; origin as lectures, 47; compared to earlier works, 63; on religion, 111-12; ethics in, 161; style in, 189

Confidence Man, The (Melville), 39

Confucius, 156

Congregationalist: E and Carlyle, 193-94, 199; *Corr*, 203, 205

Congregationalists, 8

Congregational Review: transcendentalism, 147; E's religion, 156; E's influence, 178; E and Carlyle, 198, 199

——, John Brown: E's religion, 156

Contemporary Review: on *Emerson* (Holmes), 131; transcendentalism in America, 149; E's mysticism, 153

——, Edward Dowden: E's style, 137; transcendentalism in England, 150; comparing *RepMen* and *Heroes* (Carlyle), 202

——, Violet Paget: E's poetry, 93; E's style, 139; E and evil, 158; E's ethics, 163; E and teaching, 164; E's influence, 173, 221

——, Juliet Pollock: E's poetry, 89; E and Carlyle, 190

——, William B. Rands: E's philosophy, 153; E's influence, 179

Conway, Moncure D.: characterized, ix, 31, 39, 40, 181; E's influence on, 31, 117; his *E at Home*, 95, 108, 113, 128, 171; E, 133; E and Carlyle, 208; see also under *FR, Fraser's, OC, PubO*

Cooke, George Willis, 130, 168; his *E: His Life*, 95, 130

Cooper, James Fenimore, 2, 185

Cooper's Journal: quotes E on religion, 47

Copyright laws, 2

Cornhill Magazine: rationalist articles in, 105

EMERSON'S IMPACT ON THE BRITISH ISLES AND CANADA

was composed, printed, and bound by Kingsport Press, Inc., Kingsport, Tennessee. The paper is Warren's Olde Style. The types are Baskerville, Bulmer, and Caslon. The book was designed by John J. Walklet, Jr.